# Plumbing

REX CAULDWELL

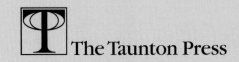

The Taunton Press

The Taunton Press
Inspiration for hands-on living®

The Taunton Press, Inc., 63 South Main Street,
PO Box 5506, Newtown, CT 06470-5506
e-mail: tp@taunton.com

Packaged by: Dolezal & Associates
Jacket/Cover design: Alexander Isley Inc.
Photographer: Rex Cauldwell

For Pros/By Pros® is a trademark of The Taunton Press, Inc.,
registered in the U.S. Patent and Trademark Office.

**Library of Congress Cataloging-in-Publication Data**

Cauldwell, Rex.
  Plumbing / Rex Cauldwell.
      p. cm. -- (For pros, by pros)
  ISBN-13: 978-1-56158-817-6
  ISBN-10: 1-56158-817-2
  1. Plumbing--Handbooks, manuals, etc. I. Title. II. Series.
  TH6291.C38 2007
  696'.1--dc22

                              2006011266

Printed in the United States of America
10 9 8 7 6 5 4 3

The following manufacturers/names appearing in *Plumbing* are trademarks:
AutoCut™, Jacuzzi®

*This book is dedicated
to my two grandchildren,
Katie and Elizabeth.*

## Acknowledgments

I would like to thank Carl, my most ardent fan, for all his ideas and input about the trades. In addition, I would like to thank the following people and manufacturers for providing products and information for this book: Nora DePalma at American Standard; Linda Carter, Senior Graphics designer at Zoeller Pump Company; All the guys at Big John; Rosemarie Ascherl at SONNHALTER; Elaine Wills at In-Sink-Erator®; Lance Hull at Oregon Copper Bowl Company; Marti Stalinski at Oatey Products; Studor, Inc.; Sioux Chief Manufacturing; Vanguard Piping Systems, Inc.; Thompson Plastics, Inc.; Zoe Industries; The Ridge Tool Company; Nibco; Fernco; Watts Radiant; and Reed Manufacturing.

# Contents

# Overview
## What the Book Covers

**M**y grandfather and Uncle Bud would be completely "bumfuddled" by today's plumbing. My grandfather "Bunt" Cauldwell (a famous baseball player and wrestler) never worked with any type of plastic pipe. Uncle Bud was around to see polyethylene, but not CPVC. Neither of them would have any idea how to plumb a house if they couldn't use metal pipe.

They would be dumbfounded by today's tools, too. Neither would have any idea how to use a RIDGID ProPress System® tool to crimp copper. And I'm sure they would get a real kick out of the new no-sweat press-on copper fittings. Because of all this new technology, I can do things they never dreamed of, and yet I'll never know as much as they did about their specialties, working with copper, steel, and cast iron. Of course, they taught me as we worked, but nobody ever learns everything that another knows.

In this book I offer what I learned from Grandpa and Uncle Bud as well as what I've picked up on my own since I left my Indiana home. I cover all service pipe (well pipe, well-to-house pipe, and city utility) and in-house water pressure pipe, as well as vent and

**PEX is covered** extensively—both brass and plastic fittings—as are various ways of connecting it.

I hope they would be able to use this book to work with the new pipe systems.

Throughout the book, I include anecdotes —true stories that show things just don't always work out the way they're supposed to. Any tradesperson will tell you that Murphy's law is hard at work in the trades. As surprising as the stories may be, all are true. I either caused the snafus or I saw them happen.

The point is to learn from mistakes, whether yours or others'. For instance, I learned that all newly cut threads are razor sharp when I reached into a can of pipe dope, pulled out a handful, pressed it onto the newly cut threads of a 2-in. pipe, and swiped it down the threads—blood went everywhere. Uncle Bud didn't stop laughing for 20 minutes. Another time, my cousin Bill and I hit a metal duct against a hot wire in a wet crawl space— bang! We crawled out, sat under a big oak tree and didn't stop shaking for 20 minutes.

drain lines (new and old) that you might use on the job. If you want to use CPVC, it's here. If you want to use PEX, I cover it. You'll find copper sweat in these pages, too.

I offer my pipe/fitting preferences for a particular job, and I give you a comparison chart so you can pick what is best for you. I show plumbing projects, such as the installation of a fixture or a submersible pump, in step-by-step photographs. If my relatives were alive today,

**Included in this book are cutting-edge products such as the Watts CinchClamp for PEX and the ProPress System by RIDGID for copper pipe. (Photos courtesy Watts Radiant, Inc.; Ridge Tool Company.)**

# Logical Layout

This book is laid out with the most logical subject first: getting water. Wells and Pumps (for country water systems) and Utility Water (for more developed areas) lead off. Once you get water to the house, you have to select the type of pipe you'll use and know how to work with it. Then you need to choose a hot water system. Do you want a standard heater or something else, such as a demand system or a recirculating system? You'll find a discussion of the pros and cons of each in Chapter 5.

## FLOWCHART OF BOOK CHAPTERS

This chapter flowchart shows that the book is set up in the order of the work to be done. First, you have to get water to the house via Wells and Pumps (Chapter 2) and Utility Water (Chapter 3). Next, you'll learn how to work with in-house pipe, which feeds into Chapters 4–8, which take you through the procedures required in plumbing a house: first rough-in, then finish. The appendix contains charts, tables, and other information that serves as reference for all chapters.

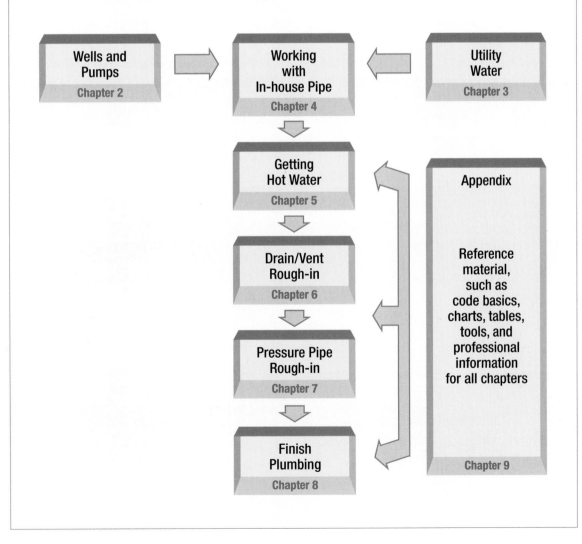

When it's time for the rough-in (Chapters 6 and 7), you'll run pipes through studs and joists. But first comes the drain/vent line system and then the pressure line system. I cover the drain and vent lines first because they have to follow a specific path and a particular slope. Even that has two steps. You'll run the pipes vertically, stubbing through the floor. Then you'll bring all the drain/vent lines together horizontally under the floor, maintaining the proper slope and selecting the appropriate pipe diameter. In Chapter 8, I show fixture installation and hookup of the drain and water pressure lines.

In the Appendix, I discuss the professional-only systems such as the NIBCO/Vitaulic NVent system for copper and the new Watts CinchClamp for PEX. And I can't leave out the RIDGID ProPress system of crimping copper. Pro-only systems are called such at the request of the manufacturer or because of the extreme expense of the tools and hard-to-find material. The Appendix also lists codes, tables, fittings, and tools.

## Safety Issues

Safety is paramount. There is no point in doing a plumbing job if you injure yourself to the tune of many thousands over what you made on the job. I speak from experience. My left ankle is mostly stainless steel, the result of falling off a house when a ladder kicked out on me. I finished that job in a wheelchair. Safety must be your number-one concern on the job, and you must be constantly vigilant.

I'll discuss safety in reference to specific tools and techniques throughout the book, but a few basic tips are pertinent to every job. Start with the proper safety gear. Wear safety glasses, and when you're not using them, hang them around your neck. Experience has shown that if they're not within arm's reach when you need

It's common sense, but most of us ignore it. If you are working above your head, wear safety glasses to keep debris from falling into your eyes.

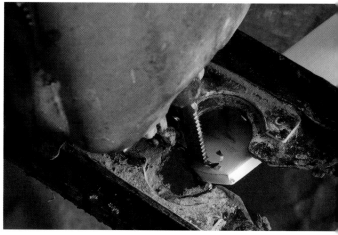

Looking down can be just as dangerous. When you're cutting a metal bracket, for instance, hot, sharp shards can shoot up, hitting your face. Not wearing safety glasses is like playing Russian roulette—eventually the odds will catch up and *your eyesight will be damaged.*

**GFCIs save lives.** The one on the right is portable, good for on-the-job safety. The recessed box with a GFCI inside is by TayMac (www.taymac.com). When it's closed, the cover will be flush to the wall.

them you probably won't use them. For large multifloor jobs, you also may need a hard hat.

Always use a nonmetallic ladder. Metal ladders are a hazard because of the possibility of hitting a hot wire. Of the alternatives, I prefer fiberglass since it outlasts wood.

Ground fault circuit interrupters (GFCIs) are necessary on any outdoor job. I know many people—yours truly included—who owe their lives to a GFCI that disconnected the electric line when a tool shorted out. If you're on a job site where only non-GFCI outlets are available, use extension cords with built-in GFCIs.

By my definition, an extension cord should, by gauge, be an extension of the in-house wiring. That means never use a cord less than 14 gauge; 12 gauge is preferable. It's a good idea always to have a 100-ft. 10-gauge cord on hand for those long runs.

## Working with Inspectors

The best approach in dealing with a building inspector is to be straightforward and honest. Never try to hide something from an inspector,

such as terminating a pipe vent inside a wall or ending an overhead bath fan exhaust between the joists. You'll most likely get caught.

Even if you get such a violation by the inspector, you will acquire a reputation for substandard work and for being dishonest. I can always spot a house built by a certain contractor in my area by removing the overhead bath exhaust cover. If I look through the fan blades and see fiberglass insulation in the vent pipe outlet, instead of a 3-in. vent pipe going outside, I know it was his job. In one instance, this contractor buried the heat-pump duct pipe, which takes the warm air to the back bedrooms. By running the metal underground, the heated air was cold by the time it reached the back rooms. There's nothing like a little air-conditioning in the middle of winter.

Back to the inspectors. If there is anything unusual about a job, ask for the inspector's opinion. Perhaps he or she has encountered a similar situation and can offer a solution. If so, everyone wins. If you're around long enough, however, you'll eventually find yourself in a

**Air admittance valves (AAV's) can be used in lieu of running a vent (the vertical pipe behind the trap) through the roof. However, this is a mechanical vent—there is a spring inside its cap—not an AAV. This installation is likely to fail to meet code during a building inspection.**

dispute with an inspector. He'll adamantly insist on one thing, and you'll just as strongly insist on another. If the disagreement is over a minor item and there's not great danger or added expense, I would advise going with the inspector. The job must go on.

Sometimes, though, disagreements are not so easily resolved. In that event, present your case logically and politely. The only thing that will change his or her mind is facts, not opinions. If you can't come to an agreement, you can go to the board of review, normally located at the state capital. You'll probably want to

avoid this approach in most cases; the process can take months.

## Working with Other Tradesmen

The most important person on a job site is the foreman, normally the chief carpenter. If you want to get on this person's good side, ask before you cut into any floor joists. The same goes for any walls or other beams or supports that hold the weight of the building. The foreman needs this information because he or she may have to build something to counter what you cut. In the worst case, if you cut the wrong board the house may come tumbling down. If you ask first, the foreman will respect you. He might even say thank you.

It's a good idea to try to get along with everybody on a job site, not just the foreman. Several crews often work on the same site, and sometimes a little competitive edge develops between the crews. There's no harm in that as long as everybody keeps it light. But insults can lead to trouble.

On one job the carpenters and the guys who were installing the exterior wall panels were really mouthing it up. It started out innocently enough, but after a while, the insults escalated, and the carpenters lost the verbal battle. Now there is one thing I have learned about carpenters over the years— they don't forget. At lunchtime one Friday, the wall-panel guys left to get some sandwiches. Pretty soon, I heard the carpenters giggling and snickering. I watched as they slowly got in their vehicles and, one by one, drove over the uninstalled wall panels stored on the lawn. The wall-panel installers never uttered an insult again.

## Learning from Mistakes

Errors generally induce grimaces and finger pointing. But mistakes also build knowledge.

One thing I've learned is how to handle blunders. If I'm on a job site and I make a mistake, I think about it for a minute and then go on working. I do the same after the second slip-up, but on the third I take a break.

Don't let mistakes make you feel ignorant; there are always others who know less. One time a foreman gave the carpenters on a job some hand-drawn diagrams and notes on stairs that needed to be constructed. The prints showed all the necessary details for those particular stairs: the width, the rise, everything. Yet he had them build the same stairs twice because they hadn't followed the plans. On the second tear-out and rebuild he realized the problem: The old-time carpenters could not read.

On another job, some new carpenters were given a photograph of a deck and told to build it just like it was shown in the picture. They built the deck at a severe angle to the house. When the foreman asked them why they would do such a thing, they showed him the picture he had given them. It had been taken at a similarly acute angle.

Expect screwups. It's the things that go wrong that break the monotony and make us remember the job years later—perhaps with a little laughter. I chuckle when I think back to my first timber-frame job. I was plumbing merrily away according to the prints I had been given. They said to put a standing tub/shower on the outside wall. So I did. I installed the drain and the pressure pipes. Then common sense set in and I couldn't stop laughing. I was building a 5-ft. shower on a 4-ft. knee wall—all according to the prints.

As shown in **this photo looking down, rainwater flowed into this uncaulked, unsleeved pipe hole through the foundation for years. The owners wondered why the basement wall was always wet. In addition, the sharp-edged hole eventually dug into the pipe, causing a pinhole leak. The entire basement flooded. This book covers many such problems.**

You might think that kind of thing doesn't happen often, but you'd be wrong. I had a similar situation on a custom bath/lavatory job that I was to plumb after the cabinetmaker installed the cabinets. He came in, installed them, and left without saying a word. That's when I saw the custom 32-in.-high white-oak vanity was built against a 3-ft. knee wall with a very low-pitched ceiling. You couldn't get near it without hitting your head on the sloped ceiling.

## In Conclusion

Using this book, you will be able to plumb a house from scratch. Whether it's the knowledge I soaked up as a kid helping my grandfather and Uncle Bud or the experience I've gathered on the job, the information here has been put to the test every day in the real world. There isn't a thing in this book that anyone, pro or not, can't handle. Now go out and get dirty.

Later chapters address seldom-mentioned issues like this one: how improperly gluing CPVC together can reduce the flow within the pipe by 50 percent or more.

# Wells and Pumps

O ut in the country, folks don't take water for granted. Water takes time, money, and skill to find. Back when I was a small child, I watched Uncle Bud use a block and tackle to pull a pump on a tripod over a well. It was slow work; so was drilling a well. The driller would set up over the well site and bang away at the rock for days, sometimes weeks, the noise traveling more than a mile. Today, drillers can go much deeper and be finished in a matter of hours. But there are still plenty of considerations when it comes to wells. In this chapter I'll cover everything you need to know before you have a well drilled, from selecting a site to choosing a driller. Because there's more to getting water than simply digging a well, I'll also show how to install a pump and tank system.

The photographs in this chapter demonstrate the drilling of a real well and the installation of a pump. They detail the ditching, and the water line and pipe, along with the selection and installation of a pump. I'll take you step-by-step through choosing materials, pointing out all the pitfalls along the way. In short, I'll give you three generations of experience to guide you around all the errors my colleagues and I have made over the years.

## Wells and Well Drillers

Typically, a well is a hole drilled in the ground with a casing approximately 6 in. in diameter. After the driller gets through the dirt and hits rock, he pulls the bit out and inserts the casing through the earth down to bedrock to keep out debris and surface water. When the casing hits rock, the driller smashes it into the rock a few times to create a watertight seal. Then he puts a smaller bit on the drill and lowers it through the casing, drilling through the rock until he hits water. The water comes from cracks in the rock so you might get 1 or 2 gallons per minute (gpm) at first. The flow will increase to 3 or 4 gpm as the bit goes deeper. When you reach the flow of water you want, you stop.

The location of your well will be dictated by code and common sense. Codes typically don't allow a well within 50 ft. of a septic tank or footings or within 100 ft. of a leach field. In addition, you need to consider that well-drilling rigs are very heavy and must remain on firm ground, ruling out sites too far from a road or on wet ground. Avoid overhead power lines and trees, and if there are buried utility lines in the area, locate them before you drill. In most cases, you'll want to get a well permit before you call a driller.

> Drilled wells are **not new.** In China, as far back as at least the third century A.D., wells were being drilled down to 300 ft. and more. The drill bits were made of iron; the pipe, bamboo.

Because of the **upright tower of the drilling rig,** do not propose a well near power lines or trees. Even in this location, several tree limbs had to be lopped off.

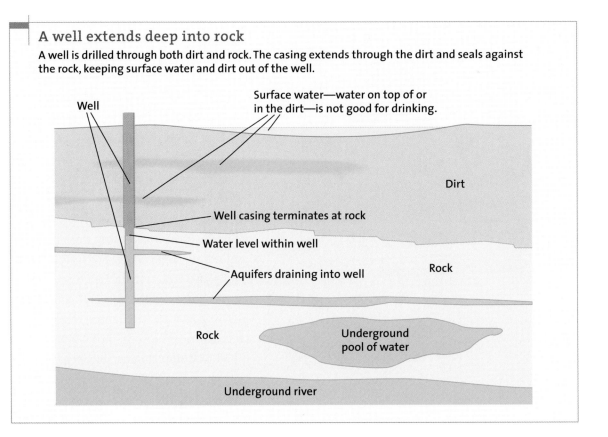

### A well extends deep into rock

A well is drilled through both dirt and rock. The casing extends through the dirt and seals against the rock, keeping surface water and dirt out of the well.

Well

Surface water—water on top of or in the dirt—is not good for drinking.

Dirt

Well casing terminates at rock

Water level within well

Aquifers draining into well

Rock

Rock

Underground pool of water

Underground river

## Typical well/tank installation

Cutaway view showing a typical submersible pump water system with wellhead for cold climates.

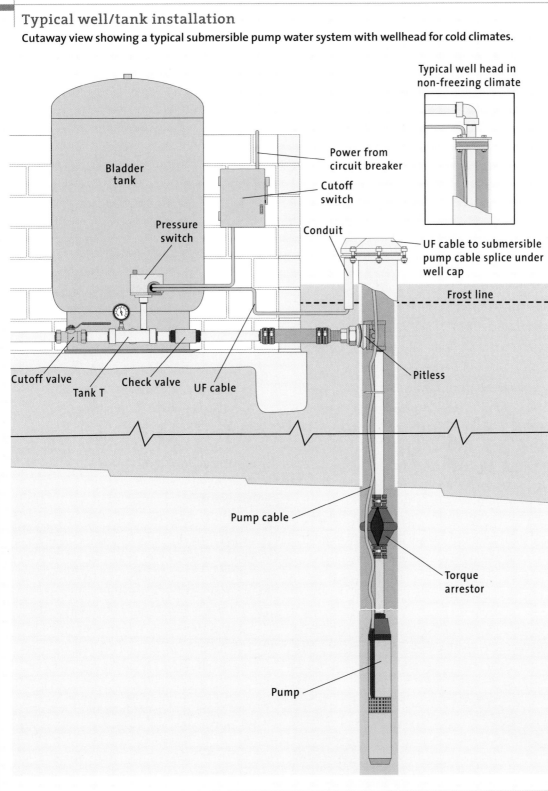

Typical well head in non-freezing climate

Bladder tank

Pressure switch

Power from circuit breaker

Cutoff switch

Conduit

UF cable to submersible pump cable splice under well cap

Frost line

Cutoff valve

Tank T

Check valve

UF cable

Pitless

Pump cable

Torque arrestor

Pump

**Pick your driller with care. Ask the important questions listed on this page to make the best choices.**

## Choosing a driller

When you're selecting a driller, do your research, and stick with a local, well-known outfit. I knew a guy who brought a low-cost driller in from out of state to save a few bucks. The well caved in, and the driller skipped town. Usually, unfortunate situations like that occur because the person hiring the driller doesn't understand the process. To make sure you and your driller have the same expectations, ask these questions:

- What is the driller's availability? There is no reason to waste time on further discussion if the driller can't meet your time frame.

**Metal or plastic casing—which is best? To decide, see the comparison chart p. 13.**

- What is the cost per foot for drilling and for casing?

- Does the driller offer a choice of metal or plastic casing? If he works with only one, does it suit your needs? (See Comparing Plastic to Steel Well Casing, p. 13.)

- What happens if the water flow from the well is insufficient? A well's recharge rate is the rate at which it is replenished by water flowing through cracks in the rock. Typically, a recharge of 2 gpm to 3 gpm is the lowest that can support a house. You can get by on 1 gpm if the well is deep enough and the water comes close to the sur-face; this gives you plenty of storage to pull from while the well recharges. A well with a 6-in. casing usually pro-vides about 1.5 gallons of water per foot of depth. If the well has a static water level (the level the water reaches

How does a well driller know the gpm of the well he is drilling? He turns off the water on his rig so no water is flowing into the hole. Using compressed air from his rig, he then blows out all water that comes into the well from underground. This water falls around the drill bit and the driller uses a shovel to channel it into one stream. He can either visually estimate gpm or see how long it takes to fill a gallon jug. It's not rocket science, but it works.

## Comparing Plastic to Steel Well Casing

| Casing Material | Advantages | Disadvantages |
|---|---|---|
| Galvanized Steel | Can be used for electrical grounding. Seals well against rock. Very tough if struck. | Very heavy. Difficult to drill for pitless adapter, which connects the service pipe to the well. Expensive. Can't be cut with a torch, which leaves a jagged edge and prevents proper sealing. |
| PVC (plastic) | Low cost (sometimes included in the cost of the well). Lightweight. Easy to drill for pitless adapter. Casing is easy to cut properly for a good seal. | Bends against underground rock. Easily broken if struck. Cannot be used for grounding. Even if cut properly, does not seal against rock as well as steel. |

within the casing) of 20 ft. from the surface and the well is 200 ft. deep, you have 180 ft. of water at 1.5 gallons per foot. That's a lot of water—270 gallons—and it is being recharged at the rate of 1 gpm. Most people can live with that.

- What is the cost of a dry hole? Some drillers charge half price for a dry hole and full price for a good well. Some do just the opposite. I prefer to pay full price for the dry hole and half price for the new hole because chances are good the second hole will be much deeper.

- What is the driller's knowledge of your area? A driller who has worked in a particular region will know from experience whether there is ample water at a given depth. It always pays to ask the neighbors how much water is available and how deep their wells are to get an idea of how deep you'll have to go. Also, in some jurisdictions,

you may be able to find information on wells at the planning department.

### It's all about money

If possible, be at the well site during the drilling, especially if the area is known for low-yield wells and dry holes. If you are there, the driller will ask whether you are satisfied with the amount of water at a particular point or if you want to pay more and go deeper for a chance at more water. If you are not there, he will be the one making the decision, and you are going to have to live with it. I knew a man who moved into a brand-new house and had no water at the faucets because his brand-new well was dry. When he called the well driller, the man said he knew

Use a metal **locator to find a "lost" well. The locator will trace the underground cable. When the signal stops, dig. The well should be immediately below.**

## Well Contamination

With casing cut off below ground, wells can easily be contaminated.

Beneath this round concrete lid is an inverted culvert inserted in the ground. Inside the culvert is the top of a well. Surface water flows into the culvert (through it and under it) during a storm and then into the well. This is against code.

Beneath this concrete lid is a concrete box. During rainstorms, water flows into the box through underground cracks in the concrete and around the lid. From there, surface water flows into the well. This is against code.

This 4 ft. in diameter well site was left open through a blocked-off area around the well casing. The tall center pipe is an air intake to the well. During a rainstorm, water flows into the hole through the alleged seal (it's a seal in name only...it leaks like a sieve) and into the well. This is against code.

What can go wrong—Your driller tells you he hit a pocket of water underground and you have plenty of water. A couple of months later, however, the well goes dry. What happened? The driller drilled into an underground reservoir that fills very slowly. Once you use up the water in the pocket, you have to wait a month or two (or until the rainy season) for it to refill. The solution? Drill another well in another location.

it was dry—it was dry when he drilled it. Why hadn't he drilled another? Because nobody was there to authorize the second well.

## Pressure Tanks

A pressure tank stores the water the pump sends up from the well. As the water enters the tank, it compresses the air above it. When you turn on a tap, the air pressure in the top of the tank pushes the water out, sending it to the tap. Just before the air has pushed all the water out of the tank, the well's pump will start and bring in more water. Without a pressure tank, the pump would wear out very fast because it would turn on every time you opened a tap or flushed a toilet.

## Why underground seals leak

A supposedly watertight, underground seal (A1) fits into the top of a buried well casing. The many holes in its top (for pipes and wires) (A2) allow surface water to enter, contaminating the well and its water.

When a torch is used to cut a metal casing (below ground), the slag that is left around the cut (B1) will not allow the underground seal to make a watertight connection against the casing's side (B2), and contamination will occur.

## Designing a better tank

Before bladder tanks became widely used, the 40-gal. galvanized tank was the standard water storage vessel. But it had a couple of problems. A 40-gal. tank held only 6 gal. to 8 gal. of usable water and the pump would turn on after a few gallons were used. With most of the water never leaving the tank, fresh water was always mixing with stale water. A bigger problem was that, over time, the trapped air in the tank dissolved into the water, waterlogging the tank. The pump would constantly turn on and off, burning out the motor. To counter this, air continually had to be shot into the tank.

Many attempts at an automatic solution came to market, but none worked well. I remember one in particular that had a little round sticker on it the size of my thumb saying CAT, for "captive air tank." Whenever I saw the sticker on a job, I would smile and rap my knuckle on the top of the tank. A dull thud would tell me it was waterlogged. I never came across one that wasn't ruined. Another major

Cutaway view of a bladder tank. Water enters the bladder from the bottom while air is trapped above it. (Photo courtesy Flexcon Industries.)

## How a tank waterlogs

Waterlogged pressure tanks are the bane of using common galvanized tanks. When the air in the tank is absorbed by the water, the tank becomes waterlogged. Without air in the tank to keep the water pressurized, the pump will have to turn on and off frequently, eventually burning out.

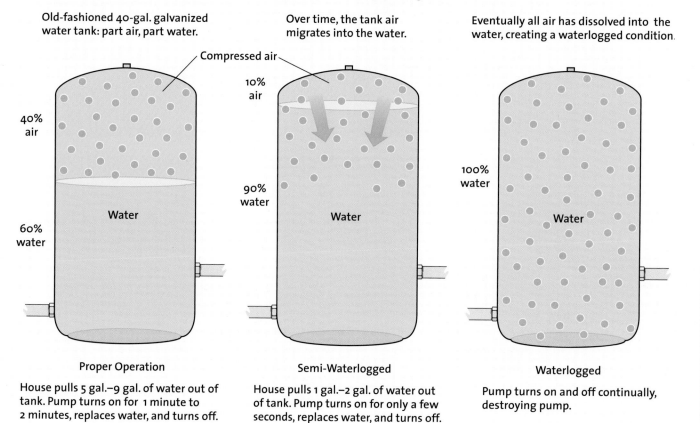

Old-fashioned 40-gal. galvanized water tank: part air, part water.

Over time, the tank air migrates into the water.

Eventually all air has dissolved into the water, creating a waterlogged condition.

Compressed air

40% air

60% water

Water

**Proper Operation**

10% air

90% water

Water

**Semi-Waterlogged**

100% water

Water

**Waterlogged**

House pulls 5 gal.–9 gal. of water out of tank. Pump turns on for 1 minute to 2 minutes, replaces water, and turns off.

House pulls 1 gal.–2 gal. of water out of tank. Pump turns on for only a few seconds, replaces water, and turns off.

Pump turns on and off continually, destroying pump.

Rather than connecting the pressure tank to the house plumbing with rigid pipe, I connect it with a flexible connector, either corrugated copper or braided stainless. This makes for a much faster hookup since I don't have to match pipe locations exactly, and it gives me two unions. Another advantage: no vibration in the house plumbing, which is a problem with rigid pipe.

failure was the side-inlet bladder. I bought 24 of these from my distributor—and lost them all to waterlogging in a short period of time. The internal bladder that separated air from water would rupture. Eventually, the industry settled on the bottom-inlet bladder system, which works very well.

**Tank size** Code requirements don't specify minimum tank size. On a low-bid job, you can get some pretty small tanks. This means you

## How a bladder tank works

Bottom-inlet bladder tanks have taken over as storage vessels for pressurized water. They cannot waterlog.

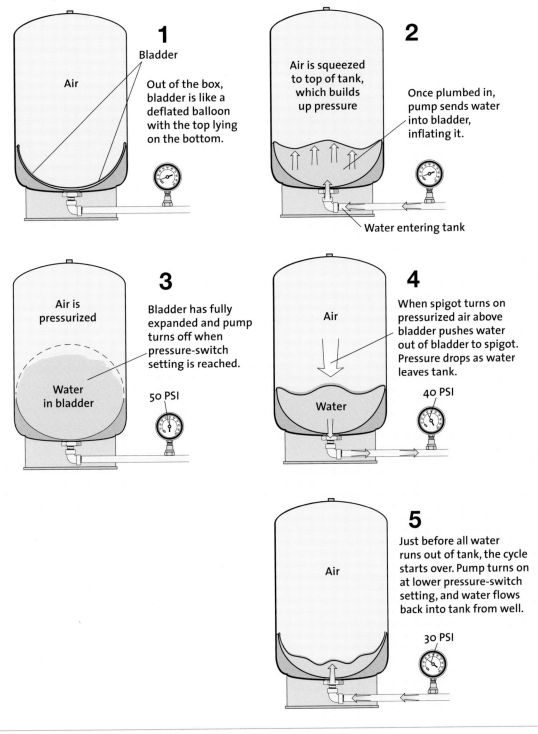

**1**

Bladder

Air

Out of the box, bladder is like a deflated balloon with the top lying on the bottom.

**2**

Air is squeezed to top of tank, which builds up pressure

Once plumbed in, pump sends water into bladder, inflating it.

Water entering tank

**3**

Air is pressurized

Water in bladder

Bladder has fully expanded and pump turns off when pressure-switch setting is reached.

50 PSI

**4**

Air

Water

When spigot turns on pressurized air above bladder pushes water out of bladder to spigot. Pressure drops as water leaves tank.

40 PSI

**5**

Air

Just before all water runs out of tank, the cycle starts over. Pump turns on at lower pressure-switch setting, and water flows back into tank from well.

30 PSI

You can determine if a tank is waterlogged by several methods. Rapping on the tank top is one. A dull thud means the tank is waterlogged; a hollow sound means it's okay. If the entire tank, not just the bottom half, is sweating, it is waterlogged. The best way to test a bladder tank is to drain all the pressurized water from the system. If possible, rock the tank slightly, being careful not to snap the pipes. If you feel or hear any water in the tank, it is waterlogged. You can also press briefly on the air intake valve, on the top of the tank. If water comes out, it means the bladder is ruptured. If you get air, the diagnosis is unclear. The bladder could be ruptured and there could still be a small amount of air in the top of the tank.

Pressure tanks come in a variety of sizes and styles (*left to right*, 20 gal., 33 gal., and 85 gal.). Opt for the largest tank you can afford and that the well and pump can supply. (Photo courtesy Flexcon Industries.)

must either request a certain size tank or be left to the whim of the installer.

Generally, bigger tanks are better. The larger the tank, the fewer times the pump has to turn on, which extends the life of the pump. You'll also have more water when the electricity goes out and the pump can't refill the tank. Where I live, the bladder tank equivalent of the old-style 40-gal. galvanized tank is still the standard (for bidding purposes). The tank is around 3 ft. tall and 16 in. wide. But if the well can handle the extra pumping (installing a large tank on a low-yield well might pull the well dry), I suggest homeowners buy as big a tank as they can afford. Some manufacturers recommend that the tank's water-holding capacity be at least twice the pumping capacity of the pump, but this is normally ignored on low-bid jobs; larger tanks cost more money.

## Tank location

Install the tank in an area that does not freeze. A utility room, basement, and protected crawl space are all good choices. If the tank must be outdoors, do whatever is necessary to keep the tank and pipes from freezing. Build a large insulated box around the tank and the tank T or install lights or heat lamps that turn on automatically to warm the tank when the temperature drops to freezing. I've even seen people throw electric blankets over the tank and pipes. In areas that don't freeze, the site of the tank is less important. In Florida, for instance, I see pressure tanks sitting out on the lawn where the owners have to mow around them. This is not recommended, but it obviously works.

Whatever you do, don't bury a tank. The tank, along with its pressure switch and gauge, must be accessible for maintenance and trouble-

## The Debris Problem

Galvanized tanks filter debris but waterlog. Bladder tanks don't waterlog but let debris through.

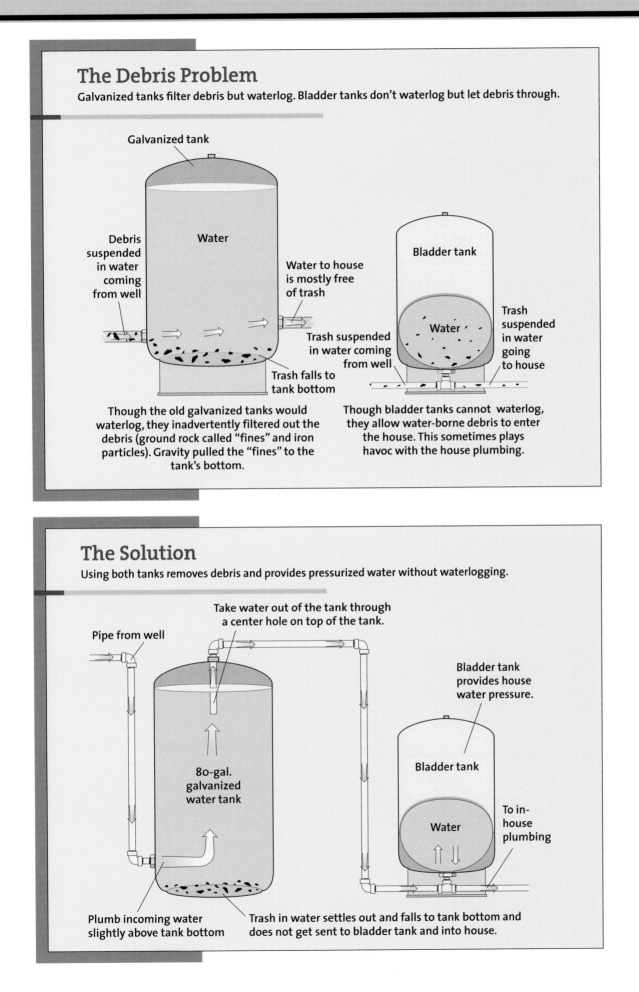

Galvanized tank

Water

Debris suspended in water coming from well

Water to house is mostly free of trash

Bladder tank

Water

Trash suspended in water going to house

Trash suspended in water coming from well

Trash falls to tank bottom

Though the old galvanized tanks would waterlog, they inadvertently filtered out the debris (ground rock called "fines" and iron particles). Gravity pulled the "fines" to the tank's bottom.

Though bladder tanks cannot waterlog, they allow water-borne debris to enter the house. This sometimes plays havoc with the house plumbing.

## The Solution

Using both tanks removes debris and provides pressurized water without waterlogging.

Take water out of the tank through a center hole on top of the tank.

Pipe from well

Bladder tank provides house water pressure.

80-gal. galvanized water tank

Bladder tank

Water

To in-house plumbing

Plumb incoming water slightly above tank bottom

Trash in water settles out and falls to tank bottom and does not get sent to bladder tank and into house.

**A chain vise** is perfect for locking down a tank T for the installation of all its individual components.

shooting. A friend of mine called as I was writing this. He has a buried tank at a well head. His complaint was intermittent low water pressure and occasional dirty water. This is an indicator that the tiny galvanized pipe to the pressure switch is rusting closed (more on that later) and that the bladder in the tank may be ruptured. When I gave him the bad news he chose to ignore the problem because he does not want to dig up the tank. Eventually, he'll have to.

### Tank T's

There are a lot of hookups around the tank: water-pressure gauge, pressure switch, pressure-relief valve, check and ball valve, the attachment to the tank, as well as incoming and out-

going water lines. You can hook all this stuff up with T's, nipples, bushings, and whatever else it takes to put it all together, or you can simply use a tank T made especially for this purpose. A tank T, either copper or brass, is the easiest and fastest solution. The best way to assemble all these items into the T is with the T fastened down tight in a chain vise.

Both short- and long-shank tank Ts are available. Opt for the short because it enables you to install a union between the T's shank and the tank (shank, union, and nipple to connect to the tank's integral elbow). A union allows you to disconnect the tank, if necessary, without having to rip apart all the plumbing and wiring. Well-Rite has a model that comes with a union if you don't want the bother of installing one.

### Check valves

Often, a check valve, or one-way valve, is installed where the water enters the tank T. The purpose of a check valve is to take the pump and well pipe off the tank pressure, which is a good idea but not required in all areas. For long

**The purpose of** a tank T is to have one place to attach the many different fittings and control items needed at the tank.

**Tank Ts come** with long and short shanks. The short shank allows you to install a union if the tank doesn't already have one—and most don't.

> Always assume Murphy's Law. Avoid putting a threaded fitting in a location where it cannot be fully tightened. Out-of-reach fittings seem to have the highest chance of leaking.

This Well-Rite tank (Online series) comes with a union, which saves the labor and expense of installing one. For that reason, it is preferred by many professional plumbers.

runs to the house—say, over 500 ft.—it is also a good idea to put a check valve, where the pipe from the house connects to the pitless adapter at the well casing. Doing so will keep the return-pressure wave (created when the pump turns off) from bouncing back from the bladder and hitting the pump. In some jurisdictions a dual-check valve, an anti-backflow device, is required to keep house water from feeding back into and contaminating the well.

In the worst case I had, a house was located more than 1,000 ft. from the tank, up a very steep hill. (In this situation, the tank could not be in the house.) I knew the pressure wave coming back down the hill when the pump turned off would be phenomenal so I installed three check valves along the way.

A pump has to have a check valve in its pump head to keep the water it just pumped from being pulled back down by gravity once the pump turns off. This valve is either internal or external, screwed in separately. Most internal check valves don't work well so it is common practice to screw a high-quality check valve into the top of the pump. Screw the male adapter of whatever pipe you are using into the top of the check valve. I use rolled polyethylene pipe; thus I screw a stainless steel male insert adapter into the top of the check valve.

Adding a second tank into the system for additional water storage, like the tank on the right, is as easy as cutting a T into the existing house line.

A lot of people like to install an outside hydrant on the incoming water line to the house. For installation of outside hydrants, and the special brass fittings I use to install them, see Chapter 3.

## Pressure Switches

The pressure switch controls the electricity to the pump by switching both legs of its 240v line. The controlling factor of the switching is water pressure. Through a small pipe from the tank T to the switch, the pressure switch senses low-end pressure and causes the pump to cut in, or turn on. When the high-end pressure has been restored, the pressure switch cuts out, or turns off, the pump. Most manufacturers set the two pressure switches with a 20-psi differential (20/40, 30/50, 40/60), which allows the pump to run long enough for the water to cool its bearings. Larger tanks, because of their size, allow the pump to run longer without the need of a 20-psi differential. At my house, where I have a large tank, I sometimes lower the pressure differential to 10 psi. This makes a world of difference in the shower and keeps my wife from complaining about water pressure fluctuation in the line.

### How Pressure Switches Work

A pressure switch tells the pump when to turn on and off. Electrical current is wired to the two outer screws (photo 3) and the pump is wired to the two inner screws. The pump cycle starts when pressurized water enters the bottom of the switch and forces up contacts mounted under the two springs beneath the adjusting nuts (photos 1 and 2). When the water pressure overcomes the spring pressure, contact breaks between the two screws and the pump turns off. When the water pressure falls, the contacts close and the pump turns on.

## Adjusting a pressure switch

You can adjust the pressure switch to the water pressure you desire. This is where you can get the extra pressure to finally make that shower massage work its magic on your sore back, or get the water up to the second-floor shower with enough pressure so you can have something more than a dribble. You can also adjust it if you want to compensate for the pressure loss in a water-conditioning system.

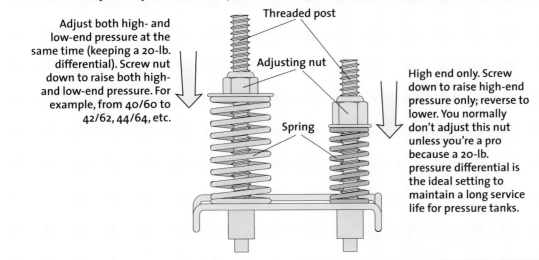

Adjust both high- and low-end pressure at the same time (keeping a 20-lb. differential). Screw nut down to raise both high- and low-end pressure. For example, from 40/60 to 42/62, 44/64, etc.

Threaded post

Adjusting nut

Spring

High end only. Screw down to raise high-end pressure only; reverse to lower. You normally don't adjust this nut unless you're a pro because a 20-lb. pressure differential is the ideal setting to maintain a long service life for pressure tanks.

A common 40/60 Square D pressure switch has one nut each on the two threaded posts on the back of the switch. The tall one controls both the high-end and low-end pressure at the same time. Thus on a 30/50 switch, as you turn the nut down, the pressure will go up to 32/52, 34/54, 36/56, and up, always keeping a 20-psi differential. You can take the switch up to 60/80 psi with a few twists of your wrist.

The nut on the short post controls the cut-out only. To reach a 10-psi differential, raise the pressure to 60/80 by turning the nut on the tall post clockwise, and then turn the nut on the short post counterclockwise to lower the high-end cutoff to 70 psi. Anything above 70 psi will kick in the water heater's T&P valve and make it start to sputter and drip (see Chapter 5).

The air pressure in the bladder tank, which is set by adding or removing air through the air valve on top of the tank, should always be 2 psi less than the system cut-in pressure. In

If the pressure **switch has an arm on it, it is a low-pressure cutoff switch. Avoid these if at all possible. They are for wells with little water, designed to save the pump by removing power to the pump when the water pressure goes below 12 psi. They rarely save the pump, and if the electricity goes out, the system will not restart automatically.**

this situation, with no water pressure in the system, the air in the tank should be set at 58 psi. The bigger tanks come with around 40 psi to 44 psi of air precharged. Smaller tanks come with about 32 psi. Manufacturers assume you will fine-tune the air pressure in the tank at the job site. That's why I have an air compressor on my work truck.

## Water pressure: How much is enough?

In the old days any water was good enough. Cooking, bathing, and washing the laundry in a handwringer washer or washtub were done outside or in the basement. As all three of these functions moved indoors, we needed water pressure.

The early pumps gave us around 20 psi to 40 psi of in-house pressure. But as more and

This is, or was, the ¼-in. galvanized pipe used to connect the tank T to the pressure switch. It rusted solid, ruining the pump, and snapped off at the threads.

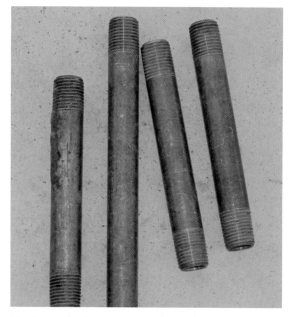

Use brass nipples to connect the tank T to the pressure switch to eliminate the rusting problem.

more appliances used water, we increased the pressure to 30 psi to 50 psi, which came with better designed pumps. For multistory houses, I design for 60 psi to 70 psi.

## Pressure switch pipe

The water pressure reaches the pressure switch through a ¼-in.-diameter pipe from the tank T. This is often the weak link in the system. The pipe's small diameter means it easily can clog up with rust if you use galvanized.

On one service call, I found the house completely flooded; water was coming out the front door. Within six months of installation, the pipe to the pressure switch (installed on a low bid) had rusted closed, causing the pump to remain on. The extreme pressure blew the pipe off an insert fitting in the house. It only had one clamp, and it probably was not as tight as it should have been. The well then proceeded to dump its entire contents into the house. To avoid a situation like this, use a non-rusting-brass nipple to the pressure switch, and double-clamp all insert fittings.

Another thing when installing a pressure switch is to ensure that the brass nipple is long enough for the bottom of the pressure switch to clear the pressure gauge. In cold climates, if the nipple isn't insulated, it will be the first pipe to freeze solid around the tank. If the pipe freezes, pressure changes won't register in the pressure switch and the switch will be stuck in the cutoff position. If this happens, hold a torch or hair dryer near the pipe until it thaws. You will know when it is thawed—you will hear a loud clack as the switch kicks in.

## Low-yield wells

If a well runs out of water and the pump stays on, because it cannot get the water to build up enough pressure for the pressure switch to turn the system off, the pump motor will overheat and be ruined. I've even seen the pump-end melt. Some people install a pressure switch that will turn the system off when the water pressure drops below 12 psi.

You can distinguish this switch from a common pressure switch by an arm on its side that says AUTO, START, OFF. I never use these switches. They rarely, if ever, save the pump, and they are no help when the electricity goes out. The water pressure eventually falls below 12 psi and the switch mechanically turns off. But when the power returns, the switch will stay off. To restore power, you have to hold the switch halfway between AUTO and ON until the water pressure rises above 12 psi. This is not easy to do—it takes very strong fingers.

Electronic low-water control boxes are also available. Though they're expensive, they work. Installed right at the pressure switch, the programmable control box monitors the current to the pump. When a pump runs dry, it pulls a different current than when it is under load. Once this happens, power will be removed from the load for the amount of time the unit is programmed for.

## Ditching

Once the well is in, you'll need to open a ditch to the house. Trenchers or backhoes are commonly used for this job. A trencher works best, but in rocky locations a backhoe is the better choice. The problem with backhoes is that they open a very large trench. I've seen people dig ditches 3 ft. wide for a 1-in. pipe. And sometimes backhoes are difficult to work with. If a backhoe has a narrow bucket—1 ft. wide, say— it can fill up with compressed dirt that will be hard to shake out of its bucket.

Common trenchers (*above*) rent for about $150 a day. They cannot be used in extremely rocky areas, however.

Tight ditching around corners and close to objects (*left*) cannot be done with a trencher. It must be done by hand.

Use a mattock, (*below*) not a shovel, for hand ditching. When the ground is frozen an inch or two deep, cut into the ground parallel to the ditch; the grass will break left to right with the mattock blade and lift up in long sections.

When ditching in very rocky areas, I slip the service pipe and UF cable into a common flexible corrugated pipe to keep them from being chewed up by sharp rocks. To slip rolled polyethylene pipe into the corrugated pipe, first unroll the poly pipe and let it straighten as much as possible. Then slit a tennis ball and put it over the end of the poly pipe. The tennis ball allows the pipe to skip easily along the ridges in the corrugated pipe.

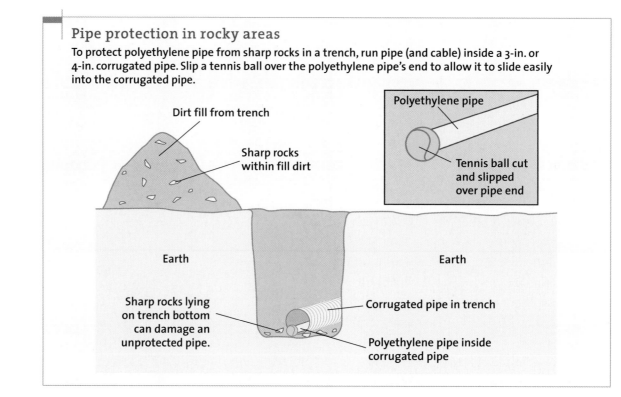

**Pipe protection in rocky areas**

To protect polyethylene pipe from sharp rocks in a trench, run pipe (and cable) inside a 3-in. or 4-in. corrugated pipe. Slip a tennis ball over the polyethylene pipe's end to allow it to slide easily into the corrugated pipe.

Dirt fill from trench

Sharp rocks within fill dirt

Polyethylene pipe

Tennis ball cut and slipped over pipe end

Earth

Earth

Sharp rocks lying on trench bottom can damage an unprotected pipe.

Corrugated pipe in trench

Polyethylene pipe inside corrugated pipe

I allow 3 ft. of extra cable beyond what it takes to get to the well cap (not the casing) and enough on the house side to reach the pressure switch. Leave enough extra pipe on the house end to get to the pressure tank. In most cases, you have to cut the service pipe within 5 ft. of the basement or exterior wall once it enters the house. I go through basements walls with my 1½-in. rotary hammer. You can rent one if you don't own one, but a simple hammer and cold chisel can get you through hollow concrete block. For more on where to "hole" a concrete block, see p. 61.

## Picking a Water Service Pipe

Water service pipe is the pipe that brings the water into the house. Many types are available, but your local jurisdiction may allow few choices. Copper, galvanized, rigid plastic, PEX, and polyethylene are the most common.

Copper is too expensive. Galvanized is too heavy, and it rusts. Rigid plastic is good, but it comes in 20-ft. sections that have to be screwed together with brass couplings or glued, which is very awkward and time-consuming for both installation and removal. I prefer rolled polyethylene. It comes in one continuous length and is easy to work with. Use high-quality, 160-lb.-test or 200-lb.-test pipe found at plumbing supply houses, not the cheap farm-grade stuff carried by many hardware stores.

If you use polyethylene pipe, you have a choice of insert fittings. From highest quality to poorest, they are stainless steel, brass, galvanized, PVC, and nylon. I use only stainless steel and brass because I have had too much trouble with the others. For a comparison of fittings, see Insert Fittings: The Good, The Bad, The Cheap sidebar, p. 55.

You can put an entire length of rolled 160-lb. or 200-lb. polyethylene (*above*) in a well or a ditch without any couplings. Other advantages: It installs faster than other pipe, and it's less likely to leak.

Before inserting or removing a fitting in polyethylene pipe, warm the pipe end with the heat of a torch (never the flame) or a hair dryer to soften it.

Many people prefer 20-ft. schedule 80 (extra-thick) rigid PVC (the pipe in both photos) as service pipe. Brass threaded coupling (*left*) screws onto the threaded service pipe. Once coupled together (*right*), a very strong connection is made between two sections of pipe. It can also be used in trenches. Schedule 80 can be purchased with or without threads.

# Drilling the well casing

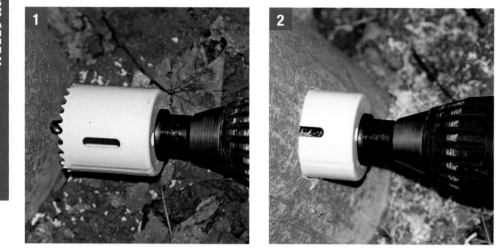

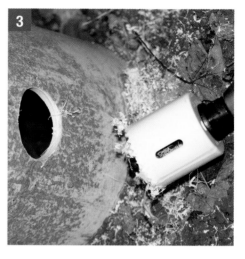

## QUICK REFERENCE

▶ **TOOLS p. 216**
For information about cordless drills

▶ **MATERIALS p. 13**
For information about casing materials

▶ **SERVICE PIPE p. 26**
For a comparison of service pipe

▶ **FITTINGS p. 55**
For information about insert fittings

**1** To drill a well casing, align a 1¾-in. hole cutter with pilot bit straight into casing.

**2** Use the pilot bit to cut through; then the skirt will cut the casing.

**3** Go very slowly. Keep the hole cutter centered so the cutter skirt cuts into both sides of the curved casing at the same time. Once hole is cut, pull the cutter out and verify hole is smooth.

## Drilling the Well Casing

Code requires the pipe coming out of the well to be underground. This is accomplished with a pitless adapter. Part of the pitless mounts on the service pipe that goes in the well, and part mounts through the casing below the frost line.

Drilling a plastic well casing for the pitless adapter is quite easy. Plastic casings allow some tolerance if you don't drill into them at a perfect right angle. Metal casings are less forgiving. You must drill metal at a perfect right angle or you will snap the pilot bit and perhaps lose a few teeth on the cutter skirt. Steel casings require a right-angle drill. Remember that right-angle drills have tremendous torque and can break bones.

# Installing a Pitless Adapter

The purpose of a pitless adapter is to allow the water pipe in the well casing to make a 90-degree turn to get to the underground water pipe going to the house. This keeps all the piping below ground so it can't freeze and allows the well casing opening to be above ground to prevent contamination.

The pitless adapter has two main parts. The first part mounts to the pipe that goes down into the well. The second part mounts through a 1¾-in. hole that you drill in the casing. This part of the pitless has two functions. The part outside the casing connects to the house service pipe. The part inside the casing contains a slide-in slot that faces upward. As the pump and pipe are inserted into the well, the part of the pitless adapter that is mounted to the pipe end will slide into the slot. (continued on p. 32)

> While you're working **on the system, cover the casing's top opening to keep out insects, animals, and debris. Once all work is completed, install a watertight cap, required by most jurisdictions, especially if the area is prone to flooding.**

### Custom-made pump puller

My custom-made pump puller breaks the pipe free of the pitless.

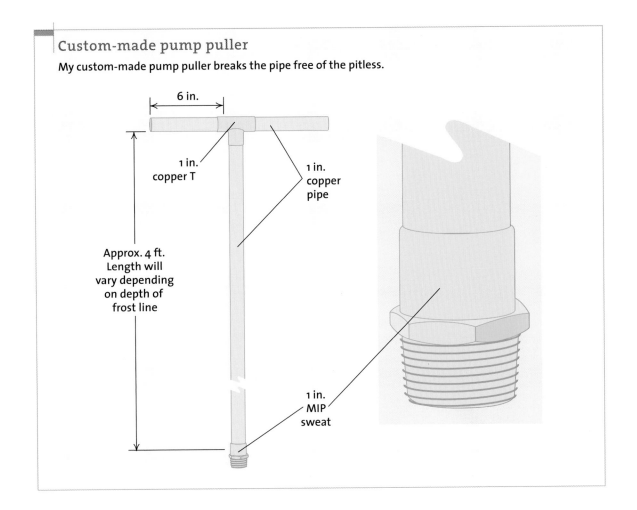

6 in.

1 in.
copper T

1 in.
copper
pipe

Approx. 4 ft.
Length will
vary depending
on depth of
frost line

1 in.
MIP
sweat

# Installing a pitless adapter

## QUICK REFERENCE

▶ **MATERIALS p. 13**
For information about well casings

▶ **PUMP PULLING p. 29**
For information about making a pump-pulling tool

▶ **FITTINGS p. 55**
For a comparision of insert fittings

▶ **ALTERNATIVES p. 44**
For information about installing the Pitless on casing extended above ground

**1** Remove the nut, curved washer, and small gasket from the large threaded end of the pitless adapter. Note the large threaded end also has 1-in. pipe threads on the inside.

**2** The top of the pitless has a 1-in. dead-end female thread. You will use it to install and remove the submersible from the well.

**3** Into this, screw in the T-handle tool (see p. 29). Gently lower the pitless, via the T-handle tool, into the casing.

**4** Use care as you lower it into the well casing, or the slide-off part of the pitless can fall into the well. (Most plumbers make this mistake only once.) Insert the large threaded end of the pitless into the hole in the casing.

**5** On the outside of the casing, replace the small gasket, curved washer, and nut on the pitless. Tighten with a large pipe wrench.

**6** Screw in a 1-in. male adapter of whatever pipe you are using into the internal threads of the pitless.

**7** | Jerk up on the T handle and pull out the removable part of the pitless.

**8** | Screw a male adapter of the pipe you are using into the female threads of the removable part of the pitless.

**9** | Cut the pipe end that is sticking out of the trench at the well head to the proper length and slip it onto the male adapter.

**10** | Tighten with at least two marine clamps.

# Installing a Watertight Well Cap

A well cap seals out animals and flood-water. In regions that do not require a watertight cap, a simple cap is satisfactory. In either case, be sure the cap diameter matches your well.

If you have a metal casing that was cut with a pipe cutter, file down the sharp edge on the interior, being careful not to cut yourself. If the metal casing was cut with a torch, make sure the pipe was cut straight all the way around or the cap may not fit properly and you may have to grind off some slag (solidified molten metal) if it extends to the outside of the casing edge.

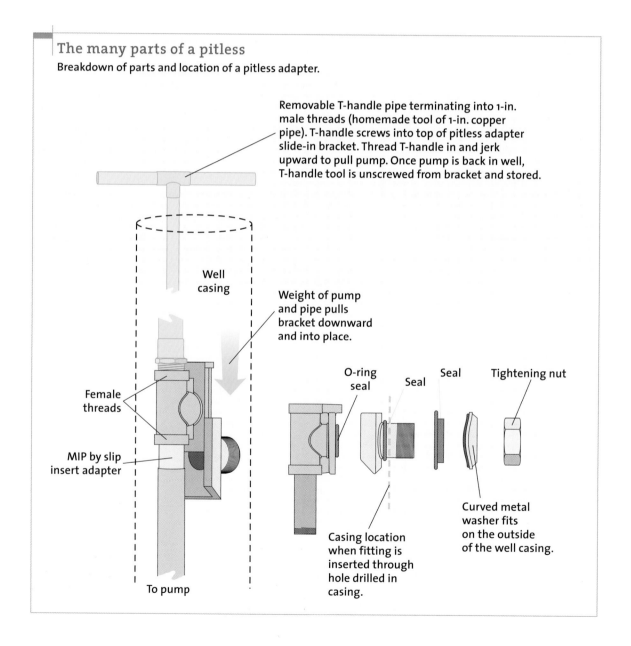

## The many parts of a pitless
Breakdown of parts and location of a pitless adapter.

Removable T-handle pipe terminating into 1-in. male threads (homemade tool of 1-in. copper pipe). T-handle screws into top of pitless adapter slide-in bracket. Thread T-handle in and jerk upward to pull pump. Once pump is back in well, T-handle tool is unscrewed from bracket and stored.

Well casing

Weight of pump and pipe pulls bracket downward and into place.

Female threads

MIP by slip insert adapter

O-ring seal

Seal

Seal

Tightening nut

Casing location when fitting is inserted through hole drilled in casing.

Curved metal washer fits on the outside of the well casing.

To pump

# Installing a watertight well cap

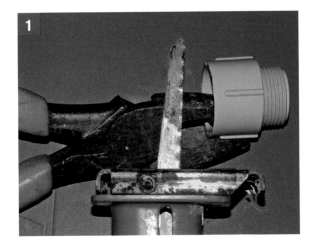
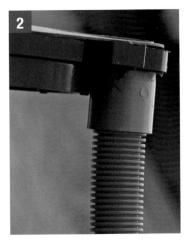

## QUICK REFERENCE

**SEALS p. 15**
For information about well seal locations

**CONTAMINATION p. 14**
For information on cutoff well casings

**LEAKS p. 14**
For information on why underground seals leak

**WELLS p. 10**
For information on wells and well drilling

**1** Use a 1-in. PVC male adapter to screw the electrical conduit into the well head's 1-in. female threads. If there are raised areas on the adapter, they may have to be cut off because of the tight fit against the well casing.

**2** Once it's screwed in, attach the flex conduit by inserting the conduit into the fitting. Rigid conduit can be used if desired (some people use a straightened piece of scrap poly pipe). In either case, the conduit should be long enough to extend down the exterior casing and into the trench. Slip the well seal bottom over the casing.

**3** Once the pump is in the well, bolt the well cap on over the casing.

## Powering the Pump

Pumps are almost always 240v. I never use a 120v motor unless I am replacing an existing one of that voltage and the service panel is full, making a conversion impossible. The lower-voltage motor draws twice the current and has half the starting torque.

Do not assume that you always match the cable gauge to the breaker, such as a 30-amp breaker to 10-ga. cable. In some cases the well is a long distance from the house—say, 1,000 ft.—and we increase the gauge of the cable to lower the cable resistance. A 1/2-hp pump 1,000 ft. from the house would require 10-ga. cable. But we would still put the system on a 15-amp or 20-amp breaker because the motor is only going to pull 5.9 amps. (For further information on required cable gauge per horsepower, see Appendix, p. 237.)

Install a cutoff switch immediately adjacent to the pressure switch and tank to turn power off for servicing.

It's also a good place to put a lightning suppressor. If the breaker is within sight of the pressure switch, it can be used instead of the switch. For more on electrical codes, see Appendix, p. 240.

Run the cable from the breaker to the cutoff switch to the pressure switch.

From the pressure switch, take the underground feeder (UF) cable straight (in the trench) to the well head. Within the well, use pump cable.

## Picking a Submersible Pump

Here are four things to look for when you shop for a pump:

- Voltage—Always opt for a 240v motor (see Powering the Pump sidebar, p. 33).

- Horsepower—This is determined by the total vertical lift from pump to water pressure tank. Though there are a lot of variables (the amount of well water, for instance), a ½-hp Jacuzzi® 7-gpm pump will typically get you down to about 120 ft. If you want 60 psi in the house, a ¾-HP pump is good to about 180 ft., and a 1-hp pump can go down close to 300 ft.

- Two-wire or three-wire pump motor (excluding ground)—A two-wire motor will have two hot wires for the 240v and a ground wire. A three-wire motor will have a run, start, common, and a ground. Go with a two-wire motor. It will be much simpler to install and be just as good as the three-wire, which requires a control box. Simply put, on a two-wire motor, if you put 240v on the two hot leads to the pump, you get water.

- GPM rating—The number of gallons per minute needed depends on how much water your well can give you and how big a pressure tank is installed. In a typical residence, I normally install a 7-gpm pump. I don't want a larger-gpm pump because, once it's on, the pump has to run long enough to cool the motor's bearings with the water. If I got a 20-gpm pump and filled the tank in a half second, the pump motor would quickly burn out. If I had a very large pressure tank and plenty of water in the well, I could opt for a higher-gpm pump. For a more in-depth look at gpm and depth, see Maximum depth for submersible pumps chart, p. 237.

As soon as I take the pump out of the box, I screw a check valve into (continued on p. 36)

On this job a code 240v (230v), two-wire, 7-gpm, stainless pump is going in. The motor is on the bottom, immediately above is the water intake, and above that is what is called the pump end.

A sea of dead pumps. To keep your pump off the dead pump pile, install it properly.

Three-wire pump motors require a control box for start-and-run operation. For 1-hp pumps and below, you can opt for two-wire motors.

# Prepping the pipe

I normally unroll the poly pipe the second I get to the job site so it loses its circular memory. I attach one end of the pipe to a tree or a fence post—just about anything will do—and unroll it. Then I weight the opposite end or tie it off to a tree to keep it from rolling back. I always make sure the ends are capped to keep out bugs and debris.

**1** | Attach the poly pipe to a fixed object. Be sure ends are capped.

**2** | Use pump cable, not UG (underground feeder cable). Break the cable end free and tuck it into the reel top.

**3** | Tape pump cable to pipe every 5 ft. to 10 ft.

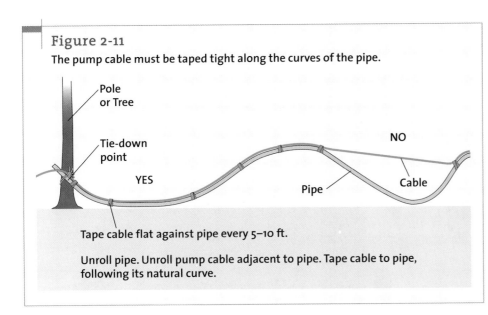

**Figure 2-11**

The pump cable must be taped tight along the curves of the pipe.

Pole or Tree

Tie-down point

YES

NO

Cable

Pipe

Tape cable flat against pipe every 5–10 ft.

Unroll pipe. Unroll pump cable adjacent to pipe. Tape cable to pipe, following its natural curve.

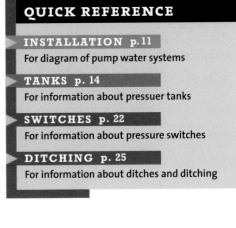

**QUICK REFERENCE**

**INSTALLATION p. 11**
For diagram of pump water systems

**TANKS p. 14**
For information about pressuer tanks

**SWITCHES p. 22**
For information about pressure switches

**DITCHING p. 25**
For information about ditches and ditching

Anatomy of a pump. When we talk about a submersible pump, we call the entire torpedo-like object a pump. But technically, the silver bottom portion is a motor. The long metal or plastic tube on the opposite end is the pump end. The webbed interface between the two is where the water is sucked in. Both the motor and pump end are individually replaceable.

the pump head and a stainless steel male insert adapter into the check valve. I then stand the pump straight up and push the polyethylene pipe down onto the male insert adapter. If the pipe opening is too tight to slip onto the fitting, I use heat from a hair dryer or torch to soften the end. When I use a torch, I aim the flame

As seen in this cutaway, the torque arrestor centers the pipe in the well casing. It grabs the casing snugly to keep the pump motor from spinning and also stops the wire from rubbing against the casing.

near the pipe rather than directly on it, and then for only a few seconds. Once the pipe is on the fitting, I tighten it using two marine clamps, placing the heads of the clamps on opposite ends of the pipe, not next to each other.

I always install a torque arrestor if I put in polyethylene pipe. Being flexible, the pipe will twist, usually within 25 ft. of the pump, every time the motor starts. When this happens, the wire rubs against the casing, and eventually it will be rubbed bare. I install a torque arrestor to prevent the pipe from twisting.

## Check your measurements

For the pipe in the well, cut the pump pipe to whatever well length you want, from pitless to 20 ft. off the bottom. (Never place a pump at the well bottom; it will pull in debris and be ruined.) If the well is 200 ft. deep and your pitless is 2 ft. below ground, cut 178 ft. (200 – 20 = 180; 180 –2 = 178) off the roll of poly pipe. How far above the well bottom you place the pump is up to you. Some people place the pump 10 ft. off the bottom.

Wherever you put the pump, be sure to do the math before you cut the pipe. It is quite embarrassing to slip the pipe in the well and have it bump bottom with 2 ft. of pipe sticking out the top of the well casing. It's another one of those mistakes you only make once.

You won't know if it's too short unless the pump isn't in the water. But this never happens because, as you slip the pipe in the well, you will feel (and sometimes hear) the pump as it hits water and make note of how many feet of pipe is in water as it goes down.

One end of the cut-to-length pipe goes onto the pump; the opposite end receives the slide-in part of the pitless, which is also connected to the T handle. Both ends lie at the well head.

# Splicing the pump to the cable

**1** Obtain a heat shrink wire kit. Of the two kinds available, I prefer the thick black one with a waterproofing compound inside. The other is thin and clear with no waterproofing compound.

**2** Tape the pump wire to the pipe. Align ground wires—green to green, etc. There's no polarity on the other two wires (assuming a two-wire pump shown here). Strip the insulation off the wires, if necessary. Crimp the two leftover wires together.

**3** Slide the tubing onto the two hot conductors (not the grounding conductor). Crimp the wires.

**4** Center the tubing over the crimps.

**5** Apply heat—not flame—to the tubing to shrink it around the crimp. The waterproofing compound should bubble out the sides. Let it cool, then tape to pipe.

**QUICK REFERENCE**

**SECURING p. 35**
For information on taping the cable to the pipe

**SPACERS p. 38**
For information about installing ropes and spacers in wells

**KWIK CLAMPS p. 39**
For information on securing pipe while resting

**INSTALLATION p. 11**
For diagram of pump-to-tank plumbing

## Ropes and spacers

I don't use ropes or spacers. Some people tie a rope onto a pump as a backup in case the pump falls off the pipe, which I've never heard an instance of happening. I have seen the rope rubbed in two on many jobs where torque arrestors were not used, so I'd avoid installing a rope down the casing to secure against the possibility of a fallen pump.

Spacers, intended to keep the pump and pipe centered in the well and prevent cable chaffing, are akin to large washers around the well pipe and do more harm than good. I once put spacers on well pipe every 20 ft. from pump to pitless and had trouble pulling the pump because the spacers kept catching on the well casing couplings and pitless. I haven't used them since.

Spacers are flat plastic pieces that keep the pipe centered in the well. You normally put one about every 20 ft. The problem with them, as you see in these cutaways, is that they catch on the pitless when you pull the pump.

## What can go wrong

You forget to slip the heat shrink tubing onto the wire before you crimp it. Sadly, I have done this more than once. If this happens, you have to cut the crimp out and start again.

Once you've made the pump splice, double-check everything. Then drop the pump into the well. If you are using a pump puller, there is no problem doing it by yourself. Otherwise, it is a good idea to have a few extra strong backs around. Be sure to have both ends of the pipe at the casing head: the pump end and the pitless end. By doing so, you'll only have to drag half the length of the pipe.

I do not insulate the ground wire splice from the water using a submersible splice kit. Leaving the splice open to the water will help to disperse lightning surges running along the ground wire before they hit the pump motor. I prefer this method over cutting the ground wire, as is commonly done, because it is against code to install an ungrounded pump.

## Putting the Pump in the Well

Put several layers of duct tape around the sharp casing edge or slip a flexible split pipe around it to avoid cutting the pipe or cable as you drop the pump down into the well.

You can also buy or rig up rollers or use a tire rim as a roller. I've used a 50-gallon drum; I placed the drum next to the well and arced the pipe over its side. Whatever you do, don't let the pipe go down at a severe angle to the casing; the casing's edge will cut the pipe and wire . The pipe must go straight down—and that means an arc must be formed as it slides into the casing opening. (continued on p. 42)

My locking clamp is a Kwik Klamp. I've seen other people use common pipe vises for exactly the same thing. They work but are awkward. I recommend a Kwik Klamp or its equivalent. They cost about $285 and are available either on the Internet or by special order through large plumbing suppliers.

## A strong back

Just how deep can one person lower a pump into (and pull it out of) a well? My limit is 300 ft., and I'm strong. (I've also ruined my back from pulling hundreds of pumps over the years.) There is a variable, though. If the water comes up high in the well, it will take a lot of weight off your back and pulling a pump up from 300 ft. will seem easy. If the water is low in the well, the pump will feel like a ton, mostly due to the weight of any water inside the pipe. My advice is to have a couple of young helpers (photo B) with strong backs available to help. In addition, keep a pipe-locking device of some sort on hand so you can secure the pipe and rest if necessary.

To take all the weight off your back, get an Up-Z-Daisy (shown in photo A at right) or another pump-pulling machine. You can order it online or through some large suppliers. If you are a pro, it's worth the $2,000 investment to save your back. Use it to pull plastic pipe only—or 1-in. galvanized down to 100 ft. One day I used mine to pull galvanized pipe (1 1/4-in. and 1-in. pipe). This was way too much weight for the machine, and when it broke, it sent a piece of metal across my left hand, breaking the bones and slicing a blood vessel.

A

B

# Putting the pump in the well

## QUICK REFERENCE

**PUMPS p. 34**
For information on submersible pumps

**TORQUE ARRESTERS p. 36**
For information about installing a torque arrester

**SERVICE PIPE p. 35**
For information on removing circle memory from service pipe

**SPLICING p. 41**
For information about making a pump splice

**1** Mount the torque arrestor and make the pump splice before installing the pump in the well.

**2** Have the pump and T handle tool with pitless located at the well head so you only have to drag half the pipe length. Slide the pump into the casing and check the fit of torque arrestor in the casing. Here, the arrestor is a bit too wide; I had to adjust it, using the marine clamps. Slide the pipe vertically into the well; it will get heavier as it goes down.

**3** Use a locking clamp (the blue device shown) to hold the pipe in place if you need to rest.

**4** As the last few feet of pipe slide into the casing, hold on to the T-handle tool and put the slide-in half of the pitless into its mate, which is mounted on the casing itself.

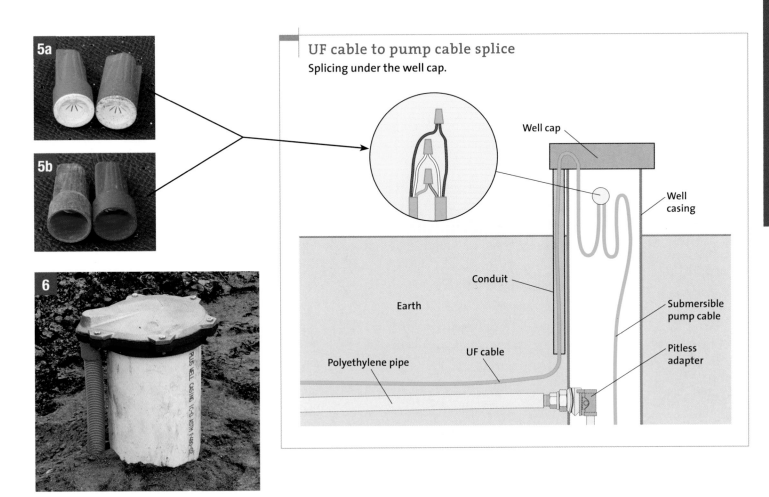

**5a**

**5b**

**6**

## UF cable to pump cable splice
Splicing under the well cap.

Well cap

Well casing

Conduit

Earth

Submersible pump cable

Pitless adapter

UF cable

Polyethylene pipe

**5** Splice the UF cable to the submersible cable under the well cap, as shown in the illustration inset. Common wire connectors, rather than heat shrink kits, can be used in the under-cap splice. I prefer the red/yellow connectors that are filled with silicone (5a). If you are using non-filled connectors (5b), keep the skirts of the wire connectors down to prevent them from filling with water.

**6** Once the splice is made, bolt the top onto the well cap over the casing.

## Jet Pumps

Jet pumps are above-ground pumps—and they can be so noisy that you'll hear them for long distances. In cold climates, we take elaborate steps to keep them from freezing during the winter. In warmer regions, you see them sitting on the ground like lawn ornaments.

The problem with jet pumps is that they require water to get water. That is, you have to fill the entire system of pipe and pump with water before you can turn on the pump. This is called priming.

Another problem with jet pumps is that all connections must be perfect. If there is a loose connection or an air pocket anywhere in the system after you put the water in the pipes, the pump will run but not pressurize, which is called "losing prime."

When installing a jet pump, always have the pressure tank adjacent to the pump. When separated, they create a water pressure wave that bounces back and forth.

Priming a jet pump can take a massive amount of water. In some cases I've had to bring in hundreds of gallons of water, using garbage cans to fill up the pipe and pump. Here's a trick that can save you a lot of water hauling. When priming a new jet pump system that has poly-ethylene well pipe, you can hand-force well water into the pipe through the check valve (continued on p. 48)

A jet pump you can see and hear. This one is a shallow-well jet, which can be identified by the single pipe going into the pump end.

## Jet pump systems

Jet pumps can be used in both shallow and deep wells. Here, they're shown for non-freezing climates.

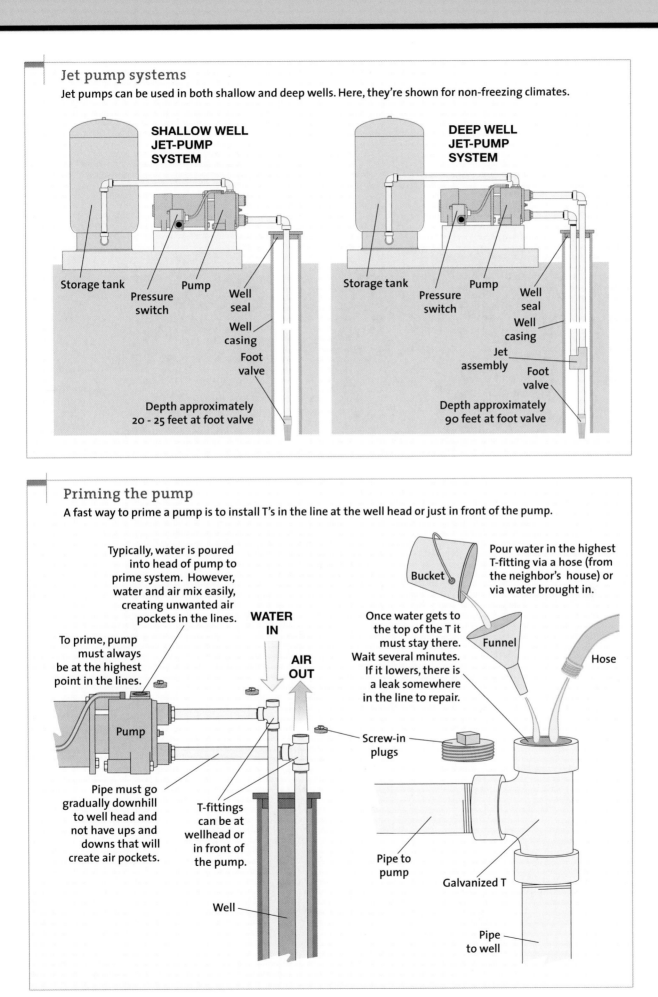

**SHALLOW WELL JET-PUMP SYSTEM**

Storage tank
Pressure switch
Pump
Well seal
Well casing
Foot valve

Depth approximately 20 - 25 feet at foot valve

**DEEP WELL JET-PUMP SYSTEM**

Storage tank
Pressure switch
Pump
Well seal
Well casing
Jet assembly
Foot valve

Depth approximately 90 feet at foot valve

## Priming the pump

A fast way to prime a pump is to install T's in the line at the well head or just in front of the pump.

Typically, water is poured into head of pump to prime system. However, water and air mix easily, creating unwanted air pockets in the lines.

To prime, pump must always be at the highest point in the lines.

**WATER IN**

**AIR OUT**

Pump

Pipe must go gradually downhill to well head and not have ups and downs that will create air pockets.

T-fittings can be at wellhead or in front of the pump.

Well

Screw-in plugs

Bucket

Pour water in the highest T-fitting via a hose (from the neighbor's house) or via water brought in.

Once water gets to the top of the T it must stay there. Wait several minutes. If it lowers, there is a leak somewhere in the line to repair.

Funnel

Hose

Pipe to pump

Galvanized T

Pipe to well

# Extending the casing out of the ground

If the well casing is cut off below ground, surface water will likely contaminate the well. The water gets in through the air vent, around the seal, through the wire hole, or in some other manner. In many cases the bacteria have no effect on adults, but for children, especially babies, and those adults with compromised immune systems, it is a problem.

To avoid well contamination, extend the casing above ground. If you have a steel casing cut off below ground, it is possible to weld another section on to it. However, I insert a new piece of plastic well casing over the existing steel casing and seal it with concrete. If the buried casing is plastic, all you have to do is glue another section onto it. Either way, the first part of the job is to pull the old pump and then dig down to and expose the old casing and a few feet of the pipe going to the house.

### Expose cable and pipe to house

Dig down and expose several inches of the old metal casing (plastic pipe must be able to slip down and over metal pipe). Pull the pump from the well and set it aside. Cover the top of the casing (not shown) to prevent anything from falling in. Expose 2 ft. to 3 ft. of old water line to house.

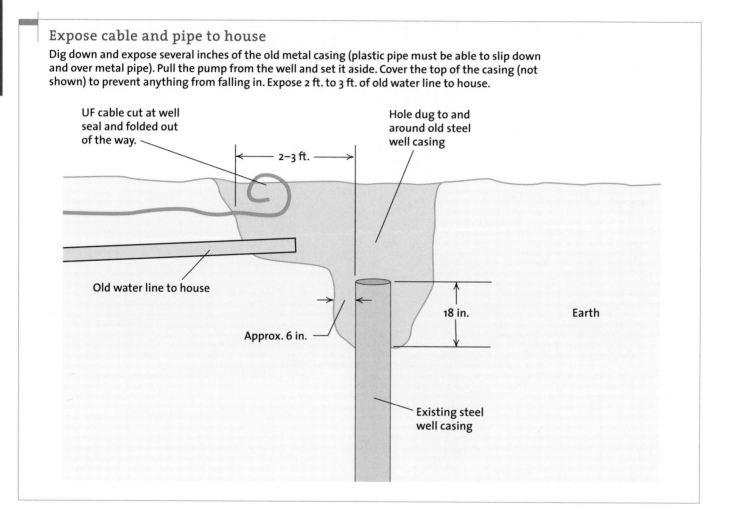

UF cable cut at well seal and folded out of the way.

Hole dug to and around old steel well casing

2–3 ft.

Old water line to house

18 in.

Earth

Approx. 6 in.

Existing steel well casing

**What can go wrong:** When digging out a buried casing, you can damage the pipe or wiring going to the casing. This is easy to do so you must be very careful.

## Insert new casing over old

Slip new PVC casing over old steel casing.

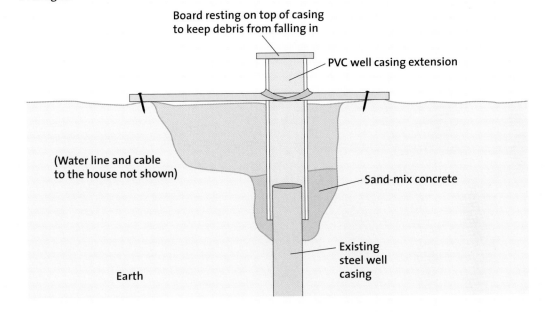

2x4 supports hold
PVC casing vertical

New piece of PVC well casing

Overhead view

Duct tape

Spike

Spike

Hole dug around casing

Old water line and
cable to house

18 in.

Slip new PVC casing
over 12 in. of
old steel casing

Existing
steel well
casing

Earth

## Pour a support structure

Mix some sand concrete and pour it around new PVC and metal casing interface. Let the concrete set up overnight and remove wood supports. Put the cap on the casing hole if it will be left unattended overnight.

Board resting on top of casing
to keep debris from falling in

PVC well casing extension

(Water line and cable
to the house not shown)

Sand-mix concrete

Existing
steel well
casing

Earth

# Extending the casing out of the ground (cont'd)

### Install pitless

Insert pitless on casing at same height as service pipe to house.

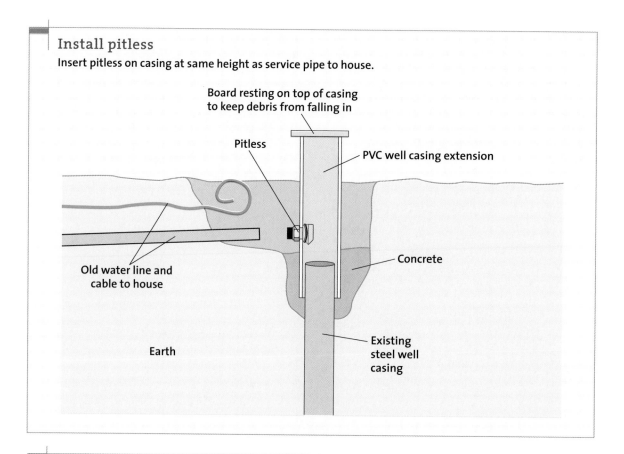

Board resting on top of casing
to keep debris from falling in

Pitless

PVC well casing extension

Old water line and
cable to house

Concrete

Earth

Existing
steel well
casing

### Install new pipe and attach to pitless

Screw a male adapter (assuming polyethylene pipe) on the pitless. Match fitting size to pipe size (normally 1 in.). Slide pipe onto fitting and fasten with two marine clamps. Insert the other half of the pitless onto the pipe end pulled from well. Fill the hole. Insert the pump into the well, making pipe connection at the pitless. Add on pump cable as needed to reach casing top.

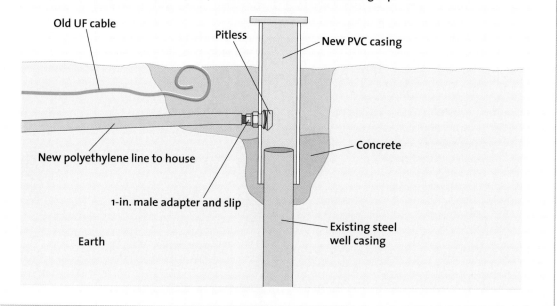

Old UF cable

Pitless

New PVC casing

New polyethylene line to house

Concrete

1-in. male adapter and slip

Earth

Existing steel
well casing

## Install conduit and splice cable

Run old UF cable through conduit into the well cap. Splice the cable to the new submersible pump cable.

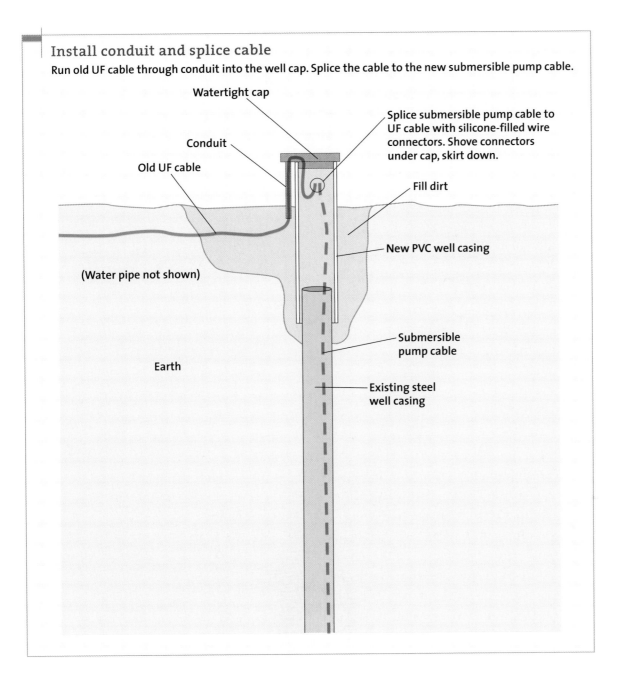

Watertight cap

Splice submersible pump cable to UF cable with silicone-filled wire connectors. Shove connectors under cap, skirt down.

Conduit

Old UF cable

Fill dirt

(Water pipe not shown)

New PVC well casing

Earth

Submersible pump cable

Existing steel well casing

Always use marine clamps, not hose clamps. Hose clamps rust and eventually break apart. I once pulled a pump whose clamps had rusted away. The only thing holding the poly pipe to the pump was friction. Fortunately, I got it all out before it came loose.

(assuming you have access to the well head). Lift the pipe (it is not yet connected to the pump) high overhead. Then lower it real fast into the well. In other words, smash the foot valve through the water. As the jet hits the water deep in the well, the check valve will open, allowing water into the pipe. Once the water is in, it cannot come back out.

If you have the muscle, you can force water a considerable distance up the pipe toward the the wellhead, greatly reducing the how much water and effort you'll use to prime the system.

If you pour water into the pump through a small opening in the pump head, which is common practice, the water goes in and the air comes out through that hole—all at the same time. This is slow and tends to create air pockets in the line and pump head. But there's a better way: At the well head, or just before the pump head, use galvanized T-fittings with screw-in plugs. Prime the system using the T-fitting, not using the pump head. This enables you to pour a lot of water in faster and allows the air to purge itself more easily, eliminating air pockets. Of course, this method works only for new systems where you can plumb in the T-fittings during

installation. For old systems you have to live with whatever the original plumber installed.

When all is said and done, the water has to be at the top of the pump head or the top of the T-fitting. And it has to stay there.

I normally wait 10 minutes to 15 minutes after the installation is complete, watching the water level closely.

If the water level slowly lowers, either you haven't completely filled the pipes or the system is leaking. Try adding more water and waiting again. Don't even think about turning on the pump until you've fixed the leak and the water won't drop any more.

The most common leak is at the foot valve in the bottom of the well—which means you have to pull the pump.

Take note: It should go without saying that the jet pump must always be installed at the highest location. That is, the pipe leaving the wellhead needs to go uphill to reach the pump (assuming the pump is not on top of the wellhead and is already at the highest point).

For rigid in-well plastic service pipe, always use the thickest you can find (typically gray schedule 80 PVC). On the opposite end of the scale is schedule 20 (it can be any color). It is almost paper thin and should never be used. The problem with schedule 20 is that the plastic gets brittle after a few years of use. Such thin-wall pipe can snap or crack easily. Expect this to happen at the least opportune time, such as when you are pulling a pump.

# Utility Water

**M**ost people in cities and suburbs take water for granted. You turn on the tap and out comes the water. The utility company does all the work, placing main lines down the streets and the laterals to the houses and installing the water meters. But that doesn't mean the home owner is without responsibility or the need for knowledge.

With an older system, you have to know enough to maintain the line from meter to house. If you are installing a system for a new residence, you have a lot of decisions to make. You must choose the type of service pipe from the meter to the house, for example, as well as the diameter of pipe, the type and placement of cutoff valves and anti-backflow devices, and the best way to get through a footer or basement wall. You may want a filter, and perhaps you need to increase the water pressure.

In this chapter I discuss utility water and all the components in the service line. I compare the different types of service lines and show you what valves to use. For polyethylene service pipe, I tell you what fittings are my favorite and which ones I wouldn't use even if they were free. I illustrate how I sleeve a pipe going into a house, how to boost water pressure within the house, and how to avoid common pitfalls when installing a cartridge filter.

A numerical readout of a water meter indicates the number of gallons of water that flow through the meter to the house.

Underneath this old-style cast iron lid lies the water meter and is where you cut off the water line to the house.

Water meter for residential installations (*top*). Interface fittings (*bottom*): Make sure you get the gaskets for the end nipples.

# Water Meters

Water meters are typically located underground somewhere between the house and the street. Look for a small lid buried in the yard. New lids are made from strong plastic; older ones may be cast iron.

The home owner is responsible for installing and maintaining the service line on the house side of the meter. This does not mean you will not be working with or handling water meters. If the meter's output fitting (which mates the meter to your pipe) leaks, for example, you'll have to fix it and sometimes property owners install a meter on the private water line. If a rental house is tapped into a home's water line, for instance, you will have to plumb a meter into the line to the rental house so the landlord can charge tenants for the water they use. In a private subdivision where a well supplies several houses, meters will enable the home owners' association to charge for water use.

It pays to be familiar with the water meter. The meter's display, usually visible from the top, indicates how much water has flowed through

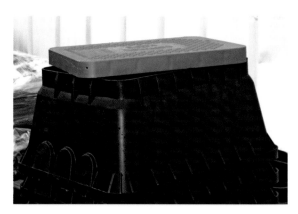

When this newer-style plastic water meter box is installed, only the green lid will be visible.

it to the house. This might be a needle, analog, or digital.

The output of the water meter, typically ¾-in. or 1-in. male thread, is where the pipe will start. In the old days, ¾ in. was the standard for city water. Today, with our abundant water-fed appliances and multiple bathrooms, I usually suggest owners put in 1 in., assuming the utility gives a choice.

On the input side of the meter is a cutoff valve. It has a flat bar handle that can be turned

Most states have given utilities, both public and private, the right of condemnation. That means they can take your property or create easements to install water and sewer lines. In addition, a small private water utility can put in a water/sewer line and charge all those who live along it, whether the property owners tie into the system or not. It happened to me in Indiana.

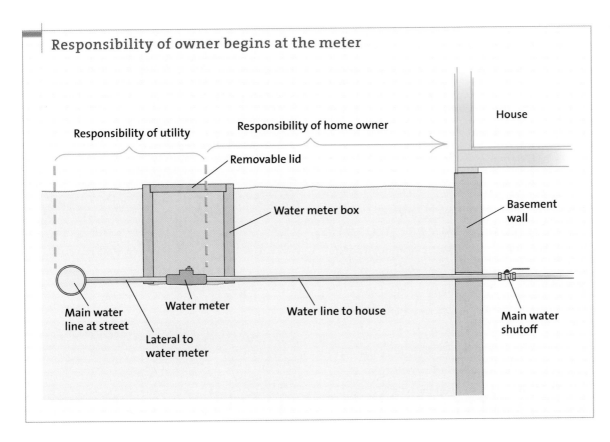

## Responsibility of owner begins at the meter

Responsibility of utility

Responsibility of home owner

House

Removable lid

Water meter box

Basement wall

Main water line at street

Water meter

Water line to house

Main water shutoff

Lateral to water meter

The responsibility of the owner starts on the house side of the water meter. The owner must arrange to fix—and pay for—any repairs to this side of the water system.

on and off with a 28-in. T-handle tool, called a curb key, available at most hardware stores and supply houses. In a pinch, you can use an adjustable wrench or a basin wrench to turn the valve, but it takes a lot of elbow power.

Home owners are sometimes surprised to find out they have no water meter (but the utility bills them anyway) or that their house shares a meter with others. These situations usually occur in older houses, and it's best to avoid them. In one case I know of, a single meter fed three residences. One owner went out of town in the middle of winter, leaving his house unheated and pressurized. The water line in his house broke and leaked for quite some time, resulting in a bill of more than $1,000. The utility split the bill among all three owners— a shock to all of them.

The long handle of a curb key (*left*) reaches down into the meter box. The key grips the cutoff valve and turns it on and off.

# Massive Water Users

When you're plumbing a house, ask about the family's need for water. Does it need a larger-than-normal water line or a lot of water for a short period of time, in the morning, say, when everyone wants to take a shower? For most houses, the utility's standard line should be able to handle such needs.

On the other hand, if a house is at the end of the utility line, or it's a very large house with a big family, the utility may not be able to keep up with the demand without a significant drop in pressure and volume because its line to the meter, and perhaps the line to the house, is simply too small. Changing them out for a larger pipe will be extremely expensive.

In most homes, you can meet large short-term water demands without resorting to service lines greater than 1 in. To do this, install several large pressure tanks where the water enters the house, usually in the basement,

**For intermittent large-volume water needs that the utility can't supply without causing a drop in the water pressure, install parallel pressure tanks. To connect into the house piping system, use tank Ts (expensive) or common Ts.**

Larger or deeper **water meters require an inverted plastic culvert as a box.**

Larger water meters, like this 2-in. unit (*top*), come with built-in backflow and water pressure devices and a bypass below the meter. A unit this size will supply a very large house. It comes with about 3 ft. of 2-in. copper pipe extending from the meter box (*bottom*) so the plumber can tie into the water meter line without having to get inside the meter box. Here 2-in. polyvinyl chloride (PVC) is used.

## Parallel pressure tanks

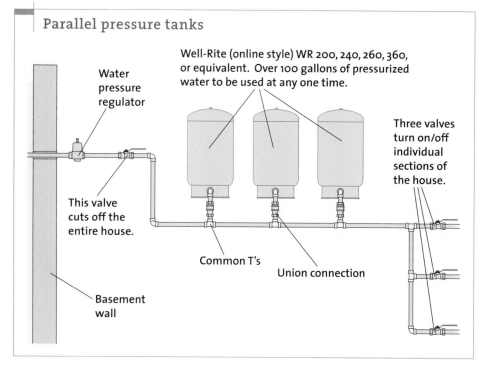

Water pressure regulator

Well-Rite (online style) WR 200, 240, 260, 360, or equivalent. Over 100 gallons of pressurized water to be used at any one time.

Three valves turn on/off individual sections of the house.

This valve cuts off the entire house.

Common T's

Union connection

Basement wall

garage, or other area that has open space. These tanks are about 6 ft. tall and 2 ft. to 3 ft. wide. They are available at most large plumbing supply houses (not at your small local hardware store). To install the tanks, simply pipe them all in parallel (see diagram, p. 52).

For a large new house that requires a massive amount of water, the utility will install a 2-in. meter with a 2-in. copper pipe output. It will be up to you to connect to the copper pipe from the 2-in. service water line.

## Service Pipe

The type of service pipe you take to the house can be polyvinyl chloride (PVC), copper, galvanized, polyethylene, or even extruded

## Comparison of service entrance pipe

| Type of Service Entrance Pipe | Advantages | Disadvantages | Comments |
|---|---|---|---|
| Polyethylene | • Moderately priced<br>• Comes in long rolls<br>• Easy to work with<br>• Noncorrosive<br>• Flexible—can make turns without fittings | • Farm-grade pipe is low quality.<br>• Deteriorates over time when exposed to UV rays<br>• Cannot be laid on rocks<br>• Retains a circular memory | • My favorite |
| Copper | • Comes in rolls or sticks<br>• Not affected by UV<br>• Cannot crack like plastic | • Very expensive<br>• Rolls easily kinked<br>• Aggressive water can eat through pipe over time.<br>• Should not be laid on rocks | • I don't use because it corrodes easily in aggressive water. |
| Galvanized | • Can be laid on rocks<br>• Able to take significant abuse | • Expensive<br>• Requires special knowledge and tools<br>• Cut threads rust easily underground and must be protected.<br>• Comes in 21-ft. lengths<br>• Will rust/corrode from within, reducing its interior diameter | • Outdated |
| PVC | • Easy to work with<br>• Noncorrosive | • Cracks<br>• Comes in 10-ft. to 20-ft. lengths<br>• Tends to leak at threaded joints<br>• Cannot be laid on rocks<br>• Needs fittings to turn corners<br>• Easy to mix/confuse pressure fittings with DWV fittings | • I do not trust PVC for water pressure since male adapters must be glued. Schedule 40 does not come threaded. You must use schedule 80 and then use brass couplings. |
| PEX | • Easy to work with<br>• Noncorrosive<br>• Can be one continuous roll<br>• Flexible—can make turns without fittings | • Hard to obtain in some areas<br>• May require special fittings and tools<br>• Cannot be laid on rocks<br>• Affected by UV | • I have never used PEX for service pipe, but it would be my second choice after polyethylene. |

polyethylene (PEX). PEX, which replaced polybutylene (PB) on the market, is much the same as its cousin polyethylene and just as good. Some plumbers prefer PVC, but I don't. I've seen too many female fittings crack and leak. Copper used to be the standard, but it can only be used in areas where the water is not aggressive. Galvanized has a nasty habit of filling up with rust. I use it only for conduit under driveways and walkways.

Plumbers normally put in the pipe they feel most comfortable with, and for me that is polyethylene at 160-lb. or 200-lb. grade (thickness). I bring in a 1-in. pipe from the meter to the house. (If you know the house under construction is going to use a significant amount of water—more than a family of four might need—and a water meter is not in yet, request the utility install a water meter with 1-in. female threads. If you don't, it will be ¾ in.)

Polyethylene pipe can be either iron pipe size (IPS) or copper tube size (CTS). IPS poly pipe has a larger diameter than does CTS pipe.

I normally use the IPS pipe. Conversion from one to the other can be tricky and requires special fittings, which are available at large plumbing supply houses.

To determine the length of service pipe you will need, measure from the meter to just inside the house. Codes normally require the service pipe to terminate within 5 ft. of where it comes through an outside wall. (continued on p. 58)

**High-density polyethylene** (here, by Vanguard) is a very strong pipe that resists UV damage. Both of these polyethylene pipes, with different diameters, are listed as 1 in. The larger one is listed as IPS and normally should be used; the smaller, which utilities and some hydronic heat systems employ, is CTS.

**The best service** pipe (up to 1½ in.) is common rolled polyethylene (160 lb. or 200 lb.). The entire run from meter to house can be done without couplings, it doesn't rust or corrode, and it's easy to install. For larger diameters, use PVC.

**Galvanized service pipe** often corrodes from within, reducing the water flow to the house. This street elbow was full. The rust in the center of the hole broke away as the elbow was removed from the system.

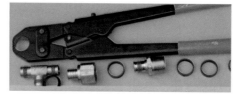

**Crimp rings can** be used on 1-in. CTS pipe. Common crimp fittings (*top*) are suitable, but Vanguard makes the Failsafe gasketed fitting (*bottom*) just for this purpose.

**This transition fitting** (*top*) connects 1-in. IPS pipe (using marine clamps) to CTS pipe using 1-in. crimp rings (*bottom*).

# Insert fittings: the good, the bad, the cheap

There are a number of insert fittings for polyethylene pipe. The worst are the white or translucent ones made from nylon. Nylon is so soft that pipe wrenches grind it away until not much is left. If you tighten nylon fittings with an adjustable wrench they will bend until they're oval and the wrench will slide off. I've seen male adapters bend 45 degrees.

The best insert male adapters are made from stainless steel. Brass insert fittings such as T's and 90s are very good, but quality varies.

I've found leaks through galvanized insert adapters after simply tightening the fitting. The wrench's teeth cut severely into the fitting's body because there are no flat shoulders for the pipe wrench to grab. If the fitting doesn't leak, it will most surely rust heavily at the teeth cuts. This is why I switched to heavy-duty brass and then stainless steel male adapters.

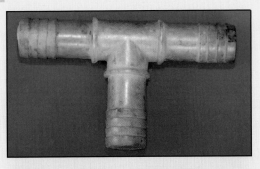

Avoid nylon insert fittings like this one at all costs.

Galvanized fittings are only pretty when new. Over time, they rust heavily.

The male adapter PVC insert fitting with a full shank of barbs (top) does not have squared shoulders for a pipe wrench. The one with just a few barbs (bottom) does. You simply can't win with PVC male adapters.

The pipe wrench teeth marks are readily apparent on the shoulder of this galvanized male adapter. Wrenches cut away the zinc, which causes the fittings to rust and possibly lead to leaks.

Someone tried to stop the leak on this PVC male adapter by adding a second clamp. But the fitting was too short for a second clamp so he tried to pinch off the leak by putting a second clamp in front of the fitting. It didn't work.

# Insert fittings: the good, the bad, the cheap (cont'd.)

Both PVC male adapters on this valve were screwed all the way in, and yet they leaked like gangbusters. By the look of them, they never stopped.

Note the lack of barbs on —these PVC insert fittings. This is why they leak so often.

Long-shank insert adapters are used when more than two clamps are needed to hold the pipe. Use these when the depth of a pump exceeds 300 ft. in a well.

To keep a galvanized fitting from rusting, wrap it with electrical tape, What the water cannot touch, it cannot rust. However, the fitting will still rust from the inside.

Here we have **two brass male adapters**. Only the one on the left is good. The one on the right has no shoulder and has metal partially lathed off.

**This insert fitting** is worth its weight in gold when you need it. It is a brass union insert male adapter. It's used when you have no "play" in the polyethylene pipe and it must be fitted onto a male adapter.

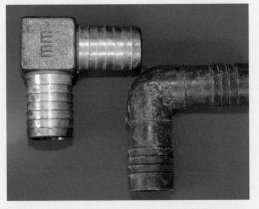

A **brass insert elbow** (*left*) is a more desirable leak-proof and crack-proof fitting than one made of PVC, especially when it's buried. Note the number of barbs.

**Stainless steel male** insert adapters like this one are best.

This is to keep it from being used as water pipe in the house, where it is not approved. Copper and galvanized are the exceptions.

If you use copper or galvanized pipe, it must be part of the grounding system. Assuming there is at least 20 ft. in contact with the ground, code says the metal water service line must be used as a ground rod. It also must have a ground rod as a backup. (Despite the code, in my opinion, metal water lines need to be grounded, not used as the primary ground.) In addition, the point where the ground wire connects the service panel to the water line must be within 3 ft. to 5 ft. of where the pipe enters the building.

When using polyethylene pipe, be wary of the fittings. Some work fine, some work great, and others I would recommend only to my worst enemies. For a comparison, see the table on p. 59, opposite.

### Service pipe leaks

A water bill that suddenly increases or that seems excessive for the amount of water use often indicates a leak. To detect a leak, turn off all the taps in the house and watch the water meter. The dial should not move. If it does, you have a water leak at the meter, along the water line to the house, or in the house. If the dial on the water meter doesn't appear to move, you can't necessarily breathe easy. Keep the water off and check it again in a couple of hours; you might have a slow leak.

Most leaks occur in-house—a running toilet, for example (sometimes you can hear this leak if all is quiet). To determine whether the leak is inside the house or out, turn off the main house cutoff valve. The meter should now stop. If it doesn't, the leak is outside. Look for soggy ground or, in the winter, for a spot where the snow has melted. Don't depend entirely on either signal, however. The water may be going deeper underground, not coming to the surface.

Usually a leak will be at the meter itself or in the line going to the house, especially if it is old galvanized. You'll probably see some standing water around the meter. If there is no water,

Metal water service pipe has to be connected to the service panel ground bus. This prevents it from becoming a conductor if a hot wire accidentally touches it and allows the breaker to kick. The connection is normally within 5 ft. of where the pipe enters the building.

## Comparing insert fitting material

| Insert Fitting Material | Advantages | Disadvantages | Comments |
|---|---|---|---|
| Nylon | • Low cost | • Soft<br>• Easily damaged by pipe wrenches | Do not install under any circumstances. |
| PVC | • Low cost | • Cracks easily<br>• Male adapter may have no shoulder for the pipe wrench | These fittings are getting smaller and cheaper. I won't install them in a pressurized system. |
| Galvanized steel | • Moderate cost | • No raised area on a male adapter for a pipe wrench to grab onto<br>• Wrench teeth must cut into the zinc coating, which weakens the fitting<br>• Will rust. Once installed, wrap the fitting with electrical tape—the fitting will not rust, at least from the outside. | These fittings are cheaper because they have only a thin zinc coating. I've had fittings rust through within six months. |
| Brass | • Doesn't corrode like galvanized steel<br>• Doesn't crack like plastic<br>• Male adapter has a shoulder for the pipe wrench | • Expensive<br>• Will corrode if the water is aggressive<br>• Some manufacturers did not design a shoulder for a pipe wrench; wrench's teeth have to cut into fitting as it is tightened. | Good fittings. Avoid brass male adapters that do not have raised shoulders for a pipe wrench. I had one fitting that was cut all the way through by a wrench and leaked. |
| Stainless steel | • Doesn't corrode or rust<br>• Doesn't crack like plastic<br>• Male adapter has a shoulder for the pipe wrench | • Expensive | The only male adapter insert fitting I now install—unless I can find good brass fittings with raised shoulders. |

the house valve is off, and the dial on the water meter is moving, the leak is in the line to the house. The entire line should be replaced.

## Sleeving the Pipe

Code normally requires a sleeve that is two pipe sizes larger than the interior pipe (for example, a 1½-in. sleeve for a 1-in. pipe). The purpose of the sleeve is to keep the service pipe from coming in direct contact with rough-edged concrete, which can cut into the pipe. In addition, sleeved pipe is more easily replaced.

If a wall is going to be poured, install a sleeve before or during the pour to eliminate the need to drill later. (When you pour the concrete, cover the open ends of the pipe with duct tape.) For solid concrete walls that are already up, use a coring bit.

When the sleeve is in place and the pipe is in it, the job is still not finished. *It is absolutely imperative* that the dirt under the pipe is tamped, and tamped hard, several feet out from the wall. If the dirt is simply thrown in the hole, there is a high chance of pipe (continued on p. 62)

# Sleeving the Pipe

I use my 1½-in. hammer drill with drill bit–type spline bits to get through hollow concrete block or slabs. For going through thick, solid concrete, you can rent core bits.

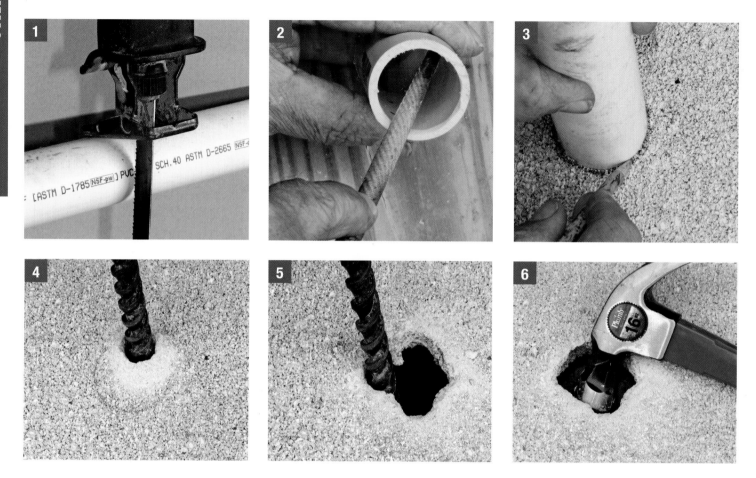

**1** | Cut the PVC sleeve to the width of the block (normally 7⅝ in.).

**2** | File the inside edge down with a rat-tail file.

**3** | Place the pipe's end against the hollow core of the block where you need to punch through and draw a line around it.

**4** | Drill a hole on the line.

**5** | Follow through by drilling several holes around the line.

**6** | Use a hammer to knock out the hole to fit the pipe.

7 | Repeat steps 5–8 for the other side of a block wall. Slide the sleeve into the block hole.

8 | Slide the pipe through the sleeve.

9 | Caulk around both pipe and sleeve.

## Cutting through hollow-core block

**To cut through common hollow-core block, always break through one of the hollow cavities, not the solid area. Follow these dimensions.**

Common 8 x 8 x 16 hollow-cavity concrete block

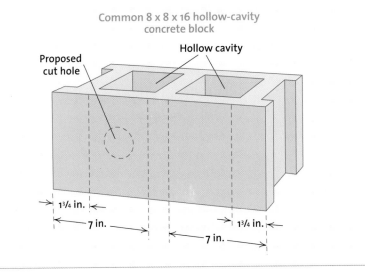

When taking the **service pipe** into the basement, be sure to tamp the soil down heavily under the service pipe where the pipe goes through the wall. Not doing so can cause pipe failure within 3 ft. of the basement wall.

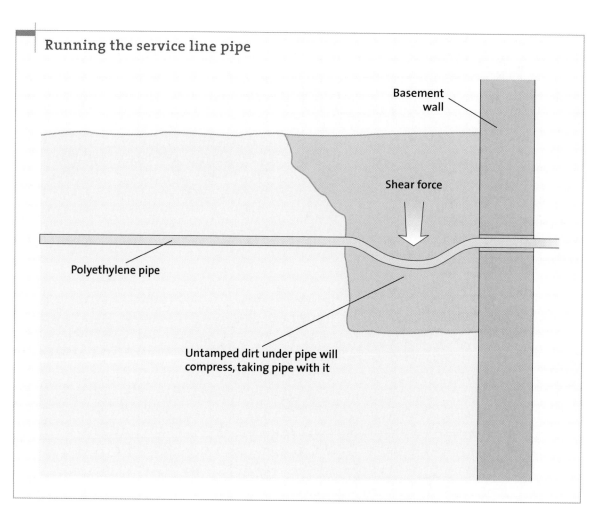

**Running the service line pipe**

Basement wall

Shear force

Polyethylene pipe

Untamped dirt under pipe will compress, taking pipe with it

shear as the dirt under the pipe settles and the pipe is pushed down by the dirt overhead. This shear will eventually split the pipe.

## Valves

Many valves have been developed for plumbing over the years. Today, for common on/off valves, we need only be concerned with two types: **ball** and **gate**. Two other types of valves are required in some areas and are perhaps even more important: a **dual-check** and a **pressure-relief valve**. Their function is not necessarily on/off but is just as important if not more so.

### Ball and gate valves

The main cutoff valve is always a ball valve or a gate valve, according to code, as is the on/off valve above the water heater. These valves are called full-flow valves because they do not reduce the water flow into the house as other types of valve would.

The gate valve, however, has two major design problems: the seating of the gate into the valve body and the screw shaft itself, from handle to gate. As its name indicates, the valve opens and closes with a gate that slides up and down. If the valve is installed horizontally,

Stop and waste valve (*right*) and globe valve (*center*) have major built-in blockages (*left*) that significantly impede the flow of water.

Gate valves are full-flow valves (*left*) but are problematic. The shaft to the gate is within the water flow of the pipe, meaning it has a habit of corroding through and breaking off, usually at the worst times. The gate valves are shown in their open (*center*) and closed (*right*) positions.

All ball valves are not the same. This low-quality one, with very little metal, split right down the middle when a threaded pipe was screwed into it.

Ball valves are the best choice for the main cutoff and for other valves in the main line. They have a rotating hollow stainless steel ball connected to a lever handle. Note how thick the walls are around the female threads; this is what to look for.

debris lying along the pipe and valve bottom may stop the valve from closing all the way in an emergency. In some cases, the water coming through might prevent you from soldering a pipe. The screw shaft, which is always in the water, often corrodes. Sometimes it is weakened to the point that, as soon as the gate seats into the valve bottom, the shaft snaps, permanently closing the valve. Other times the shaft is already eaten through and, as you attempt to turn off the water, nothing happens. For these reasons, I do not install gate valves.

Ball valves are the only full-flow valves I install. Though they're expensive, they are durable, and the on/off mechanism takes only a quick twist of the wrist. When the lever handle is in line with the valve body, the handle is on,

and when it is at a 90-degree angle with the valve body, it is off (no more turn, turn, turn). You must install the valve with room for the handle to turn—you do not want a wall in the way.

All ball valves are not created equal. I've seen some of these with shoulders so thin and cheap that the female threads on both sides of the valve body would split open as a pipe nipple was screwed in. I've always thought plumbing was hard enough without having the parts fail on me. To test a valve, lift it in your hand—it should be heavy, not light. Look at the threaded shoulder—it should be thick, not thin.

## Pressure-reducing valves

Pressure-reducing valves are really regulators, not valves. Once the utility water gets into the house you will need to lower its pressure if it exceeds what your local codes allow, typically, 70 psi to 80 psi. Use a water-pressure-reducing valve. The pressure limit is adjustable so you can set it at the maximum pressure allowed by your local code.

If your in-house pressure exceeds this maximum, the water heater temperature and pressure (T&P) relief valve will sputter and drip when the water heater turns on. I had a service call once where it turned out that all the houses on a street had this problem. This just happened to coincide with a brand-new city water tank coming online, built at the top of a hill above the homes. I had to install a pressure-reducing valve in every house on the block.

Water-pressure-reducing valves have a variety of end connections, including female threads, solder, CPVC, and PEX. On the bottom of the device is a large removable brass screw. This allows you to clean the integral screen. Before there were screens on the valves, they would stick and couldn't be adjusted. If you start to lose water pressure in a house, check the removable screen to see if it is blocked. Because all the incoming water goes through this screen, it will plug up with silt if a utility crew working on the line allows debris into the system.

Do not bury this valve outside at the water meter. This device, along with the backflow preventer, must be accessible in case it has to be replaced. I normally install both valves immediately after the ball valve inside the house. This allows me to cut the water off for maintenance or replacement.

In warm climates, such as Florida, things are done differently. Because there are no freezing problems, these devices are sometimes outside of the house sticking up out of the ground like an upside-down U.

## Dual check valves

A dual check valve (an anti-backflow device) is required by most national and international codes. However, I see few installed in new housing. The dual check valve is a one-way device to keep water, once it enters the house, from flowing back out into the main water line up and down the street. Without it, tainted

Install a dual check valve right after the main house cutoff valve. It prevents in-house water from flowing back into the city water mains and possibly contaminating them.

water (perhaps from household or garden chemicals) can go back into the main city water lines, if there is a main line break or temporary low pressure, and contaminate water to other houses.

Every house water line either has or should have a backflow preventer. If city water lines are contaminated due to the lack of an anti-backflow device, a home owner may be legally responsible for the cost to remove the tainted water as well as the replacement of the lines.

Some areas also require a dual check on well water systems. Underground water can be contaminated just as easily as city water and, when it occurs, it affects a large number of people. In Virginia, for example, a community's water supply was contaminated by a chrome-plating plant. A neighboring utility extended service to the community because the aquifer was contaminated.

REMODELING

REMODELING | Installing a Remote Hydrant

Often people want an outside water hydrant in the garden or pond area, or perhaps in an area for washing cars or near a pool. With a hydrant in the work task area they don't have to pull 100 ft. of hose around. The hydrant's water line can cut into the main line to the house from the utility meter or be on a separate line from the house.

We refer to these hydrants by their installation depth. For example, I might ask for "a 2-ft. bury outside hydrant." This means the depth of the ditch is 2 ft., which is the frost line where I live here in Virginia. If the ditch is 3 ft. deep, I would ask for a 3-ft. bury. Installing one is easy. Here are a couple of tips:

There is a valve opening at the bottom of the hydrant. This drains the column of water left in the vertical pipe after the hydrant is shut off (the seal is at the bottom of the vertical column). Do not tamp dirt against this hole—it must remain open for gravity to drain out the water. Allocate one or two 5-gal. buckets of gravel for use around this drain opening.

Rather than spend time putting together a large number of fittings under the hydrant to interface with my pipe, I use only one fitting.

The hydrant pipe opening at the bottom of the column is 3/4-in. female threads pointing straight down. Plastic and galvanized fittings going into the hydrant are known to leak. Plastic sometimes cracks due to movement of the hydrant, and the galvanized easily rusts through at the threads because of water trickling down from the hydrant. That's why the only fitting I use (for polyethylene pipe) is a solid brass insert T with 3/4 -in. threads pointing straight up, seen as an inset in the photo at left. It is indestructible.

For end-of-run hydrant installations, I use a brass elbow fitting.

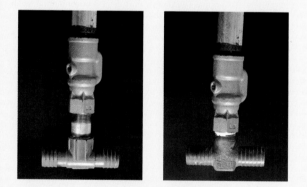

Two options for plumbing in-line outside hydrants: galvanized nipples (*left*) often rust through at the threads; the one-piece brass T. (*right*) consists of 3/4-in. male thread top center and polyethylene insert on both sides.

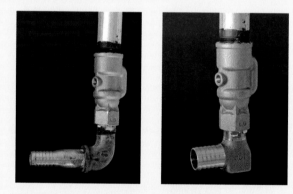

The hydrant on the left was prone to leaking after only a few years due to rusting of the fitting's threads. A better choice for plumbing end-of-run outside hydrants is a one-piece brass elbow (*right*). It has 3/4-in. threads to screw into the hydrant; the opposite end is polyethylene insert.

# Boosting Water Pressure

Some city homes have very low water pressure. Typically, these houses are at the end of a utility line and have to deal with whatever leftover utility pressure there is. Although the utility can't increase its line pressure for fear of blowing out the homes at the beginning of the line, the low-pressure problem is easy to remedy by cutting in a booster pump.

You can find premade systems that include jet pumps with little tanks, but I prefer to make my own using a Jacuzzi® 5RP2 jet pump and a Well Rite tank. The tanks on the premade systems are too small. You want as large a tank as you can afford to minimize the water pressure changes, especially in the shower. In addition, with a larger-capacity tank, the pump will turn on less frequently, reducing noise and electricity use.

Since water is forced into the jet pump by the utility, the pump does not need to be primed and it doesn't have to work too hard to raise the pressure. Given that, you can install a used pump if you desire. You'll sometimes find them in classified ads.

## Cartridge Filters

These filters are the first line of defense against debris and iron in the water. They keep the washer and dishwasher screens, as well as the aerators on the faucets, from becoming clogged.

Low-cost filters are pleated paper. I don't recommend them because (continued on p. 74)

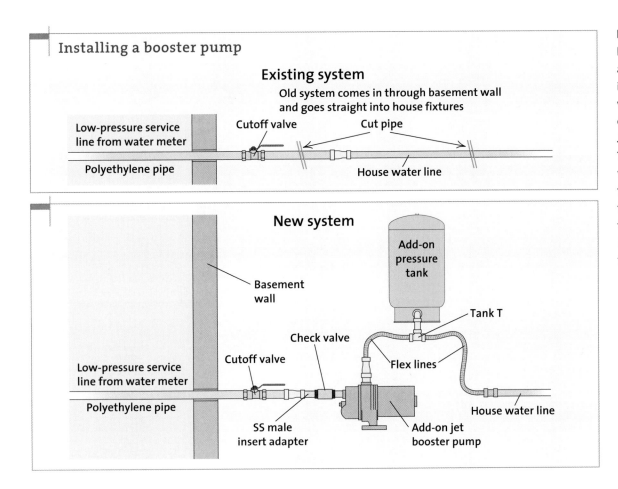

**Installing a booster pump**

**Existing system**

Old system comes in through basement wall and goes straight into house fixtures

Low-pressure service line from water meter

Cutoff valve — Cut pipe

Polyethylene pipe

House water line

**New system**

Add-on pressure tank

Basement wall

Tank T

Check valve

Flex lines

Cutoff valve

Low-pressure service line from water meter

Polyethylene pipe

SS male insert adapter

Add-on jet booster pump

House water line

For those who have low city water pressure, a booster pump will increase the in-house water pressure considerably. I usually use a Jacuzzi 5RP2 jet pump. The top diagram shows where to cut the pipe to install the pump and tank on an existing system. The diagram on the bottom illustrates the finished installation.

# Preparing a used jet pump for a booster pump

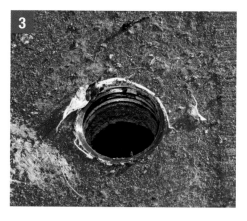

## QUICK REFERENCE

**CHECK VALVES  p. 51**
For information about turning the house water off

**PRESSURE  p. 67**
For information on increasing water pressure

**VALVES  p. 62**
For information on valves

**JET PUMPS  p. 67**
For information on jet pump installation

**1** Examine the used pump for physical damage. This pump has a broken gauge.

**2** Using a small adjustable wrench, remove the gauge by turning it counter-clockwise.

**3** Once the gauge is removed, look into the small threaded hole to see that it's not plugged up with rust. If it is partially plugged, as this one was, punch it out with a piece of wire.

**4** Attach a check valve and an interface fitting (in the front of the pump's head) for the service pipe you are cutting the pump into. Here, I am installing a stainless steel insert adapter to interface with polyethylene.

**5** The galvanized pipe coming out of the top of the pump's head (which goes to the house plumbing) was cut so I have to remove it. Adding heat to the female bushing will expand the bushing, breaking the rust bond between the bushing and the pipe for easier removal.

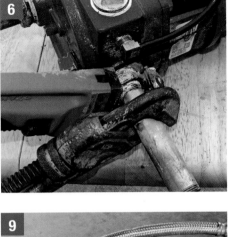

**6** The heated bushing has now expanded and the ¾-in. pipe will easily come off.

**7** I install a new ¾-in. galvanized nipple in the pump head and add a ¾-in. flexible stainless steel braided pipe for the interface.

**8** Using an adjustable wrench, install the new gauge.

**9** Once all the broken pieces have been replaced on the pump, plumb in the finished product.

they often disintegrate in the water system, sending pieces of paper through the lines. Among the many other kinds, I recommend only string filters or the solid block filters that look like white carbon filters. Both are moderately priced and do their job without adding more debris to the water. You will know when they get clogged—the water pressure will drop.

Carbon filters remove the finer grains of debris in the water, including iron particles. A 5-micron filter (the lower the micron number the finer the filter) will get out almost everything, but you will need to replace it quite regularly at $5 each. Most people settle for 5-micron filters. These get most of the iron out, and don't need replacing as frequently. I suggest starting with a 5-micron filter, and if the iron still gets through (you'll know because the toilet tanks and bowls will be stained red), then work down to a 1-micron filter. In the worst case, you will have to abandon the cartridge filter and install a backwashing filter type of water conditioner.

When you select a filter, look for one whose head is labeled BYPASS, OFF, FILTER (or ON). When the filter is on the BYPASS setting, the water flows through the head and not the filter. OFF closes valves both inside and outside the filter. When it's set to FILTER, the water flows through the filter before it goes to the house. Next check for a housing that unscrews readily so you can easily replace the cartridge. Finally, look for a filter with metal—normally brass or stainless steel—inserts for the water lines.

Mount the filter close to where the water comes into the house. And remember, you have to be able to get to the filter to change it, so its location should be about chest height and not behind an immovable object.

The most common mistake I see when someone puts in a cartridge filter is that it is not

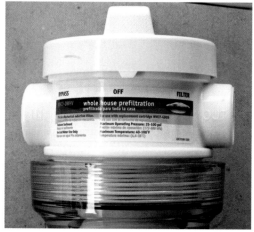

**When shopping for a cartridge filter, look for one that has an OFF-BYPASS-FILTER setting on its head, brass inserts, and a housing that is easily removed.**

properly secured. If it is not properly secured, you cannot change the filter. (See "Securing a Cartridge Filter," p. 71, opposite.)

## Replacing a filter

To change a filter, first turn the head to OFF or BYPASS. Release the water pressure by pressing the big red button on top of the filter head, if it has one. Otherwise, do what I do: Turn on any cold-water spigot in the house to release the pressure and then turn it off again. If you have a hard time unscrewing the filter housing the pressure has not been released.

# Securing a cartridge filter

There are three rules for installing a cartridge filter: secure it, secure it, secure it. If it's loose, you cannot change the filter. I use common angle brackets to secure a cartridge filter.

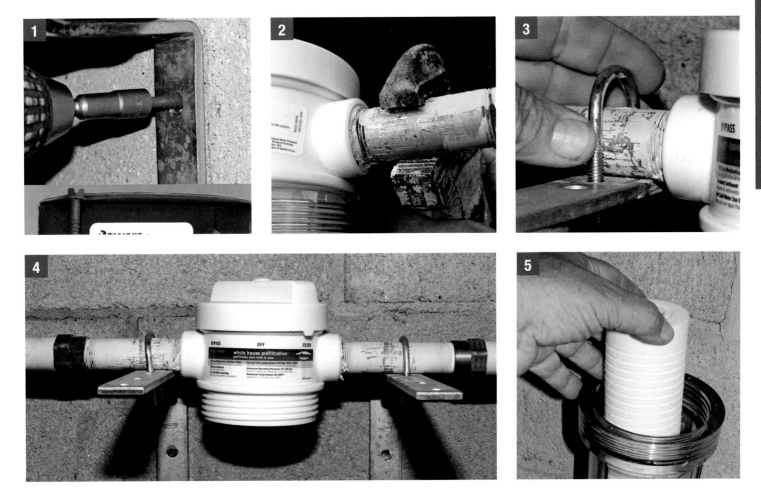

**QUICK REFERENCE**

CURB KEY p. 50
For information about turning the house water off

BALL VALVES p. 63
For information about ball valves

CARTRIDGES p. 67
For information on pleated paper filters

WATER USE p. 67
For information on increasing water pressure

**1** In concrete, use $5/16$-in.-drive hex-head $1/4$-in. concrete screws. In wood, use $5/16$-in. hex-head screws. Place the brackets about 9 in. apart. If against drywall, secure angle brackets into the studs or on a 20-in. $1 \times 8$ or $2 \times 8$ board.

**2** Screw a long $3/4$-in. nipple tight into the female threads on both sides of the filter. Copper pipe needs no nipples.

**3** Place the nipples on top of the mounted angle brackets and use horseshoe bolts to tighten them down. Drill bracket, if necessary.

**4** Keep the filter head a couple of inches away from the wall.

**5** Install cartridge of choice. The most-popular cartridges are 5-micron filters.

## Parallel filters

**M**ost plumbing experts agree that the common cartridge filters used and available everywhere are too small in surface area to make them suitable for a residence. Their opinions are verified by the many times it's necessary to change out a filter. Fortunately, larger cartridge filters are available at professional stores. Some of these are super wide, others are super tall. The problem here is that these filter media cartridges are more expensive than the common ones and often are hard to find.

To double the time between cartridge change outs, all all that's necessary is to plumb two filters in parallel. As one filter clogs up, water will go through the other. This system allows you to keep the advantage of using the commonly available filter cartridges and save money.

The one cartridge filter at the pro store that does make sense is the slender one that is twice as tall as the more-common cartridge filters. This model uses two common cartridge filters stacked one above the other. Using it allows you to install just one filter housing but have the capacity of two filters inside—both of them the commonly available cartridge filters.

# Working with In-house Pipe

**Y**ears ago, when my uncle taught me the trade, galvanized and copper were the only pipes he put in people's houses. Sometime later, along came CPVC, or plastic pipe. After that came polybutylene, or PB. Now we have PEX.

Why all the different pipes? Because there is no such thing as a perfect pipe—though they keep trying to invent one. Galvanized had problems. Copper was better, but it had other problems, which CPVC solved. PB was the first truly flexible pipe, but it was eventually banned in the United States. PEX, a polyethylene derivative, replaced PB, though it is a little stiffer. The perfect pipe exists only in dreams. A good plumber learns to work around a particular pipe's disadvantages to give the customer a good plumbing job.

In this chapter I show you how to work with the multitude of in-house pipes commonly found in residential plumbing. I discuss the advantages and disadvantages of each so you can make your own decision on which to use in your particular job (codes allowing). For an easy reference describing the pros and cons of in-house pipe choices that will guide you, see the Comparision of In-house Water Lines table, p. 238.

# In-house Pipe Choices

## Working with Galvanized

I doubt if you'll want to fully pipe a house with galvanized. That went out in the 1950s. To plumb with galvanized, you would need special equipment—pipe threaders, giant dies and pipe cutters, cutting oil, and the like. Plus, it would cost a fortune. Plumbing with galvanized is becoming a lost art. There is a lot of math involved when you have to figure how long a pipe will be after you've turned the fitting onto a pipe by a certain number of turns. Being close doesn't count when you get to the last

**Most commonly used galvanized fittings.**

| | | |
|---|---|---|
| A—Street 90 | F—Street 45 | K—Cap |
| B—90 | G—T | L—Cross |
| C—Reducing coupling | H—Reducing T | M—Reducing T |
| D—Coupling | I—Reducing bushing | |
| E—45 | J—Plug | |

# Unions

**Ever get confused** about which way to turn a union? I did, too—until I came up with this system.

**One side of a union has threads showing (on the body—not the IPS female threads), the other doesn't, and both sides of the union have female threads that screw onto a pipe. The center collar does not attach to any pipe; it screws onto the main union body. You can't loosen the union by turning either of the big flat shoulders;** these will be screwed into the pipes of the system. If you turn these, you will be physically trying to push back all the pipes of the plumbing system.

Union threads

Threads

No threads

Threads

**The only way** to loosen a union is to hold one or both shoulders and turn the collar. But which way? If you face the union threads, turn the collar clockwise to loosen. If you face the collar side, turn the collar counter-clockwise. If you want to tighten, simply go the opposite way.

No union threads: turn collar counter-clockwise

Union threads: turn collar clockwise

Union threads: turn collar clockwise

**The union test.** If you can figure out which way to turn the collar to remove them on these three unions, you're ready to work with unions on the job. Hint: Look for the threads, or absence of threads, at the arrows. Both end unions have union threads (straight arrows). If you see union threads, turn the collar clockwise (curved arrows). If there are no threads, turn counter-clockwise.

fitting and the pipe is a bit too short or too long. Galvanized is still useful in some situations. I use 1½-in. galvanized pipe as conduit under driveways and sidewalks or in situations where a pipe may come in for extreme wear and tear (like a car hitting it). Of course, we use galvanized nipples and short sections of galvanized pipe for all plumbing systems. For purposes other than plumbing, it's used as stair railing and as clothes rods in closets.

## Pipe and fittings

Most plumbing stores stock precut and threaded galvanized pipe in sections 4 ft. and under. Many old-time hardware stores will cut and thread pipe to order.

When you work with galvanized pipe, you'll need nipples and fittings of all sizes. I have a container for 1 in., ¾ in., and ½ in., with another for reducing bushings and couplings. Stay away from plastic bushings—my experience is that they crack, sometimes immediately, sometimes a year later. Over the last several years I have added brass nipples and fittings to my stock, which I use underground and in areas of high visibility.

Nipples come in ½-in. increments from all-thread up to 6 in. I keep every size in stock on my truck. Tightening short nipples—especially all-thread—is a problem. With threads along all or most of the nipples' length, there's no place to attach a pipe wrench that won't mess up the threads. Get around that by grabbing the fitting—not the nipple—with the wrench. If that's not possible, use a smaller pipe wrench, which has a narrower jaw. In worst-case situations, I have had to grind down the jaw of the pipe wrench. There will be times when you simply have to screw up the thread to get the nipple in—and then hope for the best.

**You'll be using galvanized and brass fittings which-ever piping system you use. Keep separate containers for 1-in., ¾-in., and ½-in. fittings, and another full of reducer bushings.**

Cut pipe faster by cutting at the threads; when they are cut into the pipe, they reduce the thickness of the metal walls you cut through.

The biggest problem with galvanized pipe and fittings is keeping rust and dirt out of the threads. Never install a nipple or fitting that has rusty or dirty threads. If you do, the nipple won't thread deep enough into the fitting and it may leak. To keep dirt out of a pipe nipple, wrap electrical tape once around it. If the nipple comes in a plastic wrap, leave it on until you need the nipple. To get the rust and dirt out of nipple threads, use a circular brass wire brush that fits into a cordless drill. A bench grinder with a wire brush works well for cleaning male threads, but it is not portable. To clean female fittings, use an old wire brush or tap.

## Thread lube

Regardless of the type of pipe—galvanized, brass, or copper—if it has threads, it needs some type of thread lube. The lubricant's purpose is twofold. If the male and female threads seize before the fitting is tight, there will be a leak. The lube allows the nipple to go deeper into the fitting, avoiding the problem. In addition, the compound keeps the threads from rusting together so removing the fitting will be less problematic.

Choose between a paste, which comes in a can or tube, or Teflon tape, available on rolls in ½-in. and ¾-in. widths. When Teflon tape first came out it was locked in safes to keep employees from stealing it. Now, it's commonly available in plumbing and hardware stores. The problem is that it's made so thin, you can see through it, which almost makes it useless as a thread lube. Also, you have to wrap the tape clockwise (as you face the threaded end of the pipe) or it will unwrap as the fitting is turned onto the threads. And I always have problems with it because it tends to bunch together and twist into a string once

Tape or paste? I prefer paste. Tape is too thin, it shreds easily, and it stretches into string.

It always pays to have a variety of pipe nipples on hand because you never know ahead of time the length you will need. They come in ½-in. increments from 6 in. to all-thread.

Always protect the threads of the pipe from damage. Otherwise, they will become banged up and rust like the one on the right.

If the pipe is being used as an electrical ground, call an electrician to install ground rods or separate grounding electrodes

## EZ outs

EZ-outs are those weird-looking things that we use to remove a broken pipe or a stuck bushing from a T or other fitting. You need a variety of sizes to deal with different-diameter fittings.

The two most common EZ-out designs are the tapered straight-in kind and those with spirals for threads. To use the former, simply smash it into the broken pipe and then turn it counter- clockwise. (You may need lots of leverage). If the EZ-out catches, the broken fitting will either disintegrate or come out in the threads. If it disintegrates, you will need a tiny screwdriver to clean out the female threads. The spiral EZ-out is best. As you turn it counter-clockwise, its threads bite deeper into the broken fitting until it comes out or breaks apart. Any type of EZ-out is important to have if a galvanized pipe breaks in a water heater's cold or hot outlets or if a plastic water heater drain valve snaps off in the heater. You have to either get the fitting out or buy a new water heater.

There are two problems with EZ-outs. First is the length: If the EZ-out bottoms out on the fitting before it unscrews it, you won't be able to remove any lodged-in piece. You can try a smaller-diameter, shorter EZ-out, but that rarely works. You have to drill out the broken fitting, being careful not to destroy the female threads, and pick the metal out of the female threads. The second problem is removing a broken fitting from the EZ-out once you get it removed from the fitting. If it is really stuck, you have to heat it to expand it and then try to screw it off.

I keep a lot of EZ outs on hand for whenever a pipe breaks off inside a fitting. I prefer the spiral type—they seem to work better than the square kind.

You'll need a handle to tighten the EZ out. You can use the tap-type handle, but it doesn't have much leverage. An adjustable wrench is the most common choice.

Once out, the broken piece is sometimes hard to get off the EZ out. After heating and expanding it, I use a pipe wrench to get it off.

it is off the roll. Then I have to cut that part off and throw it away. But paste is not perfect: It can get messy, and it's impossible to get out of clothes. When I work with paste I always have a rag handy to wipe my hands and the fitting. And yet, I still sometimes look a mess, with dried white paste on my hands and clothes.

Use heat to expand and remove a rusted-on galvanized fitting from a pipe or nipple.

Sometimes you have to cut into the threads of the nipple to install it as is the case for this all-thread. Here, we can only hope for the best. Sometimes it leaks, sometimes it doesn't.

When working with nipples, whenever possible use a pipe wrench that has a jaw width narrow enough that it doesn't cut into the nipple's threads.

When old galvanized pipe needs to be replaced, it's best to change all the pipe, not just parts of it. If you don't, the recip saw you use to cut out the pipe will break loose iron particles in the pipe and send them throughout the plumbing, damaging washer solenoids, clogging screens, and generally wreaking havoc.

Both of these pipes are rated at ¹/₂ in. The galvanized pipe is significantly larger than ¹/₂ in. (the copper pipe is exactly ¹/₂-in. interior diameter.) The galvanized pipe is larger because rust will build up in it and reduce its interior diameter.

## Working with Copper

Besides galvanized, copper is the pipe that we old-timers cut our teeth on. It has been getting bad press in recent years because aggressive water eats it up. This is news only to the younger generation. It's always been a problem with copper in some areas of the country. The solution is simple: Do not install copper if you have acid or active water unless you condition the water with an acid neutralizer first. If you have an old system and the pipe is getting pinhole leaks, simply replace the system with a non-copper pipe or put copper back in along with an acid-neutralizer system.

## Grades of copper

Copper comes in rolls (called "soft copper") and sticks ("hard" or "rigid copper"). Soft copper is often referred to as "tubing," and hard copper is generally called "stick pipe." There are three grades, or thicknesses, of copper: K, which has green lettering on the pipe, is the thickest, followed by L (with blue lettering), and M (red lettering), which is the thinnest. Grade K is too expensive for common residential use. Grades L and M are the common choices. Low bidders usually use the thinnest copper.

**Most commonly used** copper fittings. A—Reducing 90, B—Coupling, C—Reducing coupling, D—Elbow or 90, E, H, and L—Reducing T, F—Drop-ear elbow, G—T, I—45, J—Male adapter, K—Street elbow, M—Street 45, N—Female adapter

## Bending copper

Soft copper is meant to be bent, but it often kinks. When a pipe kinks, it's best to discard that section. If the bend is just slightly oval, you can salvage the pipe if you have a good flaring tool. To prevent the problem in the first place, use a spring-type bending tool that slips over the pipe. It spreads the bending pressure over a longer section of pipe to prevent kinking. I've also used electrical conduit tubing benders. For tiny copper tubing use a copper bender (available at all plumbing stores) made just for that purpose.

## Diameter references

Copper comes in both inside-diameter (ID) and outside-diameter (OD) references. Plumbers use ID references, while HVAC installers use OD for the same pipe. The common ½-in. copper pipe used in residential plumbing is referred to as ⅝-in. tubing in the HVAC trade.

## Cutting copper

Cutting copper with a toothed blade usually leaves a mess of jagged metal and a rough edge—unless a very fine-toothed blade is used. A tubing cutter is a better choice. Even this isn't perfect though: Its cutter head leaves a ridge on the inside of the pipe, which needs to be removed. You are supposed to use the little knife that is hidden within most tubing cutters, but I always wind up gouging the pipe and never quite getting the edge smooth. Instead, I opt for a stepped drill bit commonly used in the electrical trade to cut steel and open up conduit holes. I simply pop it into my cordless drill and push it into the cut end of the pipe. It gives me a nice smooth ream-type cut.

Avoid poorly designed tubing cutters. You'll know you have one if it tracks around the pipe.

Save your old (bent wire) copper cleaning brushes for cleaning up threads on male and female threaded fittings.

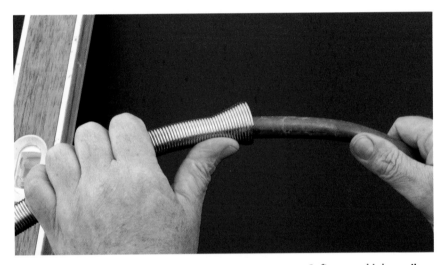

Soft copper kinks easily when it's bent. To prevent this, use a spring-type pipe bender that slips over the pipe and spreads the bending stress over several inches.

There are three grades or thicknesses of copper pipe. From left to right: M, the thinnest; L, the middle grade; and K, the thickest.

A newly cut pipe (*left*) is not quite ready to use. Tubing cutters leave a rounded ridge on the inside of the pipe that needs to be reamed out (*right*).

# Flaring copper pipe

Flaring copper pipe is just another way to splice or tap into soft copper. To flare pipe, use a special tool to bend the end open like a flower. The fittings made to mate with the flared pipe are called flare fittings. They can be used for both water and gas.

A flare fitting has a 45-degree taper on its nose.

Avoid thin-walled caps (*left*). Instead, use only thick-walled caps (*right*).

To flare, I use only a high quality Ridgid flaring tool (*top*) that breaks over and ratchets as the perfect flare is obtained. To allow the numbers (½ in, ⅜ in., etc.) and alignment indents on the tool to be easier seen in dim light, I filled their depressions with red fingernail polish (*bottom*).

Beware of cheap anodized aluminum flare fittings. They corrode severely and should be banned.

Use only heavy-duty solid brass flare fittings.

The cutter head should stay in one track and shouldn't wobble. If the pipe has multiple tracks or the head wobbles, throw the cutter away.

The length of the handle is very important in tubing cutters. You need both short- and long-handled cutters. A long handle gives you leverage, but you'll want a short handle in tight spots so it doesn't hit other pipes, the joists or the wall as it goes around. The cutter with the shortest handle is General's snap-around AutoCut. RIDGID's mini–tubing cutter is the standard of the industry, but its tightening wheel is poorly designed. As all plumbers know, you have to use pliers to tighten it because it hurts your fingers, but we use it because we need it. My favorite tubing cutter is a Reed's. It has a button you push to zip the cutter head immediately up against the pipe—no more turning of the handle.

Despite their different designs, all tubing cutters have two problems. They cannot cut a small piece of copper off a pipe end, and they cannot cut flush to a wall. To cut such pipe, I use my mini reciprocating saw. Its thin blade and fine teeth minimize jerking, and its short stroke keeps it from hitting the wall.

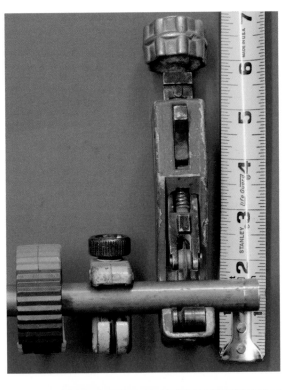

A few personal tubing cutters. Left: a snap-around AutoCut™ made by General Pipe Cleaners. Center: a common RIDGID mini cutter (you'll need pliers to turn the tiny thumb wheel); get the model that cuts both ½-in. and ¾-in. pipe. Right: a Reed cutter. The longer the handle, the easier the cut, but long handles can get in the way of other pipe and joists, making mini cutters and AutoCut necessary tools.

The Reed cutter has a pushbutton that allows the cutter wheel to go straight to the pipe without a turn of the handle. When the lever (painted yellow) on the handle is up (photo 1), the cutter operates as any other cutter; turn the handle and the cutter head mechanism goes in slowly toward the pipe. When the lever is pushed down (photo 2), this gear mechanism is released and the entire handle and cutter head can zip straight in to the pipe (photo 3). Release the button (it will pop back up) and start turning the handle for the cut (photo 4).

A single cutting track is what you want. A cheap or broken tubing cutter will not make one track around the pipe as seen here, but will wobble and leave several tracks.

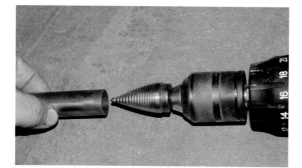

The blade that **folds out on some tubing cutters (*bottom*) is used to ream out the inside of the pipe, but I have never had much luck with it. Instead, I use a stepped bit that is designed to cut steel. I simply install it in my cordless drill and press it onto the pipe (*top*).**

## Sweating a pipe

There are three rules to properly sweating a joint: cut clean, ream clean, sand clean. Using a good cutter will make a good clean cut. And using my method of reaming assures you of a good ream. That brings us to properly cleaning both the pipe and fitting. Many people think that just because a new fitting is bright and shiny, it is clean. It is not. It still has oils and oxides on the surface. To be truly clean, it must be wire-brushed or cleaned with sandpaper, which we call plumber's cloth.

Before you sweat a pipe, obtain the proper solder and flux. If you get the flux too hot (and that is easy to do), it burns and blackens. Have the sweating temperature too cold or too hot and you mess up the sweat joint. Plumbers will tell you only other plumbers do this. I'll be one of the few to admit it: I have screwed up a few sweat joints in my lifetime. Well, maybe even more than a few. But that was before I found my famous duo. (I came across a flux that is hard to burn and tins the joint. Tinning the joint makes

A tubing cutter, **no matter how good, cannot cut really close to the edge of a pipe because of design limitations.**

A mini recip **saw can cut a tiny sliver off a copper pipe (*left*) as well as cut a copper pipe flush to the wall (*right*).**

the solder flow faster and more evenly. The solder is just as great. Compared to common off-the-shelf solder, its working temperature spans a wide range, which means overheating or underheating are unlikely, and it has a lower melting point.) Now all my sweat joints go off like clockwork. (continued on p. 89)

You must get all the water out of a copper water line before you solder it. Otherwise the water will absorb the heat and the copper cannot reach the melting temperature of the solder.

## Unsweating Copper

There are times when we change our minds and have to install a different sweat fitting, such as changing a T to an elbow. To do this, apply the flame to the fitting (not the pipe, and wear safety glasses and gloves). The fitting will heat up and melt the solder that binds it to the pipe.

If solder is visible on the fitting's hub edge, it will go from a dull appearance to a shiny look, and sometimes a drop or two of solder will drip from the bottom. If needed, use a heat sink (a wet rag will do) that absorbs heat migrating down the pipe to keep the solder in other fittings from melting too. Once melted, remove the heat. You have just two to three seconds to get the fitting off before the solder hardens again. (You cannot leave the heat on, because it will burn the flux and solder, making the pipe and fitting almost unusable.) Pull the fitting off with needle-nosed pliers. Be sure to pull straight, in line with the pipe. Otherwise, the fitting will jam on the pipe.

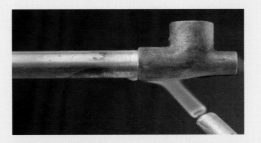

Heat the fitting for 30 seconds to a minute. It must be completely dry, with no water in the pipe.

Using needle-nosed pliers, pull the fitting straight off. If it doesn't come off, the solder hasn't melted or the fitting is binding.

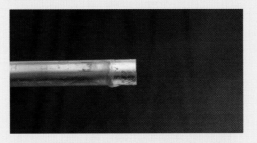

Once pulled, note the solder still left on the pipe. To get a new fitting to slide over it, you will have to heat and melt the solder again.

# Sweating a pipe

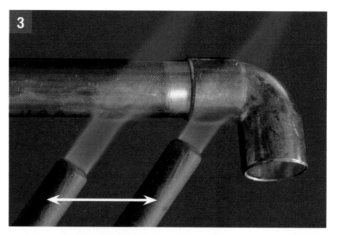

**1** Clean pipe end and then apply flux to the cleaned area. Do same to the fitting.

**2** Insert fitting onto pipe and wipe off any excess flux.

**3** Heat the pipe first, then the fitting. Move flame back and forth from fitting to pipe.

**4** Let pipe/fitting heat for a few seconds and then touch the solder to the upper part of the joint (for vertical joints, the solder will wick up into the joint). Let about ½ in. of solder flow into the joint. Remove solder.

**5** Wait 3–4 seconds for solder to set and wipe joint with a dry rag or wire brush. (Be careful—the joint will be super-hot and wear safety glasses; debris can fly up into your eyes). Let the joint air cool (do not use water), and wash it with an oil-removing dishwashing detergent.

# Terminology

One of the most common questions in plumbing is what does MIP and FIP stand for? As a master plumber, one who has heard these terms all my life, I've always assumed that those who worked in the trade knew what the acronyms represented until my local hardware-store owner asked me what they meant. They stand for Male Iron Pipe and Female Iron Pipe.

A MIP fitting has threads on its outside, such as a pipe nipple. And a FIP fitting has threads on its inside like a T fitting. It's possible for a fitting to have both—a street 90 fitting, for instance. A street 90 fitting is an elbow fitting that, instead of having two FIP threads on each end, has one end that is female and the other male. We use this type of fitting for immediate turns out of another fitting. For example, to make an immediate turn from a T fitting, either use a nipple and an elbow fitting or a street fitting. Using the former means a lot of extra labor, several more potential leak spots, and 1 in. to 2 in. extra length before the turn; a street fitting does it all in a single fitting with a super tight turn.

Taper is another term that deals with the design of fittings. All pipe-threaded fittings are tapered. That is, the diameter of the threads closest to the cut end is more narrow than the diameter closest to the solid pipe. This is to allow gradual tightening of the fitting. The one exception is the $\frac{1}{2}$-in. threaded posts coming off of some faucets as a place to attach the supply tubes. These are solid—not tapered—threads, and I don't know why. However, it's possible to get a female fitting onto the pipe—they are just tight immediately and it takes muscle to get the fitting seated fully onto the threads.

If the threads are on the inside of the fittings—or valves, T's, etc.—they are called FIPs, or Female-Iron-Pipe fittings.

If the threads are on the outside of the fittings—as in these nipples—they are called MIP, or Male-Iron-Pipe fittings.

MIP threads are tapered as shown here by the straight edge. This aids getting the pipe into the fitting and permits gradual tightening.

A street fitting such as this street elbow can have both MIP and FIP threads.

Just because the inside of a copper fitting is shiny (*top*), doesn't mean it is clean. It will still have debris, oils, oxidation, and other contaminants on its surface. "Clean" in plumbing jargon means "wire brushed" (*bottom*).

To clean copper pipe, use a wire brush or open-web waterproof sandpaper (plumber's cloth, top). Solid-cloth sandpaper (*bottom*) is normally not waterproof and, if it gets wet, will dissolve onto the copper.

This combo puts the sweating odds on my side. Use Oatey SAF FLO solder, which has a low melting point, melts more quickly, and flows smoothly in a wide range of temperatures. The flux will tin the pipe, allowing the solder to flow evenly throughout the joint. It has a high resistance to burning.

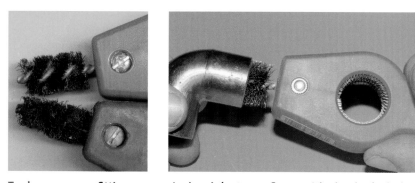

To clean a copper fitting, use a wire brush (not your finger with plumber's cloth on the end). When the brush gets bent and dirty, get a new one. You will know this time has come when you have to tilt the brush at all angles to get the fitting clean. Save the old brush for cleaning galvanized pipe threads.

# Working with CPVC

The first plastic to cut into the copper market was CPVC. This has been my pipe of choice for quite some time. Still, CPVC is not a work of art. Sometimes it is quite ugly. However, what it lacks in looks, it makes up for in fast and easy installation. Nearly anyone can install it successfully.

CPVC comes from the factory in 10-ft. sticks. Some hardware stores cut it into shorter, more manageable sticks for do-it-yourselfers. CPVC also comes in rolls for those long runs under the slab or that long ranch house, but this sometimes has to be special-ordered. As with every other pipe, when you store CPVC, be sure to cap it to keep out debris and insects. Mud dauber wasps, especially, love to build nests in it. A slip cap on each end will do the job.

All the common elbows, 45s, couplings, caps, and Ts come in CVPC. We all buy them in abundance. What most people forget are proper reducer Ts.

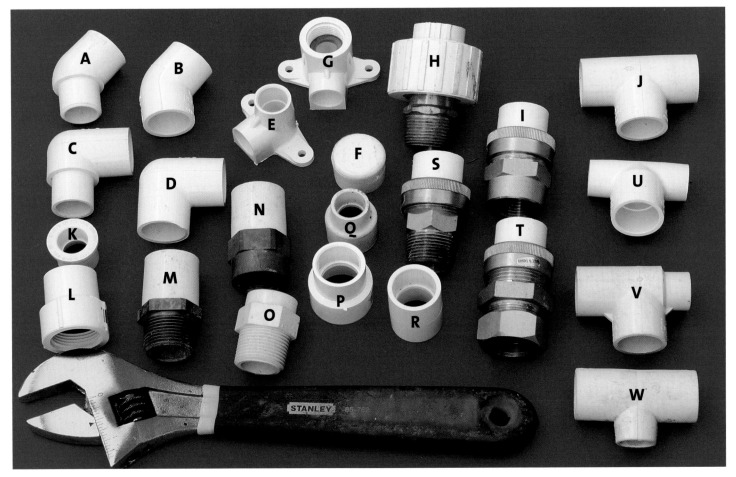

**Most commonly used CPVC fittings. A—Street 45, B—45, C—Street 90, D—90, E—Drop ear elbow; glue on both sides, F—Cap, G—Drop ear elbow, H—Union, I—Brass FIP by glue-on, J—Standard T, K—Reducing bushing, L—FIP plastic, M—Brass male adapter, N—Brass FIP, O—Plastic male adapter, P—CPVC by PVC glue-on, Q—Reducing coupling, R—Coupling, S—Brass MIP by union glue-on, T—Compression by union glue-on, U, V, and W—Reducing Ts**

CPVC is a **very popular pipe, It works well, but it cannot take even a moderate freeze without splitting.**

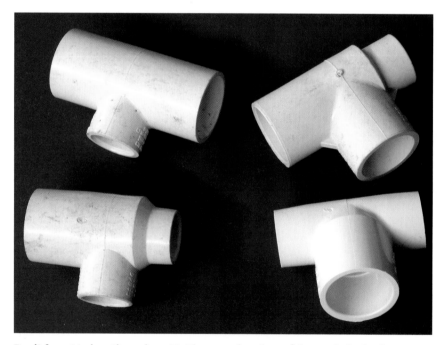

**Don't forget to buy the reducer Ts: There are four types (*shown clockwise from upper left*): the reducing T (3/4×3/4×1/2) is the most commonly used; for a simple 1/2-in. overhead tap, get lots of them. To its right a T (3/4×1/2×3/4) is used when the main line turns 90 degrees and there is a single fixture straight ahead. The T at lower right (1/2×1/2×3/4) is one of the least used—but it's a good idea to have three or four on hand just in case—and is the right choice when the main line terminates and there are two fixtures on opposite ends of the line. The last T (3/4×1/2×1/2) is used when the main line terminates and there are two fixtures ahead but at 90 degrees to each other.**

When possible, I buy my fittings in bags of 25; you'll need around 10 of each for a house. And don't forget the 3/4×1/2 bushings and caps.

CPVC's biggest limitation is that it cannot take even a moderate freeze without splitting. If you live in a warm area it's no big deal, but if you are in a freezing climate, you must take precautions to keep the pipe from freezing. Remember, insulation does not stop a pipe from freezing; it only slows the process. One of the best ways to keep a pipe from freezing is to use the type of water recirculator discussed at the end of Chapter 5.

## Cutting CPVC

I used to say that cutting CPVC should only be done with ratcheting scissors or a cutoff saw. But now I have added my mini recip saw to that short list. A cutoff saw can produce a clean, straight cut, but it is good only for new installations. The bulky tool is too difficult to raise above your head to cut pipe that's already installed. Even if you could lift it, there would be no room to use it.

Ratcheting scissors are good in renovations and new installations, but you have to be careful to get a straight cut. After a few years, CPVC can become brittle, and squeezing it with the ratcheting scissors sometimes shatters the pipe. To avoid this, I cut older pipe with my mini recip saw. Its small-toothed blade is perfect for this type of cutting. (You may have noticed throughout book that I use the mini Makita for many tasks. It is now one of those tools I cannot be without. If it dies (and mine is getting ready to die right now), I have to get a new one right away before I head back out to the job.)

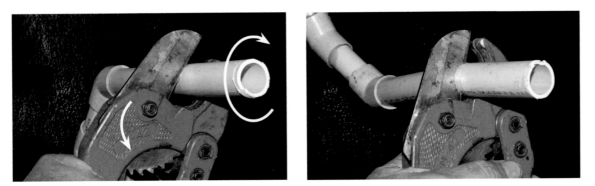

Cutting CPVC is a three-step process. First squeeze the handles and put a slight depression into the pipe (*left*). Then arc the handle down as you twist the pipe up. You may need to pump the handle as well (*right*).

Ratcheting scissors often **make crooked cuts.**

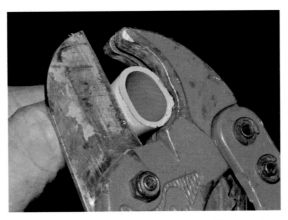

**Even sharp** blades can't cut small slices off CPVC pipe.

To cut CVPC and copper, use a chop saw with a solid blade, usually rated for steel or concrete. It gets absolutely straight cuts and can easily cut 1/8 in. off a pipe end.

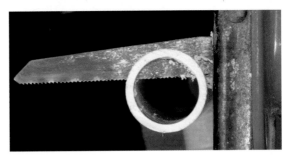

**As it does** with copper, the recip saw can shave a small piece off a CPVC pipe end. It is the preferred tool for cutting CPVC that has been installed for awhile because you don't have to worry about the pipe cracking.

## Problem fittings and solutions

The biggest problem with CPVC is leaks from its male/female fittings—and its all-plastic globe and ball valves. Due to their design, the fittings often leak. If you tighten a fitting too much, it cracks; too loose, and it will leak. Since I switched to brass/CPVC combo fittings (made by Sioux Chief), I haven't had a problem.

If you decide to pass on my advice and use an all-plastic male or female adapter, there's a trick to use to prevent the collar from being damaged as you tighten the fitting: Take a short piece of pipe and insert it all the way into the collar as you tighten. This prevents the collar from caving in or being deformed, then cracking. Also, avoid using paste on plastic threads unless the paste states that it is made specifically for that use. Many paste lubricants will weaken and deform the threads over time. Another problem with all-plastic adapters is that when you crank them

Avoid installing globe valves, whether CPVC or any other (*left*). They reduce water pressure and volume because of their interior design (*right*).

Pass up the all-plastic CPVC ball valve (*left*). Many do not turn completely off even when closed, and further tightening only breaks the handle (*right*).

down with a pipe wrench, the jaw's teeth cuts right into and weakens the fitting; many have cut a slice right into the fitting, creating a leak.

The CPVC all-plastic globe and ball valves should be taken off the market. The ball valve is sometimes very hard to turn on and off. Greasing the ball and working the handle back and forth helps somewhat. Lately, I've noticed that they don't turn the water completely off, even with the valve closed. They are now offi-cially on my banned fitting list. The globe valve has a tendency to leak around the handle stem and, like all globe valves, slows the water flow, reducing the water pressure. I know of one do-it-yourselfer who put in so many globe valves (to isolate the different branches in case there was a leak), he had no usable pressure at the distant end of the house. Common sense and most codes tell you to use full-flow fittings in the main lines.

**Avoid plastic threaded fittings (*left*). They tend to leak. Use brass adapters (*right*) to avoid these leaking problems.**

**The pressure of a wrench cracks plastic threaded adapters when they are turned into a fitting.**

To counter the **valve problem in CPVC, Sioux Chief makes an excellent metal ball valve that is designed for CPVC and is widely available.**

**Excess glue and a one-minute wait before the fitting was inserted resulted in this dam inside the pipe, which reduces the interior diameter by half.**

## Gluing CPVC

For the longest time, I stayed away from primer, preferring to sand fittings instead. I've never been a great fan of primer. It's the drippy stuff that preps the pipe for gluing. It also stains everything purple, including fingers, clothes, and floors. Then a manufacturer came out with a glue that doesn't require priming or sanding. It is now my preferred glue.

Gluing CPVC pipe might seem simple, but not to experienced plumbers. We know that it is a little more complicated than slapping on the glue and pushing the fitting onto the pipe.

> **Keep the primer can lid on extremely tight. Primer can evaporate through the smallest opening.**

Remember, if it can be messed up, we have already done it.

Too much glue can cause a blockage to form inside the pipe, significantly reducing the water flow. This happens if you wait before sliding the fitting onto the pipe. The glue softens the pipe and fitting, and when you finally slide the fitting on, the pipe edge gouges the softened inside of the fitting, forming a dam that can reduce water flow. On the other hand, if you use too little glue, you'll have a weak joint that can blow.

One time I forgot to glue a repair fitting. It didn't leak, but about an hour later, it blew off. Now I mark fittings as I glue them with a slash, and the last thing I do before I pressurize is to verify that every fitting has been marked (and glued). (continued on p. 98)

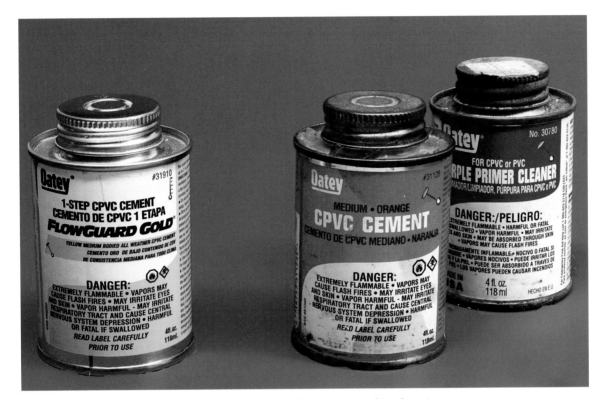

CPVC glue comes in two types: gold (*left*), which doesn't need primer (*right*), and orange (*center*), which does.

I can't mention it too often—keep primer and glue in a container that will hold a spill. This way, if something spills— and it will—the glue stays in the container and nothing has been destroyed. If you spill either on any type of carpet, it will be ruined.

# Gluing CPVC

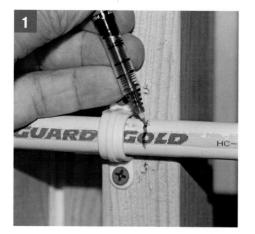

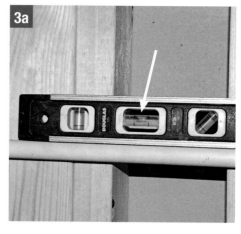

**1** Mark where cut is to be made. To turn a corner, a cut mark on this ½-in. pipe is made ½ in. back from the wall corner.

**2** Cut pipe at the mark.

**3** To make sure elbow is placed so the continuing pipe is parallel to the floor, dry fit on the elbow and a small piece of pipe, turning the corner. Place a small level on the pipe and turn the elbow until plumb. Put an alignment mark on the connection

**4** Rake off excess glue on can lip. (This glue does not need a primer.)

**5** Wipe glue onto pipe. Circle a couple of times and let the dauber absorb any excess glue.

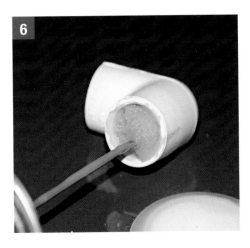

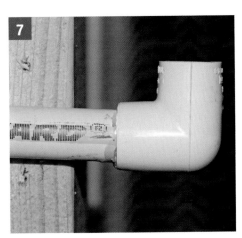

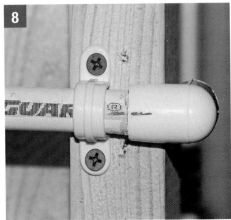

**6** Daub glue in fitting. Circle a couple of times inside fitting and let dauber absorb any excess glue as it comes out.

**7** Insert fitting fully onto pipe, 90 degrees out of alignment.

**8** Turn fitting into alignment. Hold fitting for several seconds.

## Working with PEX

PEX is simply polyethylene that is approved for inside the house. It replaced PB, although it's not nearly as flexible. Of all the pipes, PEX is the fastest to install.

Many manufacturers produce PEX. It comes in white, blue, and red (blue and red are for inside the house; white is sometimes approved for outside). I can't tell you which is the best since I don't have all the fancy equipment to test it. But I can say that all PEX, having passed the same independent tests and manufactur-

ing standards, is good. What differentiates each manufacturer is not the pipe but how the pipe is connected in the system of fittings. Crimpers are the most popular.

PEX comes in rolls and in straight sticks. I always use the latter because the rolls keep a circular memory (as all polyethylene pipes do), making it difficult to use for short straight runs. However, where long lengths are needed to minimize couplings, rolled pipe is best. Two types of PEX are available: all plastic and plastic with an aluminum center (called PEX-AL-PEX),

**Most commonly used PEX fittings. A—Female adapter, B—Reducer female adapter, C—Female adapter union, D—Female adapter union elbow, E—Drop ear elbow, F—1/2 PEX × 1/2 female thread union, G—Hose bibb (with threaded washer to the right), H—PEX to sweat adapter, I—Crimpers, J—Connector for refrigerator water supply (in-line, with tube below), K—Plastic coupling, L—Connector for refrigerator water supply (end of line, with tube below), M—Stop valve, male thread, N—Plastic T, O—Cap, P—Reducer T 1/2×1/2×3/4, Q—Brass coupling, R—Reducer coupling, S—Reducer T 3/4×1/2×3/4, T—Reducer male adapter, U—Elbow, V—Reducer elbow**

which makes it more rigid and helps to keep it in place once it is installed.

## Cutting PEX

There is only one proper way to cut PEX, and that is with ratcheting scissors. Almost any toothed cutter will leave jagged edges that will need to be cut off. When using ratcheting scissors, be careful not to cut at an angle. If you do, cut it again until you get a good straight cut. Do not use a pipe with a severely angled or jagged cut.

To interface CPVC with PEX, you can buy glue-on crimp conversion fittings in a variety of sizes.

PEX comes in straight sections in three colors, and even these straight sections can bend. (Photo courtesy Vanguard Piping Systems, Inc.)

PEX also comes with an aluminum center that makes it stay in place, once installed. (Photo courtesy Vanguard Piping Systems, Inc.)

PEX is available in large rolls when needed. (Photo courtesy Vanguard Piping Systems, Inc.).

PEX pipe, a polyethylene derivative, is a flexible pipe that can be used inside (both hot and cold) and outside the house (service pipe). For inside use, most PEX manufacturers promote a parallel system of piping coming from a manifold. This one is called a Manablock. (Photo courtesy Vanguard Piping Systems, Inc.)

## Plastic versus brass fittings

All plastic fittings in the PEX trade are made from a high-grade, sometimes medical-grade, plastic with a high tolerance to just about everything, such as chlorine. Therefore, they are just as good as, if not better than, brass fittings. In areas where the water is so aggressive it would eat copper for lunch, it's logical to assume that brass would also corrode. Plastic fittings are the preferred choice in those situations.

## Crimpers

Every year more and more crimper designs come to the market. I still have all mine from the old PB days: long-handled ones with good

PEX ball valves crimp into the water line like any ordinary PEX fitting. Never use a PEX gate valve due to the problems inherent to gate valves.

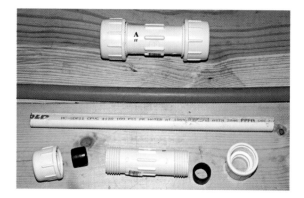

A clothes washer hose bibb can be easily crimped into a PEX system via a drop-ear elbow fitting that attaches with three screws.

A dresser coupling will splice CPVC, PEX—even copper. However, they attach only with a rubber grommet on each side (no grabber rings) and the pipe blows out of the fitting quite often. Don't use them.

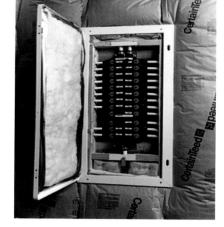

The finished product in a manifold block system. Once the door is closed, all pipes are out of sight. (Photo courtesy Vanguard Piping Systems, Inc.)

leverage, short-handled ones that fit between joists. Neither works well unless you're strong. If you are working with PEX, it would pay to hunt for an easy-squeeze crimper before carpal tunnel syndrome sets in.

The biggest problem with the crimp system is making sure the crimpers are aligned at a right angle with the pipe and the ring doesn't slide away from its proper position on the fitting, about ⅛ in. to ¼ in. from the fitting shoulder. For the latter issue, I gently squeeze the ring with pliers to keep it in place. For the former, I use short-handled crimpers, which fit better in tight areas. In dark spots, you will need a light to verify the ring has not moved.

If the pipe end has been ovaled, you will not be able to insert the fitting, let alone crimp it. Here, a rounding tool, or swage, comes in handy.

## Crimp ring types

The main difference between PEX manufacturers is the way they install fittings onto the pipe. Crimped copper rings (black) are the most common system, another holdover from the PB days. In fact, we use the same crimpers as for PB. The biggest advantage of this system is availability—the crimpers are distributed widely.

One of the newest attachment systems is a proprietary crimping system by Watts Radiant called CinchClamp. This system, which works with any manufacturer's PEX, uses a special stainless steel band with a special crimper. The advantage is that you can see the crimp ring. This may not sound like a big deal, but it is. (For more on CinchClamp, see the Appendix, p. 232).

**PEX systems come with both brass and high-quality plastic fittings for systems with aggressive water.**

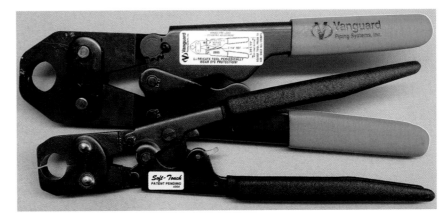

**Modern crimpers are short and close easily.**

**These old crimpers are a carryover from the PB days, but they still work for PEX.**

# Making a Crimp Splice (copper ring)

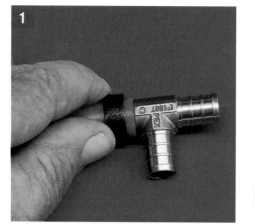

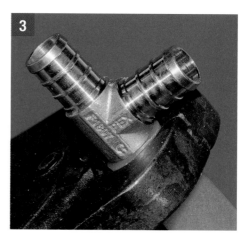

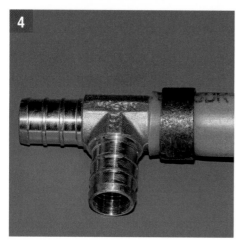

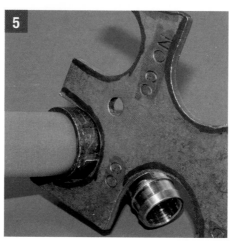

**QUICK REFERENCE**

**FITTINGS  p. 98**
Types of PEX fittings commonly used

**PEX PIPE  p. 99**
Different types of PEX pipe

**CRIMPERS  p. 100**
Different types of crimpers that can be used

**IMPROPER CRIMPS  p. 103**
Examples of crimps to avoid

**1** Slide the ring on the pipe, insert the fitting into the pipe (bump the fitting against the pipe), and slide the ring ⅛ in. to ¼ in. from the end of the pipe/fitting interface.

**2** Using pliers, squeeze gently, just enough to slightly bend the ring and hold it in place.

**3** Crimp the fitting into place, keeping the crimpers at a 90-degree angle to the pipe with the jaws

fully around the ring. Note the problem with this type of system: You cannot see the ring as you are using the crimping tool.

**4** Remove crimpers and check the ring. It should be straight and fully crimped.

**5** Use the GO/NO-GO gauge to verify proper crimp.

# Working with PB

PB is no longer allowed in new construction, according to building codes in the United States, due to leaks and lawsuits. It is still being manufactured and used in Europe and Asia (it comes with a 50-year warranty from at least one manufacturer) and is increasing in popularity every year.

Even though we no longer install it here, millions of feet of PB remain in homes and have to be maintained. PB pipe and crimp fittings are still widely available to repair existing systems. To interface with PB, Sioux Chief and other manufacturers make a variety of crimp-style brass fittings—PB crimp on one side, PEX crimp on the other. Be sure not to interchange the rings. The PEX side of the coupling must use the black copper ring while the PB side of the coupling must use the copper-colored ring. Such crimp fittings are sold at most hardware stores and on many websites.

PB, like PEX, comes in straight sections and rolls. Since you will be doing repair work only, use straight sections. It is much easier to work with. Because stored PB pipe must have been lying around for many years, there's a good chance it contains a certain amount of debris. Always verify that the inside of the pipe is clean. Simply look through short pieces. Shoot water from the hose through longer pieces to dislodge any garbage. Ultraviolet rays can deteriorate the pipe, causing it to split, so don't use any pipe that has been stored outside. PB, like PEX, can't be bent around a tight corner without an elbow fitting. You shouldn't run it close to hot objects, such a water heater flue or rub against sharp objects. Plastic PB T-fittings had a habit of snapping or cracking when the pipe going to the center tap part of the T was taken off at a severe angle, which put a lot of pressure

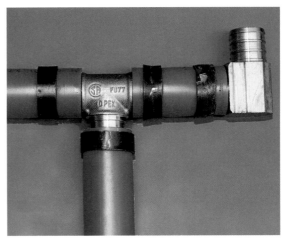

How not to crimp a copper ring. The ring on the left side of the T is too far away from the fitting shoulder. The crimp on bottom is too close to the fitting shoulder. The crimp on right is only half crimped (the tool was half off crimp ring). The crimp on elbow fitting was made with the crimpers at an angle.

This is what killed PB in the United States—leaks. In this instance, a leak was caused by a poorly made brass fitting with walls that are too thin. The teeth of the fitting compressed under the load of the ring seal even though the crimp was made properly.

To interface PB with PEX, use this special coupling by Sioux Chief. Note the different design of barbs (circular rings) on each side of the fitting: PB on left, PEX on right. You can also get T fittings.

on the T-fitting. Plastic PB elbow fittings would crack when used on a corner greater than 90 degrees. Metal clamps can cut into the pipe, so secure it with plastic hold-down clamps. Lastly, the plastic insert fittings, because they were made from a chemical called acetal, had a habit of cracking. Leaks were not confined to just plastic fittings. I've also seen many leaks when metal fittings were used, especially the T-fitting tap to the fridge icemaker.

The first rings that came out for PB were made from aluminum. Don't use these even if you are able to find them. Aluminum, being a soft material, expanded after it had been installed, especially in high-vibration areas. We would have leaks everywhere. Once the rings were re-crimped, the leaks stopped—until the rings expanded again.

Cut PB with ratcheting scissors just like you do PEX, making a straight, clean cut. Do not

**The large gray compression fittings (*above*) are perhaps the most common method of connecting different types of pipes, such as copper to CPVC (*below*).**

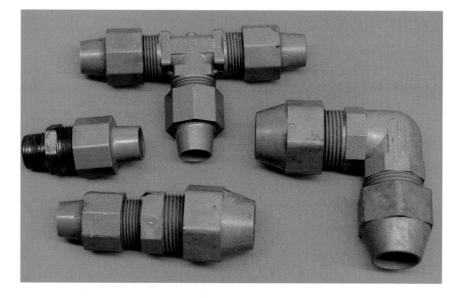

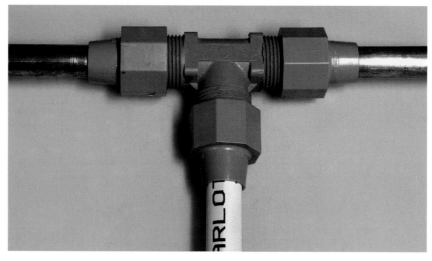

move the pipe around during the repair; an existing PB fitting could leak or the pipe could crack. While you are tapping into the old PB pipe, look around to note any fittings that may be leaking.

## Universal Fittings

Copper, CPVC, and PEX share the same outside diameter, so compression fittings are interchangeable. Some kinds have been around for a while, carryovers from the PB era. These are made from acetyl, but since they are large and thick, they don't have the trouble of the crimp fittings. These are the acetyl gray color. The new ones from the post-PB era are made from medical-grade plastic that has a high tolerance to just about everything, including heat, chlorine, and minerals.

The old acetyl fittings have no built-in stops inside so a T fitting can slide all the way onto a cut pipe and then slide back over and close the cut. Because such fittings are easy to tap into an existing line, they are perfect for renovation. They're good when it comes to maintenance, too. You can cut out a split in a copper pipe, put on a gray coupling by sliding it all the way onto the pipe and then back over the break, and have it repaired in seconds.

Due to their built-in shoulders, common brass compression fittings cannot make these simple taps and splices unless a lot of "slop" is built into the existing lines so they can be bent outward to get the brass fitting onto the pipe. Otherwise you have to cut in copper/brass unions. Also, brass compression fittings, which use brass compression rings, have a high tendency to leak. I prefer using the large gray fittings for taps.

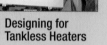

# Hot Water

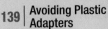
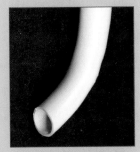
**W**ater heaters have become throwaway appliances, their large cylindrical bodies clogging our landfills. But manufacturers have known how to make a good, long-lasting water heater for years. Humphrey, a gas model made in Kalamazoo, Michigan, was 90 percent efficient—and that was in 1894. Compare that to today's gas models, which run at about 75–percent efficiency. And the tanks, electric or gas, were durable. They were made of Monel, a copper-nickel alloy. Rudd and Whitehead made Monel tanks in the 1940s and '50s that I wouldn't be surprised to find in use today.

We can't simply point a finger at the manufacturers, however. To be competitive among buyers and contractors who want nothing more than the lowest cost, today's water heaters are made from very thin, easily corroded metal with a very thin glass coating.

In this chapter I give you two solutions to this ever-growing problem. I show you how to extend the life of your existing heater and/or install a water heater with a lifetime warranty. I also reveal how to lower a hot water bill by increasing the temperature of the incoming water, detail the options of gas versus electric, and

**From home to dump. This town dumpster is nearly filled with water heaters—one week's worth.**

**Demand heaters heat water only when it's needed, but they have a host of problems.**

explain how to keep water hot at the spigot so you don't waste time and money sending all that water down the drain while waiting for the hot water to arrive.

## Tankless (Demand) Heaters

Unlike in Europe and Asia, where tankless, on-demand heaters are common, in the United States storage heaters are prevalent. These heat the water in a large insulated tank, and we use it whenever we want. It's convenient but quite wasteful. Tankless heaters heat the water as it's needed. In theory, demand heaters should be the best way to go since there's no energy wasted keeping the water hot.

In the past, tankless heaters could not keep up with the considerable hot water demands of the typical American household and they often broke down. Homeowners who installed a tankless heater had to plan their hot water use to avoid cold showers. And if the heater stopped

working, only a specially trained plumber could work on it and parts had to be special-ordered. Owners might be without hot water for a month or more. Today's demand heaters are a lot more dependable and can keep up with any household's needs if large enough units or multiple units are installed.

### Gas or electric

Tankless heaters come in both electric and gas models. The electric heaters are less expensive and easier to install, but since they heat the water slowly they are not a good choice in most areas of the house. They are fine for fixtures that don't need much hot water, such as a bathroom lav. For multiple showers or an entire house, they are impractical. A large unit will pull 150 amps, the current amount of an entire house without a tankless heater, or more.

In most cases, a gas heater, which heats the water faster, is preferable. However, gas heaters are more expensive, even without the extra cost of the flue and gas line. A stainless steel flue, which is required in some areas, adds to the final tally significantly. For an approximate example, a 12-in. straight section costs $12; a 36-in. straight section, $32. Add an elbow ($30), a bird screen, hood, and raincap ($100), flashing ($24), five support straps ($15). The total could easily climb to several hundred dollars plus labor.

## Sizing

In the past, even gas tankless heaters were severely limited in the hot water they could produce. Not today. Typical heaters range from 6 gpm at 190,000 Btu to more than double that at 13 gpm at 380,000 Btu. Prices range from $1,000 for the 6-gpm model to $4,000 for the 13-gpm one. People can get by with 6 gpm if they don't mind an occasional cool shower

spurt or if they live by themselves. Otherwise, get an 8 gpm to 10 gpm model. And remember, the gallons-per-minute the manufacturers list on their labels are best-case situations. The fine print will probably reveal something less.

### Water Heater Sizing

| Household Size | | Gas* | Electric |
|---|---|---|---|
| 5 or more | Regular demand | 50 gallons | 80 gallons |
| | High demand | 75 gallons | 120 gallons |
| 3 to 4 | Regular demand | 50 gallons | 50 or 65 gallons |
| | High demand | 50 gallons | 80 gallons |
| 2 or less | Regular demand | 40 gallons | 40 gallons |
| | High demand | 50 gallons | 50 gallons |

*Gas water heaters can be natural or LP gas and will have BTU heat inputs of 40,000 to 75,000. The larger the heat input to the heater, the faster it can heat water—as the larger wattage element of an electric water heater will allow it to heat water faster.

## The Danger of Scalding

Water temperature over 125°F (52°C) can cause severe burns or death. Children, the elderly, and the physically or mentally disabled are at highest risk. Feel water before bathing or showering. Many times the injury comes from panic. In an attempt to get away from the scalding water, people fall and break a bone.

### Temperature Settings

It is recommended that the dial be set lower whenever possible.

| Temperature Setting | Time to Produce 2nd & 3rd Degree Burns on Adult Skin |
|---|---|
| 160°F (71°C) | About ½ second |
| 150°F (66°C) | About 1½ seconds |
| 140°F (60°C) | Less than 5 seconds |
| 130°F (54°C) | About 30 seconds |
| 120°F (49°C) | More than 5 minutes |

A "low boy" water heater is about half the size of a typical tall water heater and twice its diameter. You can get them with either one element or two. (Photo courtesy Water Heater Innovations, Inc.)

When plumbing a gas water heater, keep non-metal pipes away from both heater and flue. Use either ones you make yourself or pre-made pipe assemblies like this one (made by Sioux Chief)—but skip those with the gate valve shown. Labor-wise, it's more cost effective to use the premade pipe assemblies. (Photo courtesy Sioux Chief Manufacturing)

This cutaway view shows why I no longer install gas water heaters: With only one burner at the bottom, they have to heat all the junk that collects at the tank bottom before they heat the water.

A dirt leg assembly comprises an entire array of fittings that not only allows for the trapping of in-line debris (the hanging nipple with the cap) but has a union for an easy water heater disconnect and a valve on the house side of the union to cut off the gas. I find it is easiest to assemble all this using a chain vise.

## Problems

Tankless heaters are not problem-free. The large exhaust flue in a gas model lets a lot of cold air into the building when the unit is not in use, which is an issue in cold climates. The area around the heater is always cooler than the surrounding area. The exhaust is simply a large hole in the building, which lets a lot of cold air into the living area, basement, or garage. And when windy, the air can come down the flue hard enough to blow out the pilot flame, at least in the old-style heaters. Modern heaters sometimes do not have a pilot light. Thus you may need to install some type of backdraft or draft diverter unit within the flue. Models with the highest energy rating may require 120v to power its electronics.

Another problem with tankless water heaters is that minerals may build up in the narrow water-filled tubes within the heater. If your water is hard, the minerals may render a heater useless after a couple of years—perhaps even months. At least one manufacturer has addressed this problem by including hose-bibb connections on its unit to allow a backwash solution to clean the interior of the pipes.

Because of their design, tankless heaters require a flow switch to turn on: Turn on a hot water spigot and the water flow turns on a switch in the tankless heater. This normally takes about ½ gpm to ¾ gpm. When you turn on a hot water spigot, you have to turn it on fully to kick on the flow switch and then back it off. Once you draw less than the required gpm it takes to turn on the switch, the switch will kick back off again, giving you cold water.

Bottom line: Tankless heaters provide hot water and save money, but because of their high initial costs and their other problems, they will probably never overtake storage-type heaters in the United States.

## Gas or Electric?

When buying a water heater, most people choose gas or electric according to the price of the fuel, opting for the least expensive. This is not always the best way to go. You need to consider other variables as well.

At one time I installed mostly gas heaters. Gas heats water a lot faster than electric, and in my region, the price of natural gas at that time, and even propane, was significantly lower than that of electricity.

Over the years, gas heaters have become more expensive to buy and more costly to install. In addition, gas heaters heat the water from only one location—the very bottom of the tank, like a flame heating a test tube. This means the flame has to heat through all the debris, rust, mud, and flaked-off lime lying in the bottom of the tank. Lime is the white scale

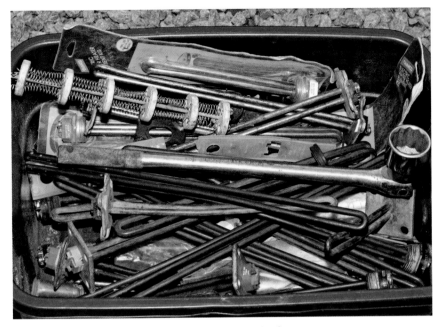

Always stock several **different sizes of elements, both of different wattages and different voltages.**

**It's a good idea to keep stocking these old open-wire elements. They insert into an open hole inside a galvanized tank. They heat cherry red, which heats the air, which heats the metal tank, which in turn heats the water. This sounds very inefficient, but it is exactly how a gas water heater works: heating air, which heats the tank, which heats the water.**

## How backdrafts happen

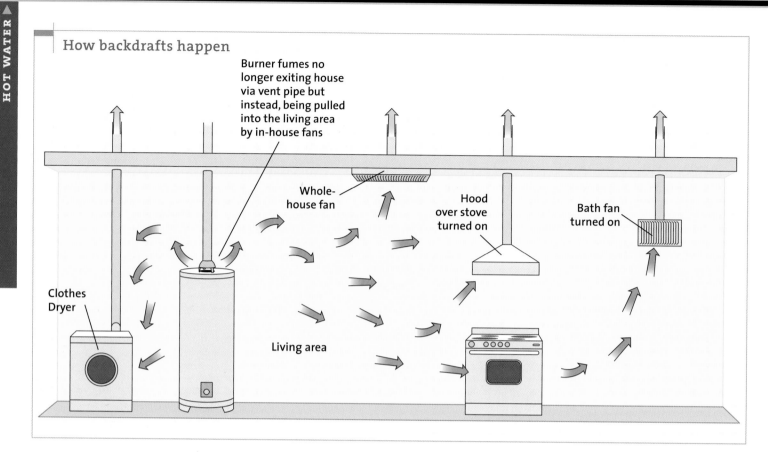

Burner fumes no longer exiting house via vent pipe but instead, being pulled into the living area by in-house fans

Whole-house fan

Hood over stove turned on

Bath fan turned on

Clothes Dryer

Living area

Gas water heaters should not be installed in living areas. The flue can backdraft, emitting poisonous fumes throughout the living area. It also burns up oxygen within the room and releases a massive amount of water vapor.

## Quick-disconnect

The supply gas line should not attach directly to water heater, but to an assembly that allows easy water heater removal.

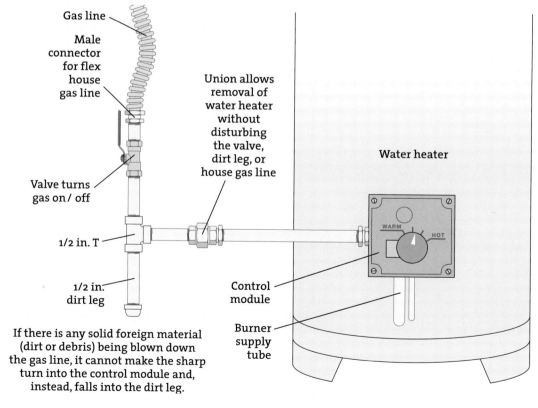

Gas line

Male connector for flex house gas line

Union allows removal of water heater without disturbing the valve, dirt leg, or house gas line

Water heater

Valve turns gas on / off

WARM    HOT

1/2 in. T

1/2 in. dirt leg

Control module

Burner supply tube

If there is any solid foreign material (dirt or debris) being blown down the gas line, it cannot make the sharp turn into the control module and, instead, falls into the dirt leg.

formed from calcium and magnesium that comes out of suspension when hard water is heated. Efficiency ratings don't account for this.

Another significant problem in some installations is that rust flakes off the inside of the vent tube (that runs vertically through the water heater), settles and clogs up the burner holes. I used to vacuum the rust out once a year. However, the newer burners are in a sealed chamber and this can no longer be done.

The most common concerns are moisture that is created within the room by the burning process, the oxygen that is removed and has to be replenished, backdrafting (which allows poisonous gas into the living area), and the risk of explosion from flammable gas. In addition, gas heaters require the extra expense of a "dirt leg", a ½-in. steel pipe arranged to keep out debris that might have entered the gas line during installation or storage from getting into the control module.

## Gas Line Myths

Many people think rolled copper can't be used for gas lines. Those of us who use copper for gas lines, along with all the thousands of utilities that also use it, know better. Rolled copper is one of the most common pipes used to pipe gas. However, one should, though it is not required, paint it yellow so it won't be confused with a water line.

Heating elements have their wattage and voltage ratings stamped on the head of the element.

Compare the larger, new-design element head size (*right*), that are starting to come on some water heaters, and the smaller common element (*left*).

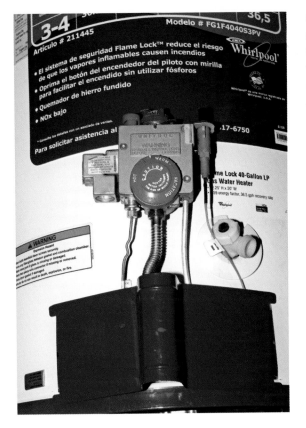

A gas water heater always has a control module directly to its front. The control module sends the proper amount of gas into the heater's burner as well as a small amount of gas to a pilot light. If the pilot light goes out, the control module cuts off all gas to the burner as a safety precaution.

## New Design Makes Gas Water Heaters Safer

**According to some** estimates, ignition of flammable vapors by gas water heaters causes nearly 800 residential fires a year, resulting in an average of 5 deaths and 130 injuries. To counter this, residential gas water heaters now have Flammable Vapor Ignition Resistant (FVIR) burners. A sensor inside the water heater can detect flammable vapor and shut off the flow of gas to the burner and pilot light. However, this is no license to store flammables around the heater. You still must keep the heater bottom high off the garage floor.

FVIR burners add to the cost of the heaters. Expect to pay at least $50 more than you used to. Before you buy a new gas water heater, find out what has to be done after the unit shuts itself off. *Some of these heaters do not automatically reset*. You might have to buy a brand-new heater or simply replace a part.

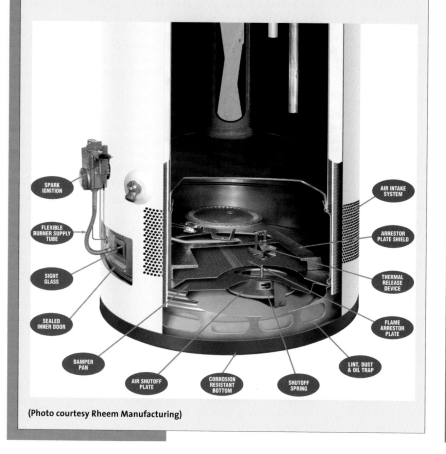

SPARK IGNITION

FLEXIBLE BURNER SUPPLY TUBE

SIGHT GLASS

SEALED INNER DOOR

DAMPER PAN

AIR SHUTOFF PLATE

CORROSION RESISTANT BOTTOM

SHUTOFF SPRING

LINT, DUST & OIL TRAP

FLAME ARRESTOR PLATE

THERMAL RELEASE DEVICE

ARRESTOR PLATE SHIELD

AIR INTAKE SYSTEM

(Photo courtesy Rheem Manufacturing)

Also, it's almost universally acclaimed that galvanized pipe cannot be used for a gas line, and this, too, is just as wrong. It's listed as an acceptable pipe in the National Fuel Gas Code. We normally use black iron pipe because it cannot be confused with a water line like galvanized pipe might be. However, such pipe rusts severely. I prefer galvanized pipe nipples and fittings as long as they are painted yellow so they cannot be confused with a water line. In any case, neither iron nor galvanized should be used underground because the moisture will rust the pipe threads.

Anyway, the use of metal for gas line is giving way to the more modern yellow polyethylene, below ground, and stainless corrugated, plastic-covered pipe in the walls.

## Elements

If you work on water heaters, you need an assortment of elements to complement the wide variety of water heaters on the market and in homes. I keep a tubful, from the old open-wire elements, to the new bolt-on, to screw-in ones.

If you have no hot water and the power is on, the problem may be due to the overload button being popped out, probably because the thermostat is set too high. When the temperature rises excessively, the heater shuts off automatically. Reset it by pushing the red button immediately above the upper thermostat until you hear a click. Then adjust the thermostat to 120°F.

You could say the element is the Achilles' heel of the water heater. Typically, only the high-end heaters come with decent elements. Less expensive models come with elements that work well only in perfect water—and we don't often find that. Hard water is the worst of all for cheap heaters, spelling death to both heater and element.

## Quality

Elements come in three categories: high, medium, and low, or good, better, best. I call them terrible, bad, and good. As you might

Older heaters used square elements with no thread. They had a flat plate and offset bolt plate. Conversion kits (*right*) are available to change a flat plate to a 1-in. threaded plate.

I use three 3/4-in. drive sockets for water heater work: 1 7/8 in. to remove the newer large-head elements, 1 1/2 in. to remove common elements, and 11/16 in. to remove anode rods. To turn all three I use a 17-in.-long breaker bar.

The thin-wall metal socket (with a screwdriver to turn it) sometimes works for element removal and might do for some do-it-yourself installations. I learned early on that if the element is rusted in, the socket will bend and slip around the element's hex head.

Using my ³/₄-in. breaker bar and a 1¹/₂-in. socket I can easily remove this rusted-in element that the thin-wall socket and screwdriver could not.

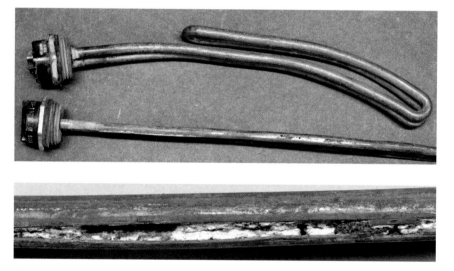

Blown elements (*above*) The top element was dry-fired, or received power before there was water around the elment; the arc is typical. The bottom element was split wide open during normal operation. Photo (*bottom*) is a close-up of the split.

guess, the elements that come in bottom-of-the-line water heaters are high density. However, there is nothing stopping you from replacing them with high-quality elements.

When selecting a high-quality element, look for these features:

- "Low density" or "ultralow density" rating. The tube is long and dull-looking, and it doubles back upon itself

- A sheath listed as "incoloy" or some other fancy alloy name. These normally come with lifetime warranties.

- A ceramic base behind the screws, which you'll be lucky to find. Plastic bases, which are common today, often melt. Then the wire pops loose, flips over and energizes the ungrounded metal jacket of the water heater, which in turn energizes the copper tubing. I've seen this happen twice. I've seen melted plastic bases too many times to count.

## Voltage and wattage

Elements come in 120v models (for the tiny under-counter heaters) and 240v units (the most common, for the larger heaters). Simply match what you're replacing. Wattages are not that exact. For any heater wired with 12-gauge cable, use any wattage up to 3500. If you have 10-gauge cable, you can install up to 5500 watts. Higher wattages heat the water faster; lower wattages create less lime within the heater,

**A low-quality** element is short. Higher-quality elements will double back on themselves, allowing more physical room for the same wattage and lowering the wattage per inch of these elements. This makes it last longer and creates less white lime on the element in hard-water areas.

**Elements with plastic** bases can melt if either of the two wires under the screw is not tight or if lightning runs the cable. We have to live with the problem, however; ceramic bases are now nearly extinct.

# Thermostats and Controls

It is important to know how the wiring inside a water heater is laid out—what connects to what— because you will remove wires as you replace a faulty thermostat.

The best way to keep from mixing the wires up is to label them—even draw a picture. Lots of times, pictorials are on the thermostat's cardboard box. If you find yourself in a situation where you have no idea which wire goes where, follow the list below for two-element water heaters (though there are several ways to wire a water heater, these steps apply to the most common method):

### UPPER THERMOSTAT WIRING

A—Connection to the incoming power. Wired internally through overload directly to D.

B—Connection to the incoming power. Wired directly through overload to C.

C—Two wires leave C: One goes to a screw of the upper element, the other to a screw of the lower element.

D—No wires connect here. It has power from A. D is a switch, sending power internally through the thermostat to either E or F. Power goes to F if thermostat senses cool water; otherwise, power always goes to E.

E—Connection to lower thermostat screw G.

F—Connection to second upper element screw.

### LOWER THERMOSTAT WIRING

Point G to H is connected internally when the thermostat senses cool water, allowing power to reach the element.

G—To E of upper thermostat

H—To the second bottom element screw. Power flows to the bottom element only when the lower thermostat senses cool water and turns its power on.

Upper thermostat

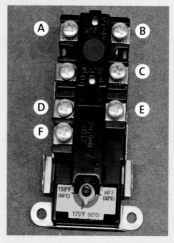

Lower thermostat

To verify voltage is on at the heater, you can make measurements at the splice box, at the overload, at the thermostat, and on the element itself. However, just because you have 245v across the two screws on the element doesn't mean the heater is working—the element could be blown.

The top element and bottom element operate independently. That is, if one is on, the other has to be off. Of the two, the bottom element works the most. The top element only kicks in if the water heater completely runs out of hot water. Thus, the top element can be blown and you would never know it until the heater runs out of hot water, the top thermostat kicks in, and the top element tries to turn on. With the top element blown, the thermostat locks on it, and the heater ceases to function altogether.

which, in hard-water areas, can blow out the element. If you are planning to put an electric water heater on an emergency generator, select one with the lower element wattage to take load off the generator.

## Testing elements

You should have a good digital multimeter for testing elements. The common 4500-watt element will read around 13 ohms (screw to screw), but you do not need to read the resistance scale of a multimeter to test an element. All you check for is continuity. Here's how:

- Touch the tips of the two multimeter probes together. The multimeter should beep if the switch is turned to continuity. The beep means there is continuity between the two probes. Everything is OK to test the element.

- With power to the heater turned off, touch the probes to the two screws of the element. The multimeter will beep if the element is good.

- Touch one probe to the metal tank (slightly scratch it to contact metal). Hold the other probe to one screw

Density refers to the element's watts per sq. in. High-density elements have 150-plus watts per sq. in.; medium-density units, 100 watts to 150 watts per sq. in.; and low-density elements, around 75 watts per sq. in. High and medium density are too hot—the hotter the element runs, the more likely it will burn out. Opt for low-density units. Some manufacturers describe their best elements as ultralow density.

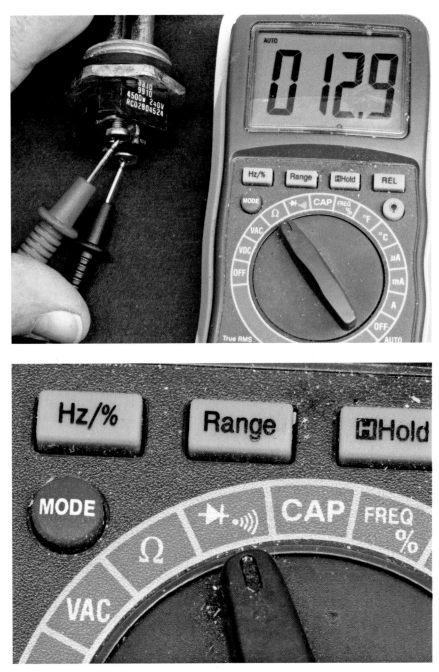

There are only two ways to test an element and both require a multimeter. Turn the power to the heater off at the circuit breaker or fuse box, then proceed as follows: (*top*) Use the Ohm (Ω) function to check the element's resistance—any reading under 20 is good. (*Bottom*) Use the most common method, checking continuity. Switch the multimeter to its "sound" icon and touch the two probes to the element screws. If a tone sounds, the element is good.

# The 60-Second (or Less) Troubleshooting Technique

**My farmer neighbor** and two other old-timers had been working on a water heater for over half a day. After numerous trips to the store for parts, it still didn't work. My neighbor asked me if I would take a look. In the country, it is an unwritten law that when you are asked to "take a look," you'd darn well better take a look.

However, there is nothing in the unwritten law that says you can't be a bit dramatic and have some fun. So there I was with three old men, staring at a water heater with both element covers off. They had changed out both elements and both thermostats several times. The power was OK—the red button reset was not popped out. I looked at their work and smiled. "Betchya I can find the problem in less than 60 seconds," I said. Nobody spoke, but their expressions betrayed their doubt. I got out my multimeter and screwdriver, and shut off the power. "Ready?" I asked. No one uttered a word. I blew at my fingertips, shook my fingers out, raised both hands like a gunfighter of the old west, and yelled, "GO!"

I tested the top element; it was blown. I relocated a wire on the top thermostat that I had previously noted they had miswired. I then checked the bottom element, and it was OK. I yelled, "Done." I was way under 60 seconds.

There was never anything wrong with the thermostats they had replaced. The initial problem was probably a bad lower element. But after they replaced it and let the water back in, they didn't bleed out all the air in the top of the tank and thereby blew the top element when they reapplied power. After that, they replaced both thermostats to no avail. As a last resort, they replaced the top element, but blew it again for the same reason. Then they thought they had bad parts from the store and kept changing things over and over until they gave up. That's where I came in.

Of course, I didn't charge them anything. Fixing the heater meant *they now owed me a favor*. In my part of the country, it is far more important to have old farmers owe you a favor than to get a small amount of money from them. Besides, how would I charge for 60 seconds' work? As a side note, from that time on both farmers plowed my driveway for free after each snowfall.

of the element. There should be no sound. If the multimeter beeps, the element tube has split and is touching the water. Leave power to the heater off. It can electrify the pipes and tank, and is dangerous.

## The element attachment bracket

When replacing a thermostat, never shortcut the installation by leaving off the attachment bracket. Some people do this, thinking the wires will keep the thermostat in place, but they won't. The spring-tension bracket keeps the back of the thermostat tight against the metal tank so the thermostat can sense the water temperature. Without it, all kinds of bad things

**The metal bracket** holding the thermostat against the tank should never be discarded or bent back, which would allow the thermostat to drop away from the tank and fail to properly sense the water temperature.

Elements

# Troubleshooting Gas and Electric Water Heaters

## Gas

| Problem | Cause |
|---|---|
| Water leaks | • Not tight enough: hot or cold supply connection, relief valve, drain valve.<br>• Leakage from basement wall, other appliances or water lines.<br>• Condensation of flue products. |
| Leaking T&P valve | • Thermal expansion in closed water system<br>• Improperly seated valve<br>• Water too hot<br>• Excessive water pressure |
| Smelly odors | • High sulfate or mineral content in water supply<br>• Bacteria in water supply |
| Pilot will not light | • Gas control knob not positioned correctly<br>• Main gas supply off<br>• Igniter tip more than 1/8" from pilot hood<br>• Thermocouple malfunction or not adjacent to pilot flame<br>• Internal problems |
| Burners will not stay lit | • Thermocouple malfunction<br>• Dirty or clogged air intake screen<br>• Flame arrester openings blocked<br>• Not enough air in room<br>• Defective gas control |
| Not enough hot water | • Heater not lit or thermostat not on<br>• Thermostat set too low<br>• Heater undersized<br>• Low gas pressure<br>• Incoming water is unusually cold.<br>• Leaking hot water pipes or fixtures<br>• High temperature limit switch activated<br>• Water lines reversed |
| Water too hot | • Thermostat set too high or malfunctioning |
| Water heater sounds | • Condensation dripping on burner<br>• Banging sound—normal expansion within heater |
| Sizzling, rumbling | • Sediment or calcium in bottom of heater tank |
| Sooting | • Improper combustion |
| Vent gas odors | • Lack of supply air<br>• Improperly installed vent piping<br>• Downdraft<br>• Poor combustion |

## Electric

| Problem | Cause |
|---|---|
| Water leaks | • Loose hot or cold supply connection, relief valve or drain valve<br>• Leakage from other appliances, water lines or basement wall<br>• Tank rusting through around screw element threads |
| Leaking temperature and pressure relief valve | • Thermal expansion in closed water system<br>• Excessive water pressure<br>• Improperly seated valve<br>• Water too hot (thermostat malfunction) |
| Hot water odors*** Caution: removal of the anode(s) will void warranty. | • High sulfate or mineral content in water supply<br>• Bacteria in water supply |
| Not enough or no hot water | • Power supply to heater is not on.<br>• Blown element<br>• Thermostat set too low* or malfunctioning<br>• Heater undersized<br>• Incoming water is usually cold (winter).<br>• Leaking hot water from pipes or fixtures<br>• Reversed water lines into water heater |
| Hot water too hot | • Thermostat set too high or malfunctioning<br>• Thermostat has dropped away from tank.<br>• Condensaton on tank due to excessive moisture in air |
| Water heater sounds** | • Scale accumulation on elements<br>• Sediment build-up on tank bottom |
| Metal jacket shocks you | • Jacket is touching hot wire—turn off immediately. |
| Frying sound from heater's splice box | • Loose or corroded splice—turn off immediately |

*Raising thermostat above 120°F may cause scalding.
**Electric water heaters "sing" and this is normal. The sound comes from the element.
***Replace anode rod with one of different material (see text).
****When replacing a water heater, this is a common complaint because the thermostat on new heaters are set lower at the factory.

A T&P valve must be installed in a heater to relieve excessive temperature and pressure and to prevent the heater from exploding. Unlike this one, you should come off the 3/4-in. threads and bring a 3/4-in. pipe down beside the heater to within a few inches of the floor.

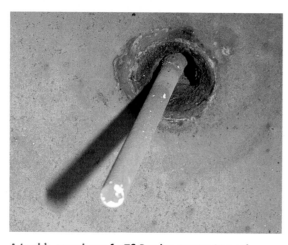

A tank's-eye view of a T&P valve sensor. Note the iron buildup around the sensor opening. If any of this breaks off and lodges in the seat of the T&P valve when you test it, the valve will not re-close and the area will flood.

Electric water heaters are required to be grounded. There is no grandfather clause for this.

can happen. Also, when replacing the thermostat, do not permanently bend the thermostat attachment bracket when you remove it because this will create an air gap between the tank metal and the thermostat sensor.

## T&P Valves

Every heater comes with, or needs to have installed, a T&P (temperature and pressure relief) valve, which will ease water pressure if the water overheats or the water pressure gets too high. If the incoming water pressure to the house exceeds 80 lb., the valve will start to sputter and drip water every time the water heater kicks on. To counter this, a water pressure regulator must be installed on the main service line to the house.

Code requires a ¾-in. pipe from the T&P valve to within 6 in. of the floor. CPVC pipe is acceptable for this. Code says the pipe cannot be reduced in size and cannot have a threaded fitting on the end that's close to the floor. If the pipe travels horizontally for an extended distance, it must slope downhill, never uphill.

All water heaters are potential bombs—and they have killed people. The T&P valve is the last-resort protective device. If the thermostat fails to shut off and the element keeps heating the water, the red overload button will sense the increased temperature and shut off the electrical power. If both fail, the T&P valve will kick in and gradually release the tank pressure in sputtering bursts. If the T&P valve also fails, the water heater will explode if the pipes to the heater do not melt, split, or somehow blow off the heater.

When a heater explodes it is like a large bomb going off. A few years ago a heater exploded in a Minnesota residence. It blew out the walls, ruined the furniture, and tore a hole in the ceiling and roof. Then the tank took off like a missile, flying more than 100 ft. into the neighbor's yard, where it hit and killed a dog. The house was totaled.

If you ever turn on the hot side of a tap and get steam, leave the spigot on and immediately get out of the house. Steam indicates that all protective devices have failed, the overheated water is starting to boil, and the water heater is getting ready to blow. If you pass the breaker box, throw the breaker off to the heater. If the heater does not explode in the next 15 minutes, you can go back in and turn off the spigot. All the hot water is now out of the heater. Turn off the heater at the breaker if you haven't done so already. Count yourself one of the lucky few and call a plumber to repair or replace the water heater. Do not, for any reason, turn the heater back on.

I do not recommend periodic testing of the T&P valve unless you have a replacement valve immediately available and the floor can stand a flood. Too often, a piece of rust will break off and get caught in the valve's seal and the T&P valve will not shut off.

## Anode Rods

Metal-tank water heaters have one or two anode rods inside. The purpose of the rods is to sacrifice themselves by corrosion, thereby preventing corrosion of the tank metal. They are typically made of magnesium (these will have a bump on the hex head) or aluminum (no bump) wrapped around a steel core wire. A rod's lifespan depends on the composition or quality of the water, but it's usually around six years. If 6 in. of wire is showing on the rod, replace it. If you let the rod corrode completely, the tank will die soon after.

You'll need around 40 in. of overhead clearance to get a new rod in. For tight locations you can sometimes buy rods that are shorter or that

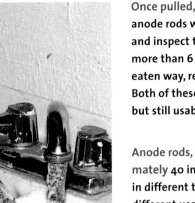

Once pulled, clean the anode rods with water and inspect them. If more than 6 in. has eaten way, replace them. Both of these are pitted but still usable.

Anode rods, approximately 40 in. long, come in different types for different uses. The top rod is aluminum, used to prevent "smelly" water. The rod in the middle is a segmented-magnesium rod. The bottom rod is a combination anode-outlet magnesium rod.

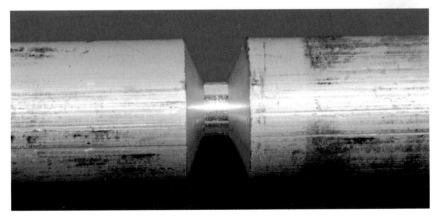

Segmented magnesium rods can bend slightly at the segments shown in this close-up, allowing you to replace an anode rod in tank installations where there are minimal overhead clearances.

# Removing an anode rod

**1** The anode rod is accessible on the heater top. To change it out, remove the plastic surround so the socket can get a bigger bite on the hex head.

**2** Using a 1¹/₁₆-in. socket and a long breaker bar handle (all ¾-in. drive), jerk the handle counterclockwise to break the anode head free. Turn counterclockwise and remove the rod.

**3** Pull the anode rod from the water heater. Typically, pull straight up—this rod was so corroded that it broke as it was pulled out of the heater.

**4** Inspect the rod. This rod obviously must be replaced. Others may not be so obvious. If over 6 in. of support wire is visible, replace the rod.

come in segments. You can also cut them to length. If the water heater uses the dip tube as part of the anode rod assembly, you will have to get an exact replacement. Try to avoid this type of design. In my region of Virginia, local suppliers don't stock anode rods anymore. If this is the case in your area, you can order these and other water heater specialty products online at www.waterheaterrescue.com.

If you smell an odor of rotten eggs on the hot water side of the faucet, something in the water is reacting to the anode rod. You will have to replace the rod with a specialty anode rod, which can be obtained from various web retailers including the one listed above. If the smell is coming from the cold water as it runs from the tap, then the problem is in the well. In that situation, replace the water heater with one such as the non-metal-tank Marathon, which has no anode rod. These are heavily marketed all across the country and should be easy to find.

**Opt for brass** drain valves and avoid plastic ones like this. Brass is always superior to plastic.

## The Six-Second Element Change-Out

Draining a water heater to change an element takes too long, and many water heaters won't drain anyway. Instead I have come up with a system that allows me to change out an element in less than six seconds. Do it right, and the amount you'll spill is a cup or less. Make an error, and you'll risk a flooded floor.

Prep work:

- Turn off the power to the heater and run enough cold water through the heater so the water is no longer hot.
- Close the main cold-water valve to the heater. If there is another valve on the hot side, close it also.
- Release residual hot-water pressure by any hot-water valve or T&P valve. This is a quick on and off. All taps in the house should be closed, and the washer should be turned off.
- Unwire the bad element.
- Have the new element (with gasket inserted over threads) and a washrag within reach
- Using a 1½-in. socket and a long breaker bar handle, break the old element free of its initial grip and loosen it until it just begins to leak.

Now start the six-second change-out:

- Using your fingers, turn the element counterclockwise and remove it. Remove the element gasket as well. Water will begin to come out the hole but will slow as it pulls a vacuum.
- Insert the new element through the water in the hole and twist it clockwise until it is finger tight. The water will stop. Use the rag to plug the hole during this process if you cannot get the element in. Warning: If the element is long and heavy, it may be difficult to hold in place with your fingers while you turn it into the heater's threads.
- End six-second change out: two seconds for unscrewing, one for removal of old element, one to insert new element, and two seconds to hand-tighten to stop the leak.

Finish the job:

- Tighten the element with a socket and breaker bar. Rewire, turn on water and check for leaks. Replace element cover and turn the power back on.

A plastic drain valve has little internal room and clogs easily.

## Drain Valves

These come in three kinds: barrel-type plastic, plastic boiler drain, and brass boiler drain.

The barrel type is the one that seems to turn forever without anything happening, and then it falls off in your hands, flooding the room. It should be banned. The plastic boiler drain isn't much better. It snaps off easily when bumped, and any small piece of iron flake, debris, or lime flake will clog the valve.

Brass drain valves have larger holes than plastic valves and will allow more water to flow

## Opt for Heavily Insulated Foam Heaters

In the old days water heaters had no insulation, and nobody cared about heat loss. Many of these are still around in Mexico. The first attempts at insulation I saw were those that used mineral wool. For those too young to remember, mineral wool is made from ground glass, and you'll itch like you won't believe if you touch it. We all gave a sigh of relief when the industry switched over to fiberglass.

But even fiberglass is now in the background. Indeed, I wouldn't recommend any water heater that uses fiberglass. Foam insulation is infinitely better

Cutaway of a superinsulated water heater (Photo courtesy Water Heater Innovations, Inc.)

because it has a higher R rating and it does not trap water like fiberglass. Foam makes the jacket rigid so it doesn't dent easily, and it gets the heater off of the cold floor. Typically, the thicker the foam the better the quality of the water heater, because a low-cost manufacturer won't waste the money for foam on their units—these are "low bid" heaters. Driving up the cost on a low-bid heater means losing the job.

If the heater doesn't mention any type of insulation, I would not recommend it—it is probably the standard six-year energy-hog/throw-away/low-bid water heater. Look for heaters that brag about their foam and how thick it is. A 2½-in. thickness is considered good and gives an insulation R rating of around 20. A 3-in. thickness is typically found on the best water heaters.

through them. Also, plastic valves do not allow straight access into the tank. With brass, you can unscrew and remove the stem and poke a screwdriver directly through the valve body. If you do this while the valve is on the water heater, it will break through any iron that has formed over the exit hole and that is blocking the water from draining. (continued on p. 130)

Plastic drain valves are fragile and can easily be broken off leaving the threaded part inside the heater. To avoid such an accident, turn the water heater so that the valve faces away from the action.

Plastic drain valves can become extremely brittle over time and can snap off flush with the tank wall if accidentally bumped. The only way to remove the broken piece still in the tank is to use an EZ out or its equivalent.

## Water Heater Leakage Checkpoints

- Condensation on metal pipes sometimes runs down pipes pooling water on top the heater. Other times, leaks within the pipes themselves drip down onto the heater. Sometimes from the valve itself. My neighbor had a pipe leak that dripped down onto their heater for years, finally rusting it out.
- Leaks sometimes occur at the point of attachment to the heater. I've had leaks at the factory connection into the heater (nipple/tank interface) and at the connections where the house pipe interfaced with the factory nipples.
- Anode rod connection into the tank can sometimes leak.
- T & P valve. Though I have never seen it happen, you can get a leak at the threaded connection into the heater if you didn't get the valve in tight enough.
- Dripping from the T & P valve. This can occur if a piece of trash gets caught in the valve seat or by the valve "popping off" because of excessive temperature or pressure.
- Leak around the heating element or anywhere in the tank because of rust–through.
- Dripping water from the drain valve or around the threaded connection into the tank.
- Water around the water heater base. This can come from any leak on the tank including rust–through. Sometimes the water heater seals itself and the pinhole leak in the tank rusts closed—only to open again later. Many times the water around the tank is not coming from the heater—but from a leak in the basement wall or floor. This is quite common when the location is near a gutter downspout.

# Clearing clogged brass drain valves

Older water heaters have a habit of rusting over and clogging the drain hole exit within the heater. When you open the drain valve, nothing comes out. If your water heater uses a brass boiler drain (instead of plastic) you can break up the clog by removing the interior of the boiler drain and sticking a screwdriver through it, into the heater, to dislodge the blockage.

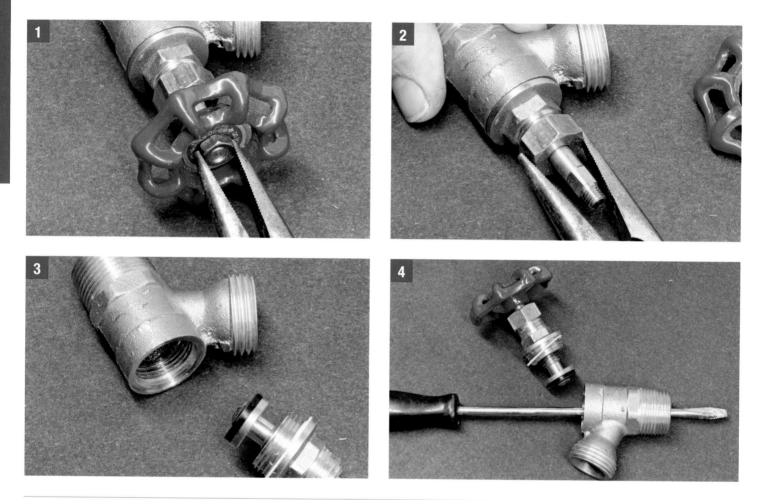

**1** Using pliers, remove the nut holding the handle onto the valve (water and power are off to the heater.

**2** Using pliers or an adjustable wrench, loosen and remove the packing nut on the valve.

**3** Using pliers or a deep socket, unscrew the step assembly from the valve body.

**4** Insert a long screwdriver straight through the valve and into the water heater body.

# Installing a full-flow drain

To install a full-size drain opening into a new heater, you will need a 6-in.-3/4-in. nipple, a 3/4-in. ball valve, and a brass 3/4-in. thread by 5/8-in. hose connection fitting.

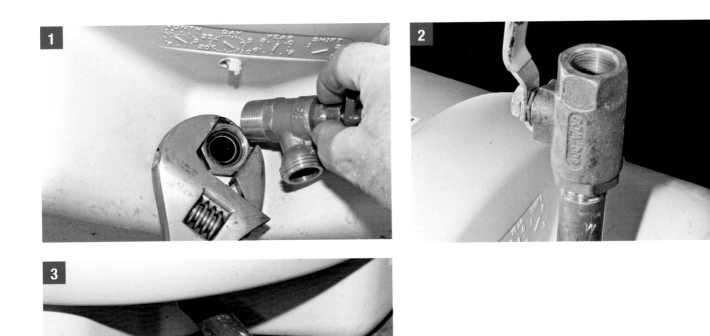

**1** Lay heater on its side and remove the old valve to expose the tank's 3/4-in. female threads.

**2** Screw the ball valve onto the nipple and the nipple into the heater.

**3** Verify handle turns properly. You can screw the hose fitting into the ball valve at any time, before or after it has been installed.

Of course, the minute you poke through, the water will start flowing out of the hole and continue until you reassemble. Don't do this if the area around the heater cannot get wet.

## The Ultimate Water Heater

The problem with conventional metal-tank water heaters is that most owners forget to change the anode rods, the tanks corrode, and another water heater heads to the landfill. Don't be fooled by lifetime water heaters that have metal tanks—they will leak. You pay a high price for the heater up front because they assume it is going to leak and you will bring it back. Thus you are paying for a second heater at the get-go.

There is an electric water heater that's warranted for the life of the house. It's called the Marathon (www.marathonheaters.com). Without a metal tank, it can't rust and leak. The Marathon has a special element that contains a resistor. It will blow fast if there is no water around it when power is applied so the tank isn't ruined. If you install a Marathon, I suggest you order an extra upper and lower element since they're not likely to be available at a local stores.

When selecting an electric water heater, look for these features:

- Nonmetal tank, if the budget allows (such heaters cost more than twice what a metal tank heater costs)

- Non-CFC-foam insulation, which doesn't give off a gas harmful to the atmosphere. Foam has a rating of about R 8 per in.

**The splice compartment of a Marathon heater is large, on the front (not the top), and with plenty of room to wire. All three features are exceptions not usually found in the majority of heaters on the market.**

- Foam thickness of 2 in. (good) or 3 in. (better)

- A high energy factor (EF), 0.94 or higher

- Brass drain valve (unless you are going to install your own full-flow drain)

- Preinstalled T&P valve

If you buy a metal-tank heater, look for low-density incoloy elements for both top and

**A non-metallic-tank water heater may last the life of the house and take a tremendous load off the landfill. (Photo courtesy Water Heater Innovations, Inc.)**

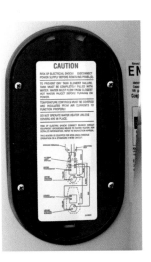

To get to the Marathon's element, you remove the bubble cover and flat plate, then pivot up the element guard.

## CONSTRUCTION FEATURES

**Energy saving pipe wrap kit**—reduces heat loss through plumbing lines.

**Temperature and pressure relief valve**—factory installed.

**Watertight grommets**—keep out overhead moisture and condensation.

**Seamless molded non-metallic inner tank**—can't rust or corrode.

**Fill tube**—high temperature material to withstand thermal storage and other high-temperature applications.

**High-tech heating elements**—upper element fused to protect tank against "dry fire". Bottom element is low-watt density, stainless alloy for long life.

**Polyethylene outer jacket**—resists dents and scratches during transit, installation and beyond.

**Envirofoam®**—a great energy saver and friendly to the ozone layer—it's made without CFCs and HCFCs.

**Filament-wound fiberglass tank**—has unmatched strength.

**Recessed drain valve**—protected from damage.

Cutaway view of a Marathon heater. (Photo courtesy Water Heater Innovations, Inc.)

## Plumbing the tank

When I install a tank, I insert two 3/4-in. brass nipples into the top of the heater and use flexible 3/4-in. braided stainless connectors to connect the heater to the plumbing system. The movable pipes create a natural union fitting and allow me plenty of flexibility in placing the heater where I want it. I also install a full-flow ball valve where the flex pipe ties into the cold-water line.

**The Marathon heater** comes with brass female adapters. I insert two brass nipples to interface with my flexible connecting pipes. When installing the brass nipples into the heater, it's imperative to use a pipe wrench—at least a 14-in. —to apply back-up or counter pressure to the water heater's female fittings—otherwise, the fittings will rip out of the tank as you tighten the nipples.

**Not all flex** pipes are alike. Avoid those with small diameters. The pipe on the left, advertised as 3/4 in., is really only 3/8 in. in diameter. The one on the right is closer to a full 3/4 in.

bottom elements. Disregard any manufacturer's claim that the top element doesn't need to be an incoloy element because the bottom element does all the work. The top element is the one that blows if the unit is dry fired; if it's incoloy, it cannot be blown. If blown, the thermostat will lock on it, not allowing it to switch to the bottom element, and the heater will not work.

### Getting more hot water

You can increase a water heater's capacity by adding a tempering tank (a tall, 80-gal. galvanized tank) beside it. Send the incoming cold water into the bottom of the tank and take the output from the top. This allows the cold water temperature to rise to the ambient air temperature before it enters the water heater and saves on energy. In cold-weather areas, depending on the location of the water heater, this temperature differential can be significant, amounting to considerable energy savings. Elsewhere it's not worth the trouble to plumb the tank in. To keep the tank from sweating, spray it with car undercoating to break the cold-metal-to-warm-air contact.

Another way to get extra hot water is to plumb in a second water heater. You can install it parallel to or in series with the first. A parallel hookup allows a massive amount of hot water in a short time. A series hookup gives you a moderate amount of hot water over an extended period. Practically, I don't think it makes any difference. I've hooked them up both ways in residential situations, and the owners were satisfied not even knowing which way I had plumbed it.

If you hook up the second heater parallel to the first, try to keep cold-water inputs and hot-

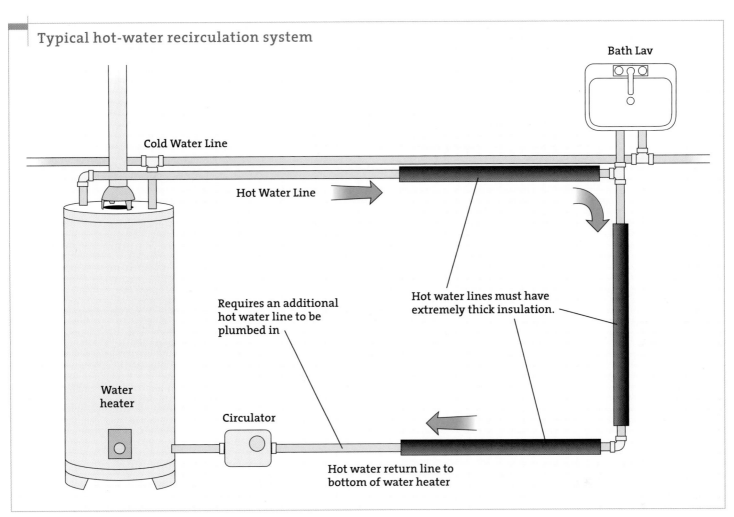

### Typical hot-water recirculation system

Bath Lav

Cold Water Line

Hot Water Line

Requires an additional hot water line to be plumbed in

Hot water lines must have extremely thick insulation.

Water heater

Circulator

Hot water return line to bottom of water heater

water outputs identical in number of turns and fittings. This keeps the heaters balanced so both run out of water at the same time. You can add and subtract balancing resistance by using the turn-off valves at the cold-water input.

In selecting a second heater, always opt for electric. That way you'll avoid the hassle and expense of running a vent line, because you cannot tie into an existing vent nor use a bricked chimney as a vent. Also, you won't need another gas line.

This recirculator system, typically controlled via a thermostat, has hot water flowing in a loop. It requires an extra hot-water line and extremely thick insulation on the pipes within the loop to avoid losing heat.

Rusted-through spot

The cutaway view (*left*) of a high-quality water heater shows where it leaked. The leak was due to a failure to replace the anode rod.

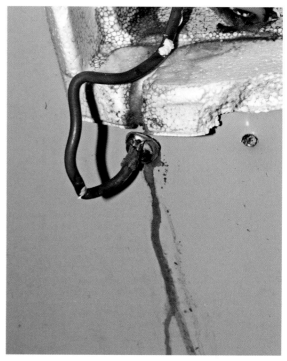

**Seen inside the** heater is a rusted-through leak spot. This corrosion, the size of a penny, ate through the steel jacket to spring a leak.

**The orange streak** is an indicator of another water heater heading to the land fill due to a tank leak.

The purpose of a water heater pan is to contain a water heater leak—the water will drip into the pan as opposed to flooding a finished floor. However, it will do little good if the drain pan overflows. That's why each water pan (some round, some square) has a drain hole in its lip for a 1 in. drain. This drain line (1 in. PVC) is what must be run outside, into the crawlspace, or to a floor drain.

A drain pan should be used under any water heater that sits on a finished floor that cannot be soaked. It will be unnoticed until there is a leak. One of my customers had just lost all of his overhead drywall due to a leaky pipe in the ceiling above. The drywall pooled the water until it could take no more, and then fell into the living room. One week later the upstairs water heater sprung a leak, and since the water had no place to drain, pooled again above the living room ceiling and brought it down again. If you have a two-story house, either use a water heater pan or you will, sooner or later, wish you had installed one.

# Hot Water Recirculating Systems

The reason for installing a recirculating system is to get instant hot water at the tap. With hot water readily available, less wasted water goes down the drain. This is especially helpful during a drought, and spares the utility from processing the wasted thousands of gallons. For country folk this is no big deal because the water comes out of the ground and is returned to the ground.

There are two kinds of recirculating systems. One type needs a new hot-water return line plumbed in from the furthermost fixture. The new line sometimes attaches to the cold-water input of the water heater; or it can attach to the water heater drain (drain is open), depending on the unit's design. The circulator typically is near the water heater or under the lav. It pumps the hot water in a loop controlled by a thermostat or timer.

The problem with this system is that you have double the length of hot-water lines, which doubles the heat loss through the pipes. If you go this route, heavily insulate the hot-water heater lines, which will be expensive. In addition, running a return line in an existing house is not always practical.

The second type of recirculating system, the one I prefer, does not have a return line but instead has a pump or bleeder valve at the furthermost fixture (normally under the lav) that sends the cooled-down water from the hot-water line into the cold-water line. The flow can be controlled by timers, thermostats, and switches, depending on the unit. This design is much more practical, especially for existing houses. The best systems will have preplumbed inlets/outlets for supply tubes. When you install

it under a sink, simply disconnect the hot and cold supply tubes from the spigot and connect to the new unit. Then add two new supply tubes from the unit back to the spigot. Now, you need an electrical outlet. Install one under the sink or run the unit temporarily off a extension cord from the bathroom outlet if the unit's cord isn't long enough. Kits, which start at just over $200, are available at most large plumbing suppliers. Recirculation units are required in some areas.

The flow of cooled-down water into the cold-water line is typically controlled by a thermostat. A higher-quality unit will have an adjustable thermostat as well as a timer and remote control to control the flow of cooled-down water.

A secondary use of these units is to keep water lines from freezing by keeping the water hot. They also prevent the cold-water line from freezing by having warm water pushed into it by the circulator. This can be a boon to owners of summer houses who have to drain every fall and still risk having a loop of water that might freeze and break a pipe. Installing this type of unit would mean no more pipe draining. Of course, if there is a power failure, the unit would cease functioning.

When selecting a recirculator, look for these features:

> **If you plumb** the water heater backwards (and this does occasionally happen), cold to hot, hot to cold, the customer will complain about running out of hot water quickly. If that's their only complaint, you're lucky—sometimes it melts the toilets' wax seals, too.

## Bleed-off type of water recirculation system

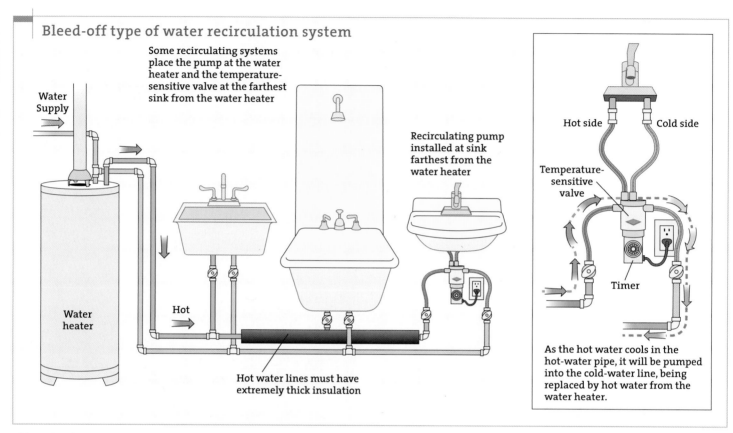

Water Supply

Some recirculating systems place the pump at the water heater and the temperature-sensitive valve at the farthest sink from the water heater

Recirculating pump installed at sink farthest from the water heater

Water heater

Hot

Hot water lines must have extremely thick insulation

Hot side          Cold side

Temperature-sensitive valve

Timer

As the hot water cools in the hot-water pipe, it will be pumped into the cold-water line, being replaced by hot water from the water heater.

**This recirculator system bleeds the cooled-off hot water in the hot-water pipe into the cold-water pipe.**

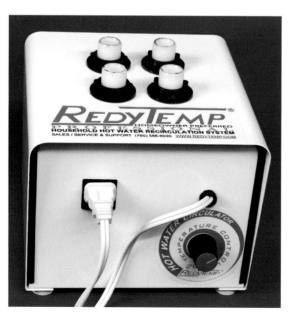

**The easiest hot-water circulator system I have installed is this Redy Temp unit. It hooks up to the supply tubes and does not require a new pipe back to the water heater.**

- A design that does not require cutting into the water lines for items such as a circulator

- A design that does not require another water line to be plumbed in

- A control mechanism that can be installed under the sink, not at the water heater

- A design that uses supply tube inlet and outlet

- A very long cord that will reach an outlet

- An adjustable thermostat and a means to control it, such as a timer or a remote control

# Gas Heater Awareness

Before you opt for a gas water heater understand its disadvantages:

- While prices vary wildly, overall, gas water heaters are more expensive than electric models.
- Gas heaters are more expensive to install, because they need a gas line and a flue, which can exceed the cost of the heater.
- Around 25 percent of the heat produced by a gas heater is wasted up the flue.
- On some models, the flame sensor, or thermocouple, seems to die early. When the thermocouple goes out, the pilot light will not stay lit. You replace the thermocouple by unscrewing the tiny nut holding the thermocouple to the control module, then unclip it from the burner and replace it.
- Gas heaters are prone to backdrafting, meaning the exhaust of the heater goes into the house as opposed to up the flue.
- Gas fumes and flame are an explosive combination. Raise the gas heater on concrete blocks at least 18 in. above the floor; gas fumes are heavier than air. Never store flammables by the heater.
- The flame produces a large amount of water vapor in the surrounding room. If you live in a cold area and the heater is in the garage, condensation forms on the warm side of the garage door in winter, producing puddles on the floor.
- Venting gas heaters is complicated and can vary from model to model. Gas condensate forms inside the flue and drains into the heater. It is corrosive and can ruin the vent and water heater. To prevent this, follow the manufacturer's venting instructions to the letter.
- The tank is designed like a test tube with a Bunsen burner on the bottom. Imagine a foot or more of debris in the bottom of the heater. The heat has to go through the trash before it can heat the water. In the center of the water tank is a flue hole and immediately below that is the burner. Burners don't work well if debris falls on top the burner and blocks the burner holes, causing the unit to burn improperly. Avoid this by keeping the burner vacuumed clean.
- Just before the control module, gas heaters require a T-shaped dirt leg with its center leg connected to a union, then to another steel nipple and the control module. Gas enters the top of the T and makes a 90-degree turn to the center leg to reach the control module. Debris in the line continues straight to the bottom leg of the T without making the turn.
- Gas heaters use metal tanks, which rust.
- Gas lines leak, often because of cheap fittings. If a flare fitting gets loose or the collar of a cheap flare fitting cracks, gas will fill the area and explode.
- If the flame goes out and the heater must be relit, you'll follow an established lighting procedure, typically 11 to 13 steps. The process is sometimes frustrating. I've witnessed poof-type (3 ft. in diameter) mini explosions at the heater when gas fumes hanging around ignited. Exercise caution whenever you work with gas water heaters.

# Installing a hot water recirculating system

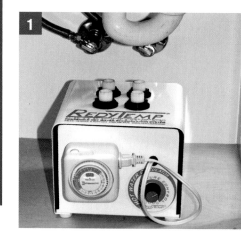

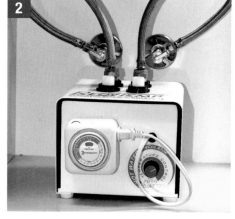

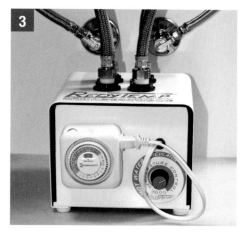

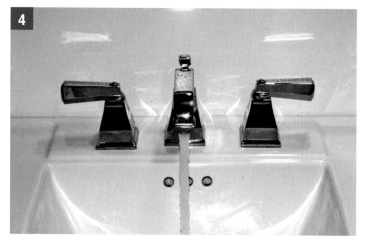

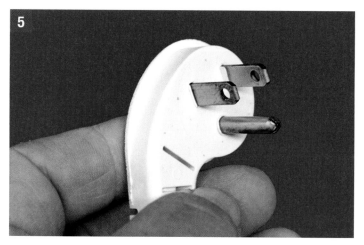

**1** Set the unit in the cabinet under the fixture farthest from the water heater.

**2** Disconnect the supply tubes from the faucet and connect them to the back two ½-in. threaded adapters on top the unit.

**3** Connect the two front ½-in. threaded adapters to the faucet with the ½-in. supply tubes that came with the unit. (Hot is on the left, cold on the right.)

**4** Turn on faucet and run water through the circulator and check for leaks.

**5** Supply power by plugging the unit into a dedicated AC outlet.

### Design considerations

Hot water recirculators do not put instant hot water at all the faucets. They keep hot water in the main line and tap line to the furthermost fixture, assuming the unit or return line is installed at the furthermost fixture. If this is the kitchen sink, for example, and there is a long tap to the bathroom, there will not be recirculating hot water in the bathroom line—only in the main line to the kitchen. This reduces the time it takes to get hot water to the lav, but there will still be a short wait depending on the length of the tap. If you have a Redy Temp–type design, you can install another one of these units at the lav to solve this problem.

## Plastic Adapters

Never install a plastic water fitting (such as a CPVC male adapter) directly into a water heater's cold or hot connections. Besides being against code, it has a high potential for a leak.

Install a pan, with drain, under a water heater if excessive damage would occur due to a leak, such as on an expensive finished floor—especially one on an upper floor.

## Timers

Don't install timers because every time you lose power you have to reset the timer. I've had many service calls where the client didn't have hot water because the timer was off. An even bigger problem is when the owner or plumber assumes the timer has cut all power to the heater—and then works on the heater wiring without throwing the breaker off. Many timers only break one side of the 240 volts; the other leg may still be

hot. In my opinion, timers save little money and are problematic. Did I mention that excessive basement moisture kills them?

A plastic fitting was installed, against code, into this water heater. As the heater's metal female threads expanded due to heat, a leak formed at the plastic male threads and ruined the heater.

This rusted water heater splice compartment was full of water due to the improper connection shown in the top photograph. Submerging the hot wires provided a short circuit that made the entire metal jacket electrically hot.

When you install a recirculating system, insulate the hot-water line as much as possible. If you live in an area that freezes, insulate both lines heavily.

The Redy Temp allows many plug-in controls to be installed on the Redy Temp, including common timers, either mechanical or electronic.

You might not be doing yourself a favor by installing a water heater insulation jacket. Some manufacturers may not want them installed if they cover and jam the T&P valve, the element covers, and the scalding warnings.

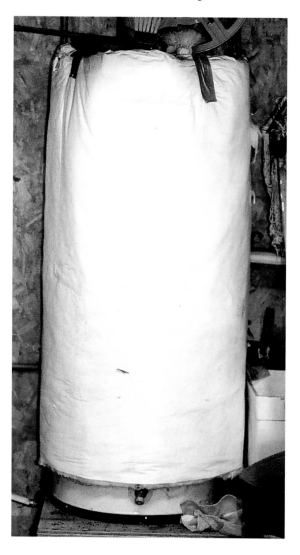

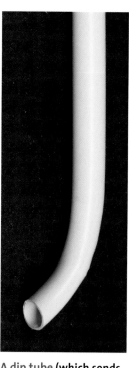

A dip tube (which sends cold water to about 6 in. off the tank bottom) can be curved or straight. The curve sends water sweeping over the flat bottom of the heater and keeps sediment from accumulating on the tank bottom.

## Dip Tubes

The dip tube is the little pipe that sends the cold water to the bottom of the heater. In the old days they were made out of glass; today they're plastic. For common metal-jacket water heaters with flat bottoms, the preferred dip tube is curved at the bottom end. This keeps scale and debris from accumulating and causing the bottom element to blow out.

People often call me saying their water heater has sprung a leak when it hasn't. There's water around the heater, but it's not from the heater. Usually the leak is coming out of the basement wall or occasionally from plumbing within the stud walls.

# Drain and Vent Rough-in

The first significant work in plumbing a house is rough-ing-in the drain/sewer lines. This means you may be in the crawl space, running pipes under the slab, or if you're lucky, in the basement. And if there are upper floors, you'll have to plumb those too. To help with the job, in this chapter I will cover slope, cutting plastic and cast iron, opening holes, and connecting the pipe using a variety of fittings.

Once you have covered all the basics, the actual work begins with the fixture layout, figuring what fixture goes where. From there comes the actual stub-out of each fixture through the floor and the vents overhead. Then all you have to do is connect the vertical stub-out pipes through the floor to the horizontal-run pipes.

## Slope

Always shoot for ¼ in.-per-ft. slope on all lines—vent, drain, sewer. This allows for slight slope variations—if you end up with a little less slope you're still okay, whereas if you design for a lesser slope and make a mistake in installation, there's no slack to make up the difference. Don't worry about too much slope; contrary to popular

**Improper slope. Too often lines are just thrown up without regard to proper support or pitch. This long, unsupported run to the kitchen with 1½-in. pipe resulted in a sag that caused the drainpipe to clog. The kitchen line tends to sag more than others due to massive amounts of hot water from the sink and dishwasher softening the pipe. The line should be larger in diameter than minimum code—at least 2 in.—and supported every 2 ft. to 3 ft., closer than the 4 ft. required by code.**

opinion, that will not be a problem. The faster the flow, the more solids stay in suspension. It's when the fluid slows down that solids drop out and cause stoppages.

As you're working, how do you know you are getting a ¼-in.-per-ft. slope or better? One way to find out, after you have hung the pipe, is to bump one end of a 4-ft. level against the lower end of the pipe and then lower the other end of the level to get a center bubble. At the center bubble, the gap between the end of the level and the pipe should be 1 in. (¼-in. slope per ft. equals 1 in. slope over 4 feet). This technique works well as long as you are a good visual estimator of small distances. I used to tape a 1-in. spacer on the end of my 4-ft. level. I would place the level with spacer against the pipe and when the bubble read level, I had my slope. Eventually I drilled out one end of my level, cut in threads for a large flat-headed bolt, and screwed the bolt in until it was exactly 1 in. above the level. Now, to get an exact ¼-in.-per ft. slope, I place the level against the pipe as I run it. When the level reads center bubble, I have an exact ¼-in.-per-ft. slope.

## Plastic Drain Pipe

The area where you work, along with cost, will determine the type of plastic you use for the

**By threading one end of a 4-ft level, and using a large bolt to turn in and out, I have an adjustable slope reference. When the bolt is out 1 in., a center bubble on the level means I have a perfect ¼-in.-per-ft. slope on my drain lines. To use the level without the bolt, all I have to do is flip the level over.**

**Foam core pipe (*right*) has the same specs and diameter as solid PVC pipe (*left*), but it's lighter and easier to use.**

drain: black ABS or white PVC. Both are durable and will outlive the home owner. ABS is more popular on the West Coast while PVC is more popular in the East. ABS can take more shock without shattering or cracking, but it often melts back together as it is cut. Each requires a different type of glue. PVC makes a surface bond (pipe to fitting) while ABS makes more of an actual fusion bond.

A new type of PVC pipe—foam core—is now on the market. It has the same physical dimensions as common schedule 40 pipe, but, with its foam interior, it's a lot lighter. I love it for just that reason. I've been using it for a couple years now and have had no problems with it.

## Cutting plastic pipe

A cutoff saw with a solid blade is the best tool to use when cutting plastic pipe. Nothing else is close. It always gives a good clean cut and allows a trim of ⅛ in. off the pipe if needed. If you don't have a cutoff saw, you can use a PVC/ABS handsaw or a recip saw. My last choice would be the trusty old hacksaw. It got its name for a reason—it rarely cuts straight and always cuts quite slowly. In other words, it hacks. Whatever saw you use, wear gloves and safety glasses.

## Hole openings

Always drill a hole for a pipe approximately ¼ in. larger than the pipe's outside diameter. This will prevent the squeaking sound as the pipe expands and contracts. The pipe is approximately ¼ in thick. Thus a 4 in. pipe is around 4½ in. OD. Add ¼ in. hole tolerance, and you

By far, the best way to cut plastic pipe is with a cutoff saw with a solid blade, such as the type used to cut masonry or metal.

If the pipe is already in place and has to be cut, use either a PVC/ABS hand saw or a recip saw.

The ¼-in.-per-foot slope or better gives us at least a 2-ft.-per-second flow down the lines. Design engineers call this the "scouring velocity." It's the speed the fluid needs to flow to aid in cleaning the lines.

To cut holes **through multiple plates,** use a self-feed bit (*right, top*).

To cut **through** a single plate, use either a hole cutter (*right, bottom*) or self-feed bit. The hole cutter will cut more slowly, be safer, cut around nails, and leave less blow-out. For a faster cut, use a self-feed bit. Always be wary of nails in the wood.

For a hole **cutter or a** self-feed bit, use a right-angle drill, because such large bits require strong torque that only right-angle drills are powerful enough to deliver.

## Saw Diameters for Various Pipes

| Pipe | Hole saw diameter |
|------|-------------------|
| 4 in. | 4¾ in. |
| 3 in. | 3¾ in. |
| 2 in. | 2½ in. |
| 1½ in. | 2⅛ in. or 2¼ in. |

have a 4¾ in. hole. As shown in the above table, different hole openings are needed for the various pipe diameters plumbers work with. You will need a hole saw and/or a self-feed bit for 1½-in. and 2-in. pipe. For larger holes, use a hole saw or a recip saw.

I always wondered if anyone else thought how illogical the process of building a house was. Carpenters go to all the trouble and expense of placing studs and joists, and then in come the electricians and plumbers who destroy everything the carpenters worked so hard to build. Bottom line: Be wary of reducing the structural integrity of whatever you are drilling through.

According to code, you are not supposed to cut a hole that's bigger than one-third of the stud's width. I'm sorry to say this is sometimes ignored by everyone on a job, including me. In reality, the only way this part of the code can be followed is if all plumbing walls are 6 in. wide or greater. For example, a 2-in. pipe needs a 2½-in. or 2¾-in. hole. By code, the stud this pipe is in needs to be at least 6 in. wide (a 2×6 wall)—not a common 2×4 wall, which is only 3½ in. wide. It is rare to see an architect plan a wall that large even where a drain line has to go.

If a wall has a hole within 1½-in. of the stud's edges, be sure to install ¹⁄₁₆-in. metal plates on the outside face of the stud. This steel protection plate keeps screws and nails from entering the wall and damaging the pipes.

Even if the hole—in this case, for a 1½-in. pipe—is drilled dead center of the stud (red line), it will extend deep into no-man's land (within 1½ in. of the stud edge, marked by the green line). Both sides of the stud must have metal plates, and such a stud cannot be used as a main structural support.

In the past you could always get a 3-in. pipe (3½-in. OD) within a 2×4 stud wall. No more. Some studs are no longer 3½ in. wide; some are now 3⁷⁄₁₆ in. and must be furred out to make them wide enough.

Sometimes rules have to be broken. That is, the pipe has to go where it has to go and at least 50 percent of a joist will have to be cut. If you find yourself in this situation, contact the job foreman. He or she will thank you. If the pipe cannot be relocated, the crew will brace the area with plywood, steel or some other method once you are finished. Never make such a significant cut into a structural beam or joist without the job foreman's permission.

## Plastic Fittings

When you're on a job, it's a good idea to have several of each type of fitting for each pipe size as well as reducer fittings. I keep mine in garbage containers, with each size in its own can—1½ in., 2 in., 3 in., and 4 in. The reducer fittings go in the container of the largest opening for that fitting. That is, a 3×2 reducer bushing will be in the 3-in. container. Using containers with wheels saves my back and allows me to easily take them where I need them.

The good news is that plastic fittings come in myriad designs and sizes. The bad news is you have to stock them all.

I keep my 1½-in. and 2-in. fittings in a small garbage container with wheels Like these; 3-in. and 4-in. fittings require larger containers.

**A street fitting is the same size as the pipe on one end and has a hub on the other. Such a fitting is designed to make a fast turn off another fitting's hub.**

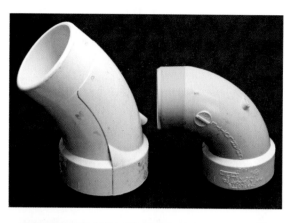

**A long-sweep elbow is 1 in. taller than a short-sweep elbow.**

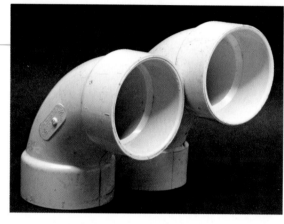

**To make a hard turn, besides a common 90-degree fitting, you can also use (*left to right*) 22-degree, 60-degree, or 45-degree fittings.**

On any particular job, you will need the following fittings for each pipe diameter:

- Elbows and street elbows—long sweeps and short sweeps
- 45s and street 45s
- 22s and street 22s
- Ts and reducer Ts
- Ys and reducer Ys

- Couplings and reducer couplings
- Reducing bushings
- Female cleanouts—hub-type, which fits onto a pipe, and insert-type, which goes into a fitting hub.
- 3-in. or 4-in. cleanout Ts
- 3-in. or 4-in. closet flanges
- 1½-in. trap adapters. These are fittings that connect the drain line to the smaller diameter P-trap pipe under the sink (lav or kitchen). One side of the adapter is a hub that slips onto a drainpipe. The other side has threads that make a compression fitting connection onto the P-trap pipe. Get both hub-type adapters (which fit onto a pipe) and insert-type ones (which fit into a fitting hub).

## Gluing

You must have a specific glue for the type of pipe you are using: ABS glue for ABS pipe, for example. Even though multipurpose glue works just fine, multipurpose glues are not allowed by code.

Large cans of PVC glue include a large dauber, or glue applicator. Use this for gluing large-diameter pipe (3 in. and 4 in.). Small and medium cans of glue have small daubers for use only on small-diameter pipe. A small dauber can't spread glue on large pipe and fittings fast enough before it starts to dry, and you'll wind up with part of the pipe and fitting hub not being covered with glue. I saw one entire system of pipe in a crawl space come falling down because of that. For several months, the crawl space became the septic tank.

Here's another tip to avoid such a problem: mark glued fittings with a hash mark to indicate they have been glued. A plumber's nightmare is to forget to glue a fitting. However, on one job, the plumber (if he was one) forgot to glue them all. I was called to this job and was in the crawl space replacing a cracked tub trap, when someone in the house flushed a toilet. As the water flowed down the drain/sewer line in the crawl space, I noticed water dripping out of every fitting along the 40-ft. line. Not a single fitting in the entire system had been glued. The system had been in place for many years, but since the water had been dripping under the house, no one had ever noticed.

On PVC, apply the primer and then the glue, first to the fitting and then the pipe. Go around twice to spread the fluid and a third time to absorb the excess that might run or pool.

## Flexible Fittings

These are those black fittings, sometimes called Fernco fittings, that look like rubber, feel like rubber, and even smell like rubber but are really flexible PVC. Simply slip them onto a pipe and fasten them with large stainless steel clamps. I keep a lot of flexible fittings in stock. Flexible fittings are, by definition, transition fittings, made for the transition from one pipe type to another—from cast iron to PVC, for example.

Those of us in the field have found a million other uses for them. They work well in connecting an entire cast iron system. When installing a new plumbing system or repairing an old one, with a flex T or elbow I no longer have to be right on the money where pipe and fittings meet. Knowing this, I can work a lot faster. Plus I no longer have to bend the pipe to get the last fitting on. I use flexible fittings for add-ons in renovations, and for cleanout fittings. You can

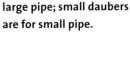

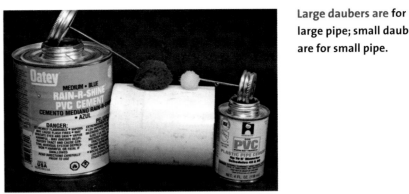

Large daubers are for large pipe; small daubers are for small pipe.

To ensure I have what I need when I need it, I keep a washtub full of flexible fittings: Ts and couplings of all sizes, even traps.

Although it's designed to interface with different types of pipes, flexible fittings work quite well connecting pipes of the same material. Here, a vent had to be cut in an existing line.

A flex elbow keeps the vibration from a sewage pump from being transferred into the house drain and vent system.

# Gluing a fitting

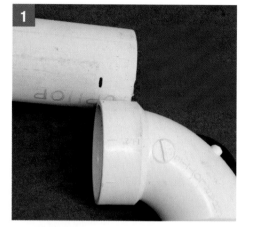

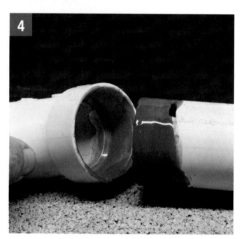

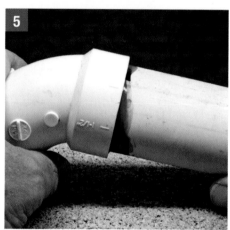

**1** Mark the pipe so you will know when it is all the way into the hub. If necessary, make any alignment marks on the pipe/fitting connection.

**2** Prime first. Rake the excess primer off the dauber by running the dauber in circles on the inside of the can's lip.

**3** Apply primer to both the fitting and pipe.

**4** Apply glue to both the fitting and the pipe.

**5** Push pipe and fitting together slightly offset from where you want the alignment to occur. Twist pipe or fitting into alignment. Hold the pipe tight for one minute.

take an elbow right off the line and easily rod with a snake downstream or upstream.

In some areas, local code restricts the use of such non-banded couplings to outside the wall and requires banded fittings inside the wall. In theory, the logic goes, a drywall screw could be driven into a non-banded coupling. I don't think that logic holds water. Sure, you can drive a drywall screw into a flexible coupling or fitting, but that same screw can go right into a plastic or PEX pipe just as easily.

When I go out on a job, for each pipe diameter I bring the following flexible fittings:

- Ts
- Elbows
- Couplings
- Caps
- Trap adapters

## Cast Iron

Cast iron, once shunned by plumbers, is once again in favor in the trade. It wasn't used for years because its lead and oakum joints required a massive amount of time and experience to install. Melted lead had to be poured into the hub fittings to seal the pipe connection. As a kid, my first job was firing up the lead pots.

With the new no hub–type and Fernco-type (with and without metal bands) coupling systems, joint connections are fast and easy. Cast iron's main advantage, and the reason some home owners are requesting it, is that it's quiet while plastic is noisy. When a long run of straight pipe is adjacent to a living area, such as an upstairs bath drain line running over the dining or living room, cast iron is the pipe of choice. To further reduce the noise, fiberglass

I use flex **couplings to connect two pipes or fittings that are slightly out of alignment.**

Be wary of **caps or any other fittings that use anodized screws instead of all stainless steel. They rust.**

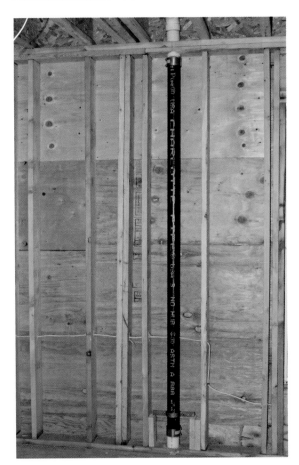

One of the **most common uses of cast iron pipe is in walls adjacent to living and eating areas. Being cast, the pipe muffles the drain's noise so it won't disturb dinner conversation.**

Cast iron pipe is heavy and must be clamped off immediately above the interface to hold its weight. The coupling on the left is a heavy-duty type of No Hub. The solid metal band coupling on the right is a Fernco Proflex.

When there is not enough room in the stud cavity for extra vertical supports, you will have to cut a slot in the studs.

Studor makes a trap and vent combined in one unit that fits right onto the standpipe of the sink. Though it works well and is being used in most countries worldwide, including Canada, it is not available in stores in the United States. It can be ordered online and used in areas that don't have codes.

insulation can be fitted around the pipe and fittings.

By far, the easiest way to cut cast iron is with a cutoff saw with a solid blade. You can also snap it off with a soil pipe cutter that sometimes can be rented. If the pipe is already in place and needs to be cut, I use a common rip saw with a solid blade. This can take me most of the way around the pipe. To finish the job, I use a hand grinder with a solid blade, always wearing gloves and safety glasses.

## Venting

The need for venting is absolute. When water runs through a line it pushes air ahead of it and pulls air behind it. If the pipe is completely filled with water as it flows, then a vacuum is formed behind the water (which can pull the water out of a trap), and the air in front will push and bubble itself out of a fixture trap, assuming there is no opening to the outside on either end.

In addition to running a vent line, I try to make the drain lines large enough so the air can flow over the drain water, or slug, from front to back as the water runs down the lines. Of course, the outside air vents in the line help keep the water flowing.

In my grandfather's day, each fixture was vented separately. Once a line to a fixture was tapped off, it made sense to take the pipe vertically to the roof. The trouble with that system was that the roof looked like a pincushion, and the process was expensive and labor intensive. Eventually, plumbers started combining vents, and in larger houses we might even have a vent stack—several horizontal vents tied to one giant vertical vent pipe—but we still would have several pipes going through the roof.

## Modern venting techniques

The Sydney Opera House, the NASA facility in Houston, and my house have something in common: air admittance valves (AAVs) in place of through-the-roof vent pipes. This valve cuts down the number of vent holes through the roof. Do not confuse an AAV with the old-style mechanical vent, which is sometimes called an automatic vent. The latter is not up to code in most areas.

A fixture AAV is installed under the sink right after the P trap. Typically, the trap will drain into a T. The top of the T goes into the AAV (the AAV needs to be around 4 in. above the trap weir (water line). The T then drains into the pipe coming out of the wall. AAVs can vent a single fixture, a group of fixtures, or an entire stack of vents. The newest type of AAV is designed right into the trap, which is mounted directly under the sink tailpiece. This is the way to go, but unfortunately this AAV is not yet available in the United States.

The Studor Redi-Vent™ (*left*) can vent a single fixture. It can vent island sinks, lavs, washers, tubs, etc., up to 6 DFUs. The Mini-Vent (*right*) can vent a single fixture or a small group of fixtures up to 24 DFUs on a single stack and up to 160 DFUs on an entire branch.

This Studor Maxi Vent, made for 3-in. and 4-in. pipe, can vent an entire stack of fixtures, up to 500 DFUs. This is normally installed in the attic. Install it 6 in. above the insulation.

Avoid mechanical vents with springs. While they're inexpensive, they are not up to code.

Once all the vent pipes have been extended into the attic, they can be joined to keep the rooftop mostly clear of vent stacks. Within the attic, combine the vents (keeping a 1/4-in.-per-ft. slope for any horizontal runs by plumbing them together. For example, if yoiu have a 2-in. bath vent, you can bring over another 1 1/2-in vent pipe and T it into the 2-in. bath vent. For such cases, use an upside-down 3-in. T with reducer bushings and extend a single 3-in. pipe through the roof.

An AAV can be in the wall but, since it cannot be hidden, you have to cut a hole in the wall to mount it in a box, like a washer box with a louvered front. For example, for a vent coming off the downstream line right after a lav and toilet and straight up into the wall, run the 2-in. vent line up into the wall for a few feet and then terminate in a louvered box that can be accessed from the bath. AAVs are perfect for add-on plumbing, log cabins, timber-frame

# What Is a DFU?

Basically, a drainage fixture unit (DFU) is a water discharge volume of 7.5 GPM and is used as a design reference for plumbing codes.

The more a pipe fills with water, the less room there is for air, creating negative and positive air pressure behind and in front of the slug of water as it flows down the drain. To keep this from happening, researchers have determined the amount of water each diameter pipe can take in DFUs (with average, not peak, use) and have listed this in a DFU chart.

But there's a problem. The researchers' formula takes into account that not all fixtures are used at the same time. If one fixture gets used more than the formula allows, or if several fixtures on one branch are used more than called for, the pipe can overfill. To complicate matters, two DFUs do not equal 15 GPM due to the probability in the researchers' formula.

Knowing this, I over-design my drain and sewer pipes by at least one pipe size. I have never had a problem with a drain/sewer system that I have designed and installed.

houses, and any place, such as a kitchen island, where getting a vent up through a wall would be difficult. Simply put, an AAV is a perfect vent for any appliance needing a vent. There is no longer a need to run individual vent lines, or even the branch-circuit (a group of fixtures on one drain line) vent line.

**Vent-only Ts** should be installed upside down to allow better airflow from horizontal to vertical.

As water flows down the pipe, it pushes air ahead of it. If the pipe is large enough, the air can go over the slug and behind it, and no negative or positive pressure is created.

## Small diameter drain pipes create problems

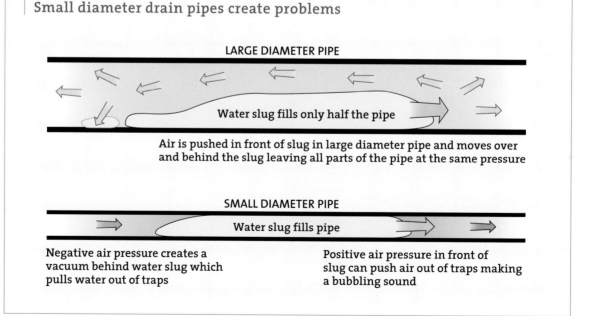

LARGE DIAMETER PIPE

Water slug fills only half the pipe

Air is pushed in front of slug in large diameter pipe and moves over and behind the slug leaving all parts of the pipe at the same pressure

SMALL DIAMETER PIPE

Water slug fills pipe

Negative air pressure creates a vacuum behind water slug which pulls water out of traps

Positive air pressure in front of slug can push air out of traps making a bubbling sound

# Fixture Layout

When planning the locations of fixtures in a bathroom, an easy way to determine distances you can live with is to make cardboard cutouts of the toilet, lav, and bath. Simply lay them on the floor to determine the amount of space needed. For example, the minimum spec distance for a toilet is 15 in. to a side wall (at least 18 in. is better) and 18 in. to 24 in. of clear area in front. Verify

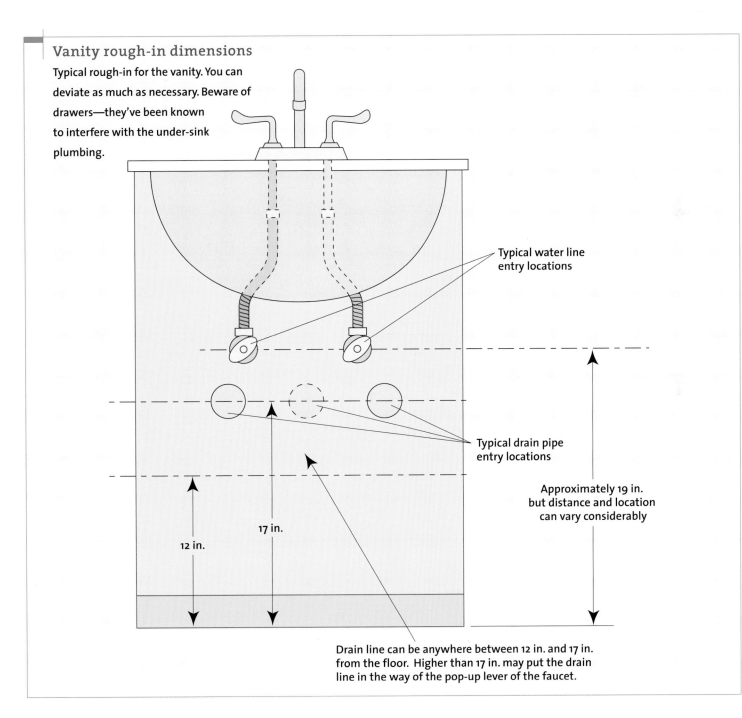

**Vanity rough-in dimensions**

Typical rough-in for the vanity. You can deviate as much as necessary. Beware of drawers—they've been known to interfere with the under-sink plumbing.

Typical water line entry locations

Typical drain pipe entry locations

Approximately 19 in. but distance and location can vary considerably

17 in.

12 in.

Drain line can be anywhere between 12 in. and 17 in. from the floor.  Higher than 17 in. may put the drain line in the way of the pop-up lever of the faucet.

## Water-line rough-in to toilet

Typical toilet rough-in for water line.

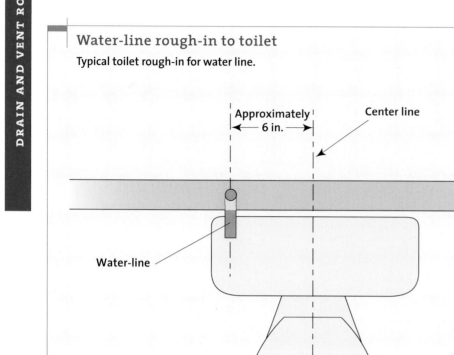

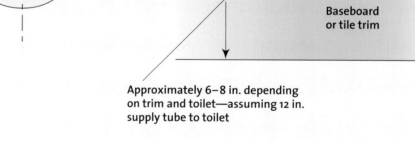

Approximately
6 in.

Center line

Water-line

Chrome trim
(escutcheon)
around pipe

Supply pipe

Chrome escutcheon
must clear trim

Baseboard
or tile trim

Approximately 6–8 in. depending
on trim and toilet—assuming 12 in.
supply tube to toilet

the room's door will open without hitting anything.

You should have the tub or shower on site before work begins. Unlike other fixtures, a tub, shower, or whirlpool needs to be in the room before framing occurs because it may be too big to move in afterwards without cutting out studs. The tub or shower may have a framing diagram you can follow. If not, put the unit in place and it should be obvious where the studs go. Wherever there is a vertical nailing lip you should have a stud. Wherever there is a horizontal nailing lip, you need a stud, every 16 in. or less. Do not put a stud where the spigot has to be placed. Leave open about 8 in. on each side of the spigot for clearance. If you have a standing shower, be sure the door will open fully without hitting anything.

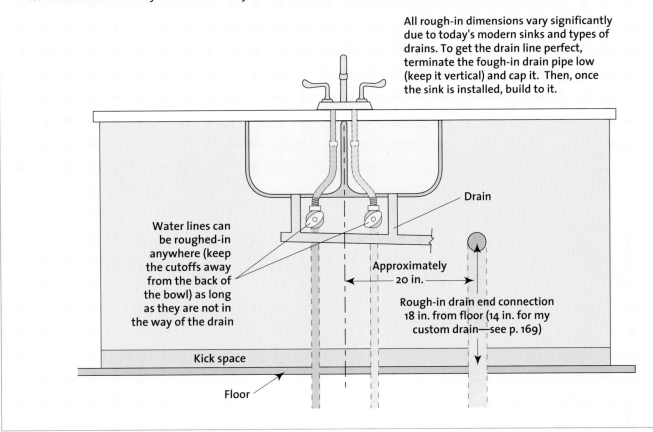

## Kitchen sink typical rough-in dimensions.

Kitchen sink water lines can go almost anywhere. Just make sure that wherever you put them that someone can get to them for maintenance and they are not in the way of the drain lines.

All rough-in dimensions vary significantly due to today's modern sinks and types of drains. To get the drain line perfect, terminate the fough-in drain pipe low (keep it vertical) and cap it. Then, once the sink is installed, build to it.

Drain

Water lines can be roughed-in anywhere (keep the cutoffs away from the back of the bowl) as long as they are not in the way of the drain

Approximately 20 in.

Rough-in drain end connection 18 in. from floor (14 in. for my custom drain—see p. 169)

Kick space

Floor

# Drain Stub-Out

There is a standard pipe layout for lavs, tubs, toilets, specific places where the drain and water lines come out of the wall or floor. These days, however, more and more fixtures require custom layouts. For a custom layout, follow the manufacturer's template for roughing-in locations for drain and water lines. If you are using AAV-type venting that Ts in right behind the trap, you may need to pull the drain rough-in pipe about 4 in. off to the side from dead center to give the extra room needed for the T.

With the exception of the toilet flange, virtually all drain stub-outs will be 1½-in. and

2-in. pipes. The stub-out is where the pipe pokes through the wall to attach the fixture to the horizontal drain flowing under the floor.

Once you know the exact fixture location, draw its outline on the subfloor with a thick marker. This will be an aid for everyone, from electrician to carpenter, who will use the mark to determine the door opening or the placement of the light switch. To stub out the drains, running the pipe from fixture through the floor, you will need to know the exact location of the fixture's drain. It helps to have the fixture on site to measure; if not, you have to go by the

The minimum toilet spec from center line to finished wall edge is 15 in. Here we have around 16 in.; 18 in. would be better.

The subfloor cutout for a tub is 8 in. to 12 in. wide and 14 in. deep from the bottom plate. Verify this for your particular tub. For a standing shower, I cut out at least an 8-in.-diameter circle under the proposed drain.

common guide to all fixtures and assume it will fit.

For the lav stub-out, work backward from the wall behind the lav to the floor (normally straight down inside the wall, or slightly off to the side and then straight down). Once the drain hole is drilled through the bottom plate behind the lav, insert several inches of drain pipe into the hole and cap the pipe. If you are running individual vents, remember that a vent pipe will be needed as well, going up. The drain pipe is normally 1½ in. on the horizontal run behind the trap, dumping into a 1½-in. or larger vertical pipe, while the vent line is typically 1¼-in. or 1½-in. pipe.

The kitchen drain stub-out is normally identical to that of the lav—1½-in. horizontal pipe

dumping into a sometimes larger vertical pipe. Install an optional vent line overhead as in the lav. AAVs are ideal in a kitchen sink along a back wall with a window overhead and in kitchen island sinks. Although some local jurisdictions still don't allow them, I see no reason why AAVs shouldn't be approved for this use.

For a tub/shower, cut out an 8-in.-wide, 14-in.-long section of subfloor from the plate where the plumbing is brought in. This hole is for the tub's drain system. I normally install the tub's drain system on the tub before I set it in place. For a standing shower, cut a 7-in. square.

When running the drain, do not worry about being exact for the drain rough-in. Just get the drainpipe in the area and stop—do not install the trap yet. Once the tub is in place connect the two. I use a Fernco flexible coupling here, which allows a few degrees of error in pipe alignment. Most important in tubs and showers, it acts as a flex joint between the shower/tub drain line and the house drain. When someone steps into a tub or shower, the bottom will flex down, sometimes as much as ¼ in. The flex joint will take the movement without bending the entire main drain line or ripping the drain out of the shower.

Installing a toilet flange will take care of the stub-out for the toilet. The fastest and most accurate way to plan and cut the stub-out is to place a template (wood or cardboard) against the bottom wall plate where the toilet is to be installed. Draw a circle within the template's flange hole and then cut out the hole. Without a template, measure 12½ in. out from the bottom plate (assuming ½-in. drywall; the center of the flange must be 12 in. from the finished wall). Then use a compass to draw a circle to cut. If you mess this up by an inch or two, you will have to buy a special toilet that will fit, which can be expensive. Typically, these toilets are 10-in. centers (for those who got the toilet too close to the back wall) and 14-in. centers for those who got the toilet too far away from the back wall.

I don't like all the fancy toilet flanges on the market. The fancier they are, the more problems they give me. A common flange with an open hole in the center is just fine. I mount the flange to the floor with the U-slots parallel to the back wall plate. If you use the long-angled slots designed for the toilet bolts, the bolts will spin as their hold-down nuts are turned. I normally mount the bolts ($^5/_{16}$-in. bolts, not the thin $^1/_4$-in. ones) to the flange with a nut/washer on top before I set the flange in the hole. Not doing so may bend the bolts as the toilet bowl is set in place. If tile is to be laid, elevate the flange off the floor the thickness of the tile and thinset underneath. Once done, duct tape the opening so no debris falls in.

The washer drain stub-out is simply the washer box, standpipe, trap, and a T or elbow. Always use 2-in. pipe. Tape the standpipe end closed to keep out debris until all is done. Cut the standpipe at 36 in. (the height of a washer) and rest the bottom of the trap on the bottom plate. The width of a 2-in. drain trap assembly from the edge of the standpipe, through the trap, to an immediate turndown with a street 90, is 12 in. Add to that half the width of a washer box, if used—normally 4 in. The minimum width of a washer drain assembly from box to turndown through the plate is more than the full width of a stud opening so be prepared to relocate a stud or drill it. However, if the drain is going against an unfinished block wall in the basement, you don't need a washer box; just mount it to the wall.

An AAV eliminates the need for running a separate vent pipe for the washer. Putting the

Typical lav rough-in. **The plumber needs to install metal plates on the vertical stud and bottom plate and use some fire-stop caulk where the pipe goes through the bottom plate.**

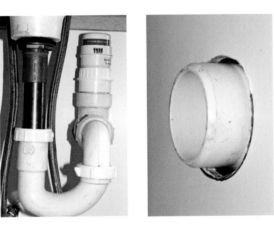

This AAV (*left*) **Ts in right under the fixture. The rough-in pipe (*right*), when installed, must be 4 in. over to the side from the center line of the sink's tailpiece to allow room for the T.**

The fastest way **to locate a flange hole is to make a template (from foam board) with a hole 12$^1/_2$ in. (assuming $^1/_2$-in. drywall) out from the back. Butt the flat edge against the bottom plate and trace around it.**

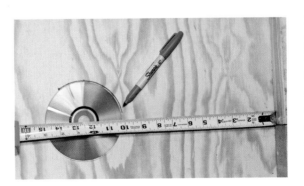

Use an old CD **as a template for a toilet flange hole. Draw around the CD, then cut inside the mark, on the mark, or outside the mark, depending on the flange dimensions required.**

This is why I do not use the designed location for toilet hold-down bolts. As all plumbers know, they spin when you try to remove them.

Attach the toilet bowl hold-down bolts to the flange first. Attach the flange to the floor with large-diameter, tapered-head wood screws—not drywall screws.

These are three types of toilet hold-down bolts: a wood-screw tipped to grab onto the floor or subfloor when the old-style cast iron flange has rusted out around its rim (*left*); the ever-popular 1/4-in. bolt (middle); and a 5/16-in. bolt—(*right*). The latter is the one I prefer. It's thick and holds the bowl more securely to the floor.

I never use flanges with plastic knock-outs. I wonder where the engineer thought the plastic shards were going to go? Once installed, the breaking shards fall directly down into the drainpipe under the flange. It's better to use those without knock-outs in the first place.

AAV in the washer box makes it accessible without installing it in a separate box.

## Running the Lines

At this point, from underneath the floor, you should see a bunch of vertical pipes coming down. All you have to do is connect them together horizontally. First, plan the lines in your mind.

Look at the distant end where the main sewer line comes in. You can go no lower than this line. Ideally, you'll be coming uphill from that spot at 1 in. per 4 ft. Look at the stub-out farthest away; this will be your ending point in reference to slope. From there to the main sewer line you need to have a slope of at least 1/4 in. per foot. If not, you may have to notch the last few joists going to the last fixtures to gain height for the main run.

The first line I run is the main sewer line from where it enters the basement or crawl space to the toilet. I want this line to be as straight as possible between these two points— no elbows, no turns, if at all possible. If you have two toilets, you can split the run between them and then Y off as you get close, or go straight to one toilet and Y off at some logical point to the second toilet. If you have to make a turn in the line, use one 45, then go a few feet, and use another. The object of all this is not to slow the movement of fluid in the sewer or drain line. Start at the main sewer line and run the line with supports every 3 ft. to 4 ft. to the toilet flange.

As you plan the proposed line, think about the fittings you will be using for tap-offs to fixtures or branches. In particular, think about vertical headroom that these fittings might need. T-Y combos are best. T fittings work fine, but they disrupt the flow of fluid by not directing the incoming branch or fixture fluid in line of the main line as it enters. And officially, by code, a T fitting on its back is not

allowed. The problem with T-Y combos, however, is headroom; they take up a lot of space and are difficult, if not impossible, to install in tight locations. This is why most inspectors allow a T fitting to be used on its back. They know there isn't room for a T-Y combo in many situations.

On the straight line to the toilet flange, pick up any additional drains you are passing. As previously mentioned, use T-Y combos whenever possible. Raise the center part of the combo slightly above the center line of the main line it cuts into so the main line cannot drain into it. This also interfaces the slope of the side tap drain coming in. Individual drains not yet tied in as you approach the toilet flange will be tied in later. (continued on p. 162)

Think before you glue. That is, lay out the lines in your mind first. If the plumber on this job had followed that advice we might see a system with a better layout and proper fittings. However, in his defense, the system works just fine as is.

Used directly under a tub or shower drain, a flex elbow trap assembly will move with the tub or standing shower and not put pressure on the drainpipe or the drain fitting.

A T fitting works fine but disrupts the flow of fluid on both the tap line and main line. If flow gets below 2 ft. per second, the solids could come out of suspension and clog the lines.

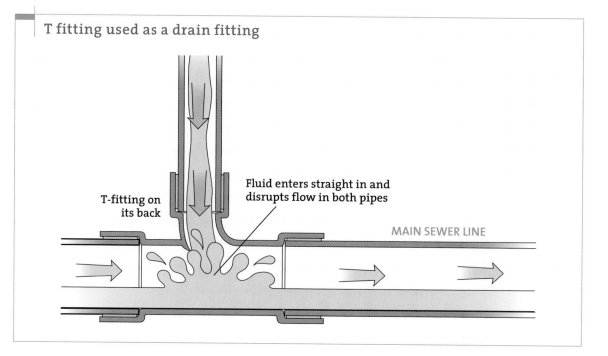

## T fitting used as a drain fitting

T-fitting on its back

Fluid enters straight in and disrupts flow in both pipes

MAIN SEWER LINE

A Y fitting or a T-Y combo (a combination of a Y fitting and a street 45) brings the fixture or branch water into the main line at an angle that does not disrupt the main flow of fluid.

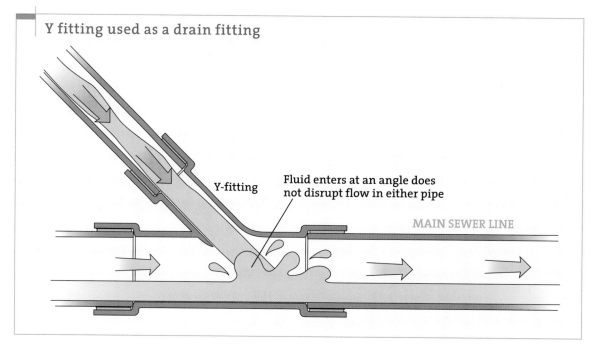

## Y fitting used as a drain fitting

Y-fitting

Fluid enters at an angle does not disrupt flow in either pipe

MAIN SEWER LINE

# Putting an AAV into the washer box

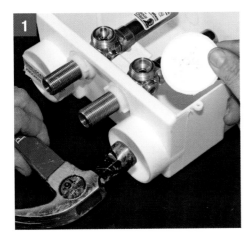

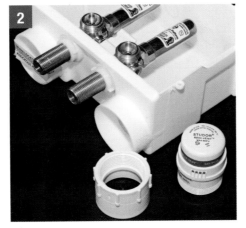

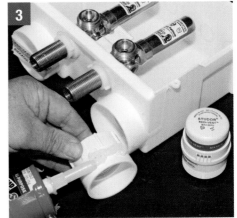

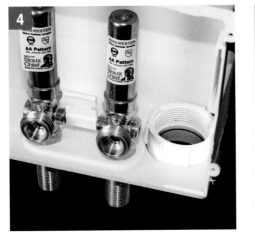

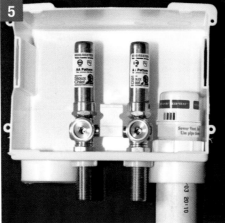

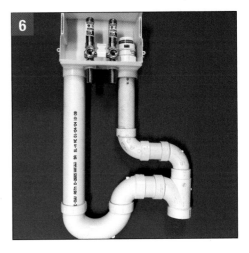

## QUICK REFERENCE

▶ AAV VENTS p. 151
For more information about AAVs

▶ STUB-OUTS p. 157
For information on washer drain stub-outs

▶ CODES p. 240
For more information about washer codes

▶ PIPE p. 89
For more information about plastic drain pipe

**1** Using a hammer, remove the knockout on whichever side of the washer box the AAV will be installed.

**2** Bring in the AAV and a 1½-in. female hub fitting (a cleanout fitting without the plug).

**3** Silicone caulk around the bottom half of the female adapter.

**4** Insert the adapter into the knockout from the inside of the washer box.

**5** Screw in the AAV from the top (use Teflon tape on the threads) and glue in the vent pipe from the bottom.

**6** Once completed, it should look like this mockup here. Install a short pipe between the trap and the T. Otherwise you create an S-trap.

**Always bring a vent line into a main line at 45 degrees or higher to keep the fluid from the main line from entering the vent line.**

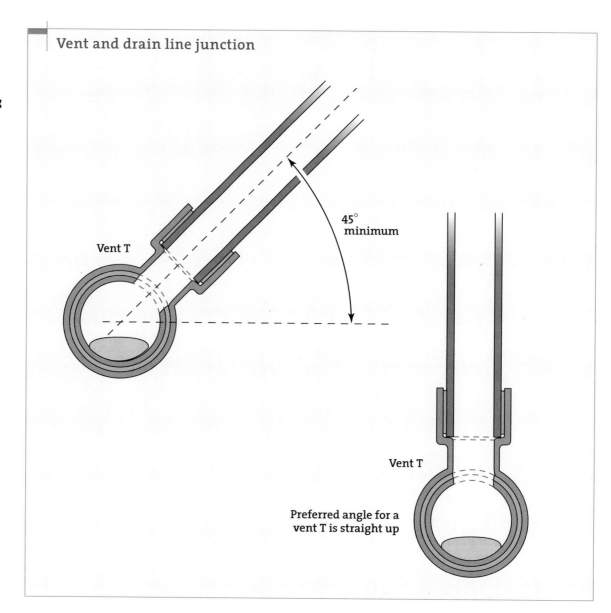

### Vent and drain line junction

Vent T

45°
minimum

Vent T

**Preferred angle for a vent T is straight up**

As you tie in the lines, keep in mind a rule of thumb my uncle taught me: Always wash the toilet line with another fixture from further upstream—this scours the sewer line, keeping it clean. In other words, try not to have the toilet as the last fixture on a particular line. If you are cutting in a vent line, always enter the line at least 45 degrees up from the horizontal to keep fluid out of the lines.

Once you've figured out how the lines will run, make sure you have all the necessary fittings and tools.

# Gluing a run of pipe

Whether a short run or a long run, putting it all together breaks down into four parts:

1. Cut and dry-fit. Allow enough pipe to go all the way into the hubs.

2. Once all fittings are pointed the right direction, mark the fitting hub/pipe interface. At first, mark all interfaces. Later you will figure out which ones don't need to be marked and which ones do.

3. If a run goes over several feet—for example, a 10-ft. length of 3-in. PVC or ABS gluing into an elbow—you'll want hangers (properly sloped) every 3 ft. to 4 ft. Position hangers so they hold the pipe in place once it's glued into the fitting.

4. Disassemble and then reassemble, gluing it all together.

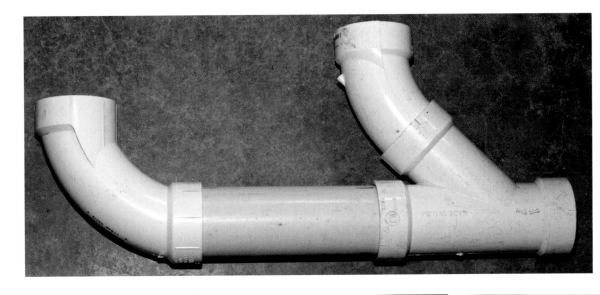

**To get all the fittings straight and parallel, dry-fit them and place the assembly on a flat surface. Push down on all the fittings' hubs until all are touching the surface. Now they are straight and parallel.**

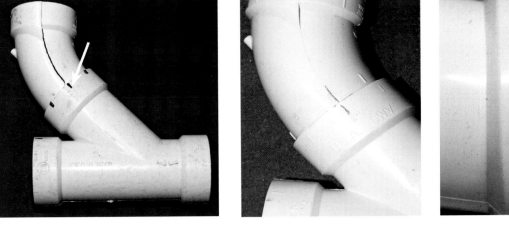

**To align a street fitting perfectly with a Y fitting, line up the mold mark on the street fitting with the raised hash mark found on the hub of the fitting into which it is being glued.**

**Alignment marks, made once the fittings and pipe are dry-fitted into place, will help keep everything straight when you start gluing it all together.**

## Pipe size

My rule of thumb is to run as large a pipe as possible. Forget about the old wives' tale that if you put in too large a line the solids will be left behind. It can't happen in residential. If the sewer line comes in at 4 in., stay at 4 in. If it comes in at 3 in., you are stuck with that. Run this large line straight to the toilet flange, stopping along the way to tie in individual drains. Wherever the large line stops (or reduces in size), install a cleanout the same size as the line. Follow the same logic on the branches: Where a branch stops or reduces in size, install a cleanout. Allow at least 12 in. of clear area behind the cleanout.

Follow the same steps above for individual drains to the fixture stub-out, keeping them as large as possible. If the tap is going to contain the water flow of one fixture only, maintain that 2-in. minimum.

If the horizontal line will carry the flow of two or more small DFU fixtures, the line should be 3 in. At times you can keep the line at 2 in., but if you do so blindly, you run the risk of filling the pipe completely with water, which causes venting problems (Read about the "probability formula" researchers used when they created the DFU-per-pipe-size chart [see chart, p. 239]. You must calculate the DFUs of the fixtures and compare that to a max DFU chart (see appendix for both). Taking the pipe up to 3 in. in the two fixture situation, however, means you never have to calculate DFUs because the pipe is always large enough for the water flow, and you will never have to worry about venting because the pipe will be big enough for the air to flow easily above the water slug as it flows down the line. This line, of course, will be flowing into the main branch sewer line going to the toilet, which will be either 3 in. or 4 in. (preferred).

Any pipe under a slab has to be at least 2 in. in diameter. The clothes washer pipe should also be 2 in. Though a long run to a kitchen sink can be $1\frac{1}{2}$ in., it's best to keep it at least 2 in. in diameter; 3 in. is better, especially if it is an island sink, because smaller pipe is prone to clogging and results in service call after call. Increasing the size, along with proper slope, solves any venting problems, as well as clogging.

If you have to get a line to a second floor bathroom, apply the same pipe-size logic and install a full-size pipe. You might have to compromise, using a 3-in. line instead of a 4-in. line, if the clearances within floor joists are limited. If the second floor has two toilets on the same branch line, try to get a 4-in line at least to the first one. If three toilets are on the same branch line, always use a 4-in. pipe and take it as far as clearance allows.

In summary, if the main sewer line enters the house as 4 in., keep that size as long as possible so it clogs less frequently and allows better venting. Don't think about reducing the main sewer line to 3 in. until after you have brought the last toilet into the line. Keep side taps to groups of individual fixtures at 3 in. and reduce to 2 in. only when one fixture is left.

## Strapping

How do you hold up all that drain line pipe? I use common galvanized strapping. It's cheap, easy to find, and installs fast. Its numerous holes allow me to adjust the pipe height as I search for the optimum slope. You can also find ungalvanized (continued on p. 168)

# A T fitting Is Not Always Code

A T fitting on its back is not an official sanitary T. In fact, it is against code. Not that it won't work—it will, as millions of installations have already determined. I don't know any plumber, including me, who hasn't used a T on its back. Bottom line, if there is no room for a Y or T-Y combo, you have to use it.

So what's the big deal? The problem is that the T does not promote the flow of fluid within the line. We want the fluid to flow at 2 ft. per second. Faster is OK, but slower is not. Solids will drop out of suspension if the fluid moves at a slower rate.

A T fitting smashes the incoming water directly into the main-line flow of fluid. This slows down both the incoming fluid from the tap as well as the main-line fluid. The solids drop out of suspension because the water flows too slowly. A T-Y combo or a Y fitting sends the tap fluid into the main line in the direction of the flow. Bottom line: a T fitting works, but a Y or T-Y combo works better, giving you less chance of a stoppage.

This is a triple screw-up. The top fitting should be a long-sweep elbow (or two 45s) and the bottom fitting should be a T-Y combo with cleanout. Also, the plumber glued ABS to PVC.

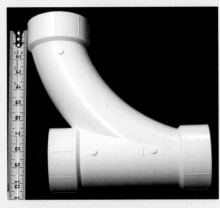

A T on its back (*right*) is not a sanitary T. Use a T-Y combo (*above*) if there is room. From toilet flange bottom to center line of pipe, a 3-in. T-Y combo needs 9-in. to make a turn. Here, the plumber had 9½ in. so there was room.

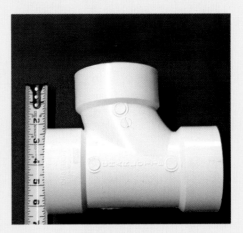

Plumbers use Ts on their backs instead of T-Y combos because of their minimal clearance to make a turn.

Whenever you make a turn from vertical to horizontal, install strapping to take the weight off the line. Here, the plumber should have used a long-sweep elbow. Note the rusted non-galvanized strapping—which is why you shouldn't use it.

When the sewer line makes a turn, install strapping to take the weight off the line. Here the plumber should not have used a sanitary T to make the turn. A Y and a 45 should have been used.

This method of strapping is called swing-under. It's fast, but pipes can move if they are bumped.

This method of strapping is called wrapping. It's secure, but it doesn't allow for minor changes of direction if they are needed.

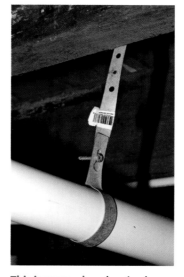

This is premade galvanized strapping.

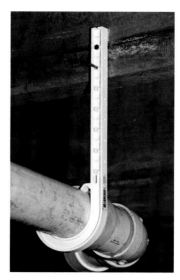

Plastic hangers for drains work, but they are expensive.

# The Cost of Strapping

One of the decisions you make is how to use strap to support a drain pipe. This may seem like a minor point, but it isn't. For example, I strap with either flat galvanized strap in a roll—it comes in 10-ft. 25-ft., and 100-ft. rolls—or with flat copper-coated strap. These cost around $3.00 per roll. You may need two to three rolls to do a house, bringing the total cost to strap every drain in the house to less than $10.00.

If you choose to use plastic J-hook-style hangers, these cost around $1.00 each. To plumb a house, you will need a dozen hangers of each size from 1½ in. to 4 in., around 50 in all. So the total for doing the job with plastic hangers is about $50.00.

If you choose instead to use the premade metal hangers, these cost around $2.00 each, or $100.00 for the house. Insulated premade metal hangers that stop vibrating pipe noise cost around $3.00, raising the price for the job to $150.00.

So, the cost of strapping the plumbing in a house can be as low as $10.00 or as high as $150.00. With flat strapping in a roll, you avoid the issue of keeping track of many different-sized pieces, one size fits all, it doesn't stretch or break, and it is much easier to adjust the pipe slightly to the left, right, up, or down.

**Insulated metal hangers.** They are the elite of the hanging systems, are excellent in every regard, but are also very expensive to install.

**Premade metal strapping** works well, but it is more expensive than rolled flat strapping.

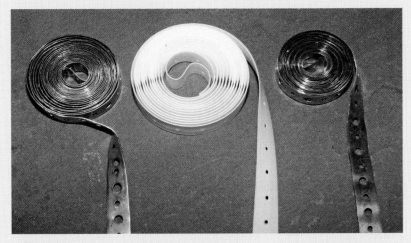

**Three different types** of rolled flat strapping. Copper (*left*) and galvanized (*right*) are the mainstays of the trade, and they'll neither stretch nor rust. The plastic strapping (*middle*) is less expensive, but it may stretch and break, so avoid it.

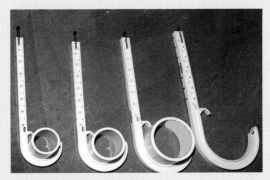

**Plastic J hooks** are also popular. The pipe snaps into the hook. They will hang at an angle unless straightened and are hard to relocate when the pipe must be slightly moved.

strapping, but don't use it. It rusts heavily. Copper strapping is fine, but it's expensive and getting hard to find.

Other types of strapping have been developed. Rolled plastic stretches and breaks; avoid it. Plastic J hooks work fine, but are expensive. I have experimented with other strapping, but I always come back to common galvanized strapping.

I use hex head (5/16 in. hex heads) screws—shooting them in through the holes in the strapping with a cordless drill—so I can change the slope of the drain lines as fast as I install them. I first hang the pipe without regard to slope, just taking the pipe in the right direction. Once I get the direction down, I adjust the strapping to give the correct slope.

There are two ways to hang the pipe using galvanized strapping. Shoot one end of the strapping into the joist, go under the joist with the strapping and shoot the opposite end of the strapping into another joist (like a pipe laying in a horseshoe). Or simply loop the strapping around the pipe one time.

## General Rules for Drain Fittings

As a reminder, here are the general rules we follow, assuming there is enough vertical room for the fittings.

- Use two 45s, separated by a short piece of pipe, as opposed to a 90
- Use a T-Y combo as opposed to a T
- Use long-sweep 90s as opposed to short sweep
- Achieve a slope of 1/4 in. per foot or more

There is one place where plumbers have to break some of the rules: at the kitchen sink where the horizontal drain from the fixture is a long distance from the fitting that takes it down to the crawl space, basement, or under the slab. Typically, a lav turns its drain down in the wall just a few inches behind the sink so there's no problem there. Unlike the lav, the kitchen drain may be offset around an overhead window. or the sink may be in an island. This is where we have problems.

In a nutshell, we do not want this horizontal-to-vertical distance (from trap to turndown fitting) to be so long that the turndown fitting is below the trap water level. If this occurs, the trap water may siphon out, leaving an air gap in the trap and allowing sewer gas to enter the house

To keep this distance short with a minimized slope, we use a common elbow or sanitary T as opposed to a long-sweep elbow or a T-Y combo.

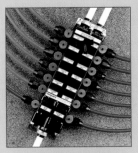

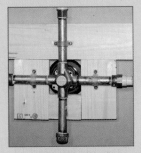
# Pressure Pipe Rough-in

The pressure pipe rough-in cannot be installed until all the drain lines are in. This is because supply water lines can make turns, up and down, left and right, without regard to slope. By contrast, drain lines must be sloped and located in specific areas. In addition, supply water lines do not have to follow the drain lines; they can go their own way.

In this chapter I follow the water line from design to installation through the joists and wall stud system. Then I create a stub-out system for the pipe at the point of use, the fixture.

## Picking a Distribution System

Before you start drilling holes to run the water lines, determine how many lines you will install and their diameter. Both of these decisions depend on the type of distribution system you use. You will also need to know where the outside water spigots will be located.

There are three basic systems that can carry water to the fixtures: series, parallel, and combination. Each has advantages and disadvantages.

## Series system

This is the most common distribution system. It is the least expensive, and installation is simple. When installing a series system, use ¾-in. pipe for the main feed water lines until you are down to the last two fixtures. Then reduce the line to ½ in. Many plumbers install ½-in. pipe throughout, resulting in a drop in water pressure at one tap when the water is turned on at another. If there is a tap off a main line that feeds two or more fixtures, keep this tap at ¾ in. until you get to the last fixture. Running two fixtures off a ½-in. pipe is allowed in many jurisdictions and works quite well. If you design to that spec, however, expect to have pressure/volume problems.

In addition to using ¾-in. pipe, install 90-degree (quarter-turn) stop valves on all the fixtures (as opposed to stop valves with handles that turn-turn-turn). Use ball valves at the water heater valves and at the main house turn-off valve.

### Properly designed series-type water distribution system

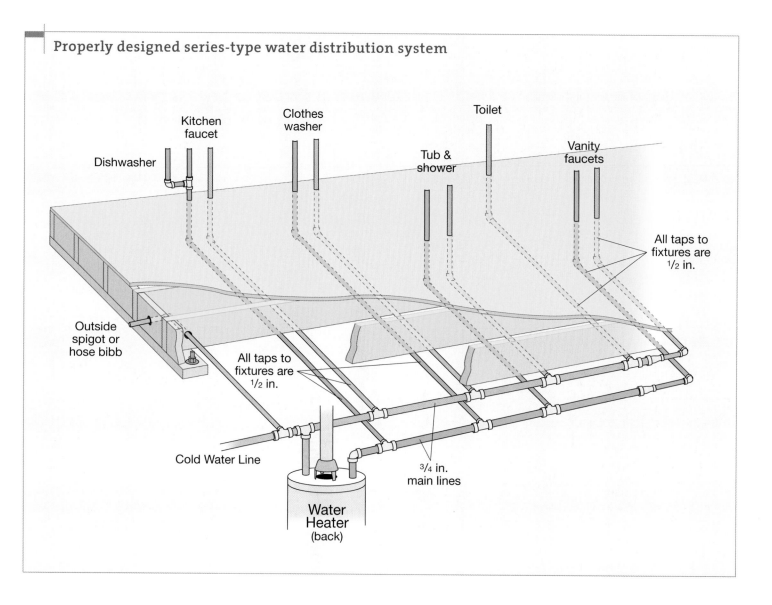

## Parallel system

This distribution system is also known as the manifold system. Install a manifold—a large hollow block or pipe—where the water line enters the house. From there, run a ½-in. line to each fixture. With an independent feed, each fixture will have plenty of water even when water is being used in a second or third location in the house.

The problem with the parallel system is that it requires a lot of pipe, a lot of labor, and a lot of drilling (which can weaken the joists). And

forget about making it look nice; it looks like a bowl of spaghetti.

Cut down on the installation time by using PEX, which is quicker than other pipe to install. Even then, you still have to organize it all. Label each pipe feed with its destination or you will end up with a tangle of pipes and not know where any of them go. Either install a ball valve to control each run, which is expensive, or buy a manifold that has the valves already built in, which I prefer. Because of all the extra pipe, the costly

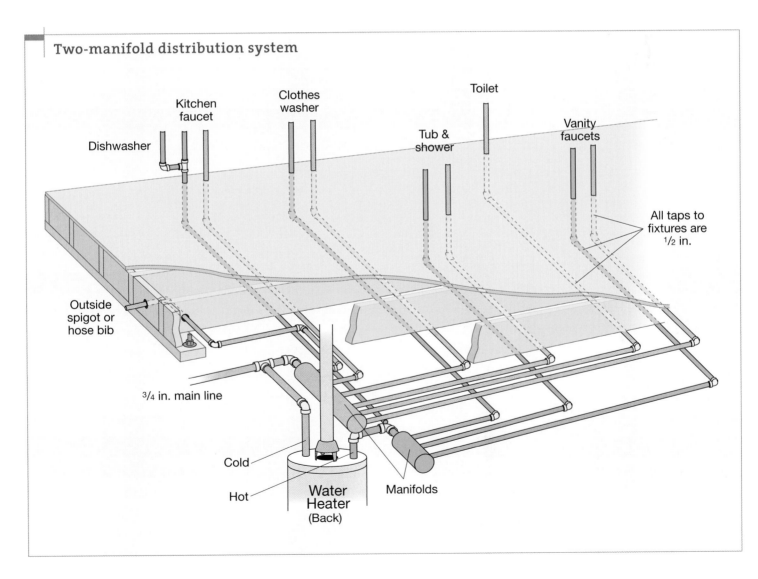

### Two-manifold distribution system

Toilet

Kitchen faucet

Clothes washer

Dishwasher

Tub & shower

Vanity faucets

All taps to fixtures are ½ in.

Outside spigot or hose bib

3/4 in. main line

Cold

Hot

Manifolds

Water Heater (Back)

A manifold block indicates a parallel system has been installed. With a ½-in. line going to each fixture, there will be no pressure/volume problems. (Photo courtesy Vanguard Piping Systems.)

manifold and all those ball valves, this system is the most expensive.

## Modular system

This is my favorite distribution system. With the modular system—also called the combination, custom, or series/parallel system—you plumb in groups of fixtures, or modules. Its only drawback is its high price tag.

Each module has a full-size (¾-in.) feed in both hot and cold. A typical one-bathroom residence will have three modules: kitchen, bath, and water heater. The clothes washer, and a half bath if there is one, can be on either the kitchen or bath module, depending on which is closest. Each additional bathroom is treated as another module. The kitchen is always independent of the bathrooms, eliminating any pressure problems between the two. After the water heater, put in a ¾-in. T and run a hot water main line to both the kitchen and bath.

As with the series system plan for branching out to individual fixtures, keep the line at ¾ in. until you have no more than one fixture to feed. Then reduce the pipe size to ½ in.

## Prep work

Once you decide on the distribution system determine the exact location of each fixture, to the inch. If you have blueprints, follow them. If not, mark a fixture's location on the subfloor with a permanent marker, indicating both the left and right sides of the fixture and its front edge, if necessary. In a bathroom, I also mark the door swing opening. For a vanity, I write "LAV" on the subfloor. I let the owner or job foreman know that this is the proposed location. That way, if something changes after I get the lines in—like the door swing or the width of a vanity—I get paid for relocating the water lines.

When plumbing a bathroom, it's always a good idea to have the vanity on-site, or at least have the specs, so you know where its drawers are located within the frame. If you don't, you might later find that the drawers are in the way of the water line pipes coming out of the wall. For a pedestal sink, you have to know the exact height and width. If the owner hasn't decided on a sink, urge him or her to do so before you lay out the plumbing.

Once you have marked the layout, you can see what studs are in the way of the pipes. The water line pipes coming out of the wall for the spigot do not necessarily have to be positioned perfectly on each side of the drain line. You can bring both out on one side of the drain if, for example, the drawers of the vanity are in the way.

## Stubbing Down

After the fixture location is set, plan the stubdowns, where the individual fixture lines go through the floor to the main line running through the joists. First find exactly where the hot and cold lines go through the floor.

## A modular distribution system

This system breaks the plumbing down into modules: kitchen and bath. Half baths are tied to the kitchen module. Additional baths have their own hot and cold feeds identical to first bath.

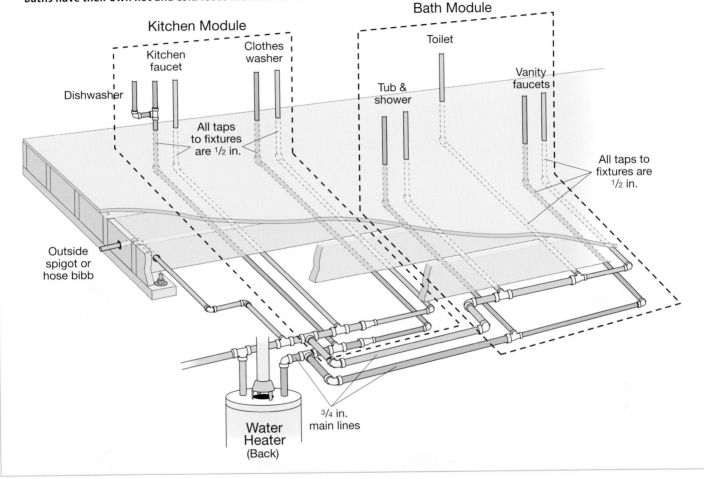

Kitchen Module

Bath Module

Kitchen faucet

Clothes washer

Dishwasher

Toilet

Tub & shower

Vanity faucets

All taps to fixtures are 1/2 in.

All taps to fixtures are 1/2 in.

Outside spigot or hose bibb

3/4 in. main lines

Water Heater (Back)

Sometimes this will be immediately behind the fixture. Other times, it may be a stud or two over or perhaps straight down through the floor. The size of this line will be determined by the distribution system you are using.

Once you know where to drill and the size of pipe to drill for, you can start drilling. If you are going straight down through the plate and subfloor, drilling is no big deal. Sometimes you have to take the pipe over to the side and pick up another fixture or get into a better position to drop down to the main feed under the floor.

Vertical stub-outs will go through the subfloor and extend into the area between the floor joists. Once all fixtures are in, you simply have to connect the dots to run the water lines.

In that case, you will be drilling a lot of studs. I use a ¾-in. bit for ½-in. pipe and a 1-in. bit for ¾-in. pipe. A sharp spade bit is fine for studs up to 3 in. thick. On thicker ones, use an auger bit with a right-angle drill. Remember, if the pipe is being placed through a stud within 1½ in. (1 in. by some codes) of a wall edge, the stud must have a 1/16-in.-thick metal plate on its edge to protect the pipe from screws and nails.

The vertical water line going down through the plate must be plumb, or vertical, as it ties into the horizontal pipe below the floor in the joists. This is very difficult to do if you are sticking the pipe up through the floor because you

## Stubbing the pipe through the floor

Once all pipes are through the floor, all you have to do is go into the crawl space and connect the dots.

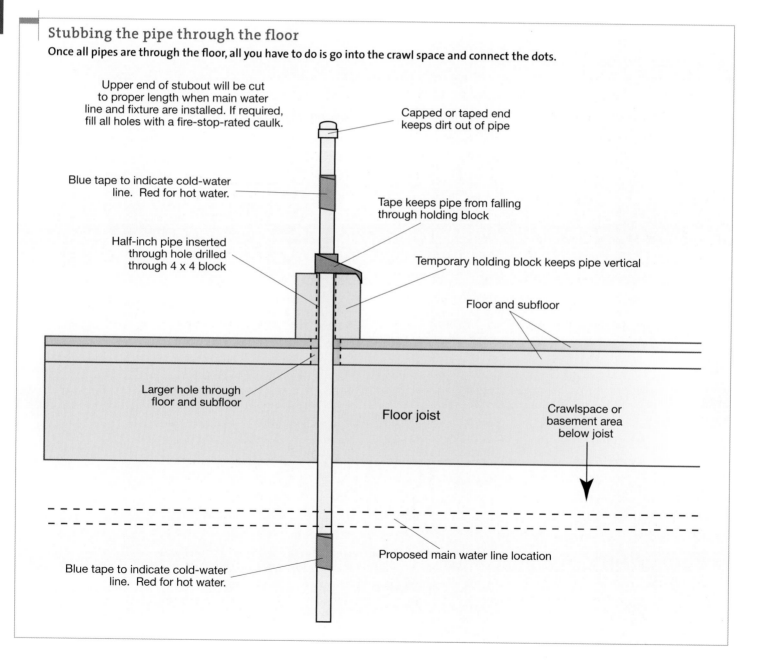

Upper end of stubout will be cut to proper length when main water line and fixture are installed. If required, fill all holes with a fire-stop-rated caulk.

Capped or taped end keeps dirt out of pipe

Blue tape to indicate cold-water line. Red for hot water.

Tape keeps pipe from falling through holding block

Half-inch pipe inserted through hole drilled through 4 x 4 block

Temporary holding block keeps pipe vertical

Floor and subfloor

Larger hole through floor and subfloor

Floor joist

Crawlspace or basement area below joist

Proposed main water line location

Blue tape to indicate cold-water line. Red for hot water.

can't see what it looks like from above. I solve this problem by sticking all pipes down through the floor first. To hold them vertical and in place, run them through a piece of 4×4 placed flat on the subfloor or plate. From underneath, all I have to do is get my main line over to them and install an elbow or T. It also pays to mark the pipe stub to indicate hot or cold. I use blue tape for cold, red for hot.

## Running the Lines

After you have all the stub-downs in place, all you have to do below is connect the dots. If you are using a manifold system, run every ½-in. line all the way to the manifold. For a series or custom system, run the pipes parallel to the floor joists; the pipe diameter will depend on the system. If you have to drill a joist, drill through its center. The hole diameter and bit choice for drilling the joists will be the same as for the stub-downs. Drill a hole large enough for only the pipe, not the insu-

lation wrap. The bigger the hole, the weaker the floor joist will be. The best approach is to run the pipe through the joist and then wrap it with insulation. I remember one plumber who cut out a little too much from a joist that supported a wood-burning stove. When the floor bowed, the plumber had to install two posts, one on each side of the hole he had drilled so that the joists could carry the stove's weight.

If you run the pipes through the joists, drilling holes in each stud for them along the way, one problem you you will have to deal with is getting the pipe through the holes. With joists spaced every 16 in. to 24 in., this is not always simple. You can bend PEX to thread it into the drilled holes. You might be able to do the same with CPVC, but not with rigid copper. To get rigid copper into the drilled holes either cut the pipe in small sections, insert the sections into the joists and then solder them back together, or figure out another way.

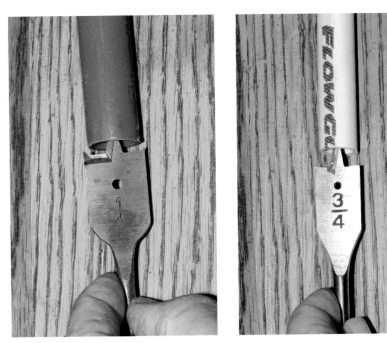

The easiest and fastest way to drill holes in studs for a water line is with sharp spade bits. Avoid drilling too small a hole for the water line. Typically, a 1-in . bit (*left*) is used for ¾-in. lines and a ¾-in. bit (*right*) is used for ½-in. lines. Going smaller than these may cause the water lines to bind in the studs and make annoying squeaks each time the pipes expand or contract. Going larger may weaken the stud.

One method I have found is to feed the pipe into the studs through a screened, crawl space vent hole—the vents that allow air to circulate in the crawl space. The screens can pop out of their holders in the vent. I drill the holes in the joists in line with the vent, slide the pipe from the outside through the little rectangular vent hole and then through the holes in the joists. But this only works when everything aligns perfectly, when the drilled holes just happen to be needed opposite the vent hole or the crawl space access door. Another technique is to drill a hole in the block wall (or outside joists) in line with the newly drilled holes in the joists. Once the pipe is in place, patch the hole. Cap or tape over the ends of the pipe before sliding it through the joists. This is perhaps the most common error made—sliding an open-end pipe through the studs and joists and having pieces of wood break off and fall into the pipe.

This must seem like a considerable amount of work to get a pipe in—and it is. The best way to avoid such folly is to run the pipe below the joists or use flexible pipe.

## Pipe Supports

If you're working with PEX or CVPC, support the lines every 2 ft. to 3 ft., if the pipe is parallel in the joist cavity, and on every joist if it runs at an angle under them. Attach copper, which is rigid, at every other joist.

Many clamps are available to support the pipes. To figure out which you should use, consider whether you are holding just a pipe or pipe wrapped with insulation. Also think about your budget. Fancy clamps such as plastic J hooks can cost as much as a dollar each. Tube talons, inexpensive plastic clamps with integral nails, are good for attaching a single uninsulated pipe. Once they're nailed in, however, they're difficult to remove. If you use these, make sure each talon is in its final location before you sink the nail. I just tap the nail and then go back later and knock it in after I have determined it is not going to be moved.

For pipe with insulation, I prefer the old-fashioned device for holding the pipe in place: inexpensive galvanized strapping. I fasten it with $^5/_{16}$-in. hex-head screws to allow fast

Drill pipe holes in rows along the length of the stud, not in a row across its width. Drilling holes across the width of the stud destroys its structural integrity. Install metal protection plates on both edges of each stud to prevent nails or screws from damaging the pipe.

Tube talons like this one are a good option to secure a single pipe though they are relatively expensive.

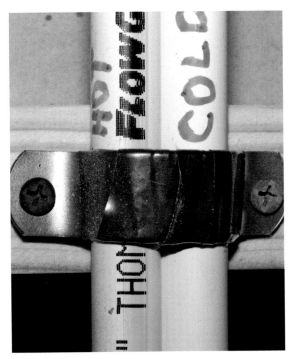

You can secure two ½-in. pipes at once with a common ¾-in. copper strap bent out to hold both pipes. Electrical tape keeps the metal from abrading the pipe.

My favorite method of securing insulated pipe is with common metal strapping. It is fast and inexpensive.

change if I want to switch its location. I also use the strapping to hold a single water line that just happens to fall between joists. For non-metal pipe, I wrap the strapping with a couple of layers of electrical tape to be sure it does not rub into the pipe.

## Stubbing Out

Once you know exactly where the vanity, tub, and toilet will be and their locations have been marked on the floor, and you know which way the doors to the room open, you can stub out the pipes to the fixture. Stubbing out means putting the hot and cold pipes in place through the wall at the proposed fixture location. For the placement of the stub-out in a typical situation, see Chapter 6. Remember, though, there is no ironclad rule. You can bring the pipes out anywhere. For example, under a kitchen sink or vanity, you do not have to split the pipes to have one on each side of the drain, as is commonly done. You can bring both hot and cold out

Copper stub-outs that interface with CPVC add more benefits. (Photo courtesy Sioux Chief Manufacturing.)

together on either side. This is sometimes necessary on vanities that have a drawer in the way on one side.

### Fasten the stub-out securely

Even though it might not be required by code, secure the pipe inside the wall or stud cavity just as it leaves the wall cavity. If it's not secured at this location, when it comes time for maintenance or replacement of the stop valve, you may have a difficulty turning the valve, and the pipe going to the valve could easily snap or twist.

If the stub-out happens to be adjacent to a vertical stud, attach the pipe to the stud using tube talons. Often, however, the stub-out will

The plumber on this job made several errors. First he did not secure the pressure pipe within the wall; he fastened the toilet flange with bent-over nails; and he did not cover the flange hole—wood, nails, and other debris could drop into the drainpipe.

This method of securing the pipe within the wall allows the pipe to be easily adjusted left to right anywhere along the metal horizontal bar. (Photo courtesy Sioux Chief Manufacturing.)

A drop-ear elbow with female threads can terminate nonmetal pipe in the wall, with copper extending through the wall for the fixture.

Common drop-ear elbows are most commonly used as anchors where it's necessary for the pipe to be super secure as it leaves the wall, such as at a shower head. They are also used as an interface fitting to change types of pipe, including CPVC, PEX, or polished copper pipe.

Copper-sweat drop-ear elbow gives support to the stub-out pipe going to the fixture.

Plastic drop-ear elbows have a tendency to crack as pipes are threaded into them.

be somewhere between the joists. Some manufacturers make a metal bracket that spans the opening and fastens to the studs, holding the pipes in place.

If you have a lot of scrap lumber lying around, an easy, low-cost method of securing the through-the-wall pipe is simply to attach a nailer across the stud cavity and secure the pipe to it with a tube talon or two. If you

are using a metal pipe with a fancy finish—chrome, gold, or brass, for example—to come out of the wall and attach to the stop-valve, you need to terminate a female threaded drop-ear elbow in the pipe cavity for it to screw into. In this situation, a low-cost method is to use a common galvanized pipe nipple painted the same color as the wall. For copper, use a sweat drop-ear elbow for a super-secure attachment within the stud cavity, tube talons nailed to the stud or nailer, or a metal bracket that spans the stud cavity.

## Hiding the pipe

There are times when you must get the pipes around the house and you don't have stud walls, typically in timber-frame houses and log cabins. In these situations, you can run 2×6 trim and rip out a hiding place on its backside for the pipes, being careful not to run a trim nail through the pipe. I usually use brass screws to hold the trim. If there are no studs in the wall that can hold a trim nail or screw, glue a board on the wall and then secure the trim to that.

To run pipes from floor to floor, hide the pipes under the stairs. If all else fails, run the pipes in a corner and cover them with a corner trim board as a last resort.

### Hiding pipes in a plenum

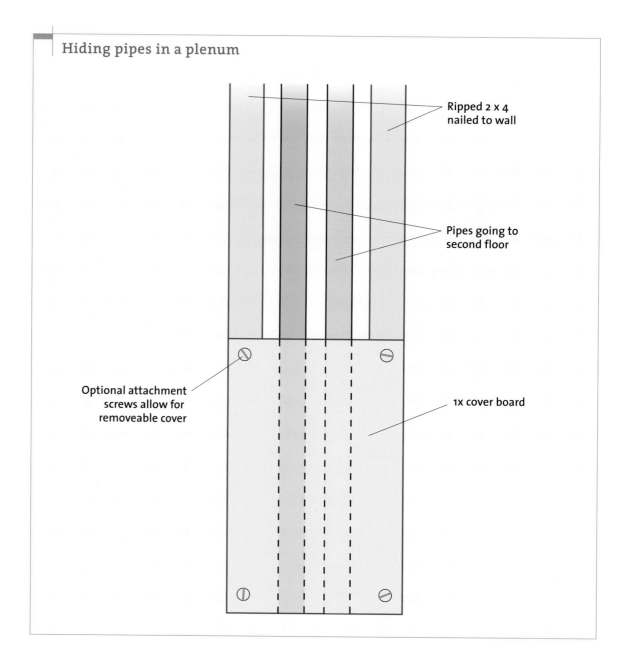

Ripped 2 x 4 nailed to wall

Pipes going to second floor

Optional attachment screws allow for removeable cover

1x cover board

## Hiding pipes behind a homemade wooden trim

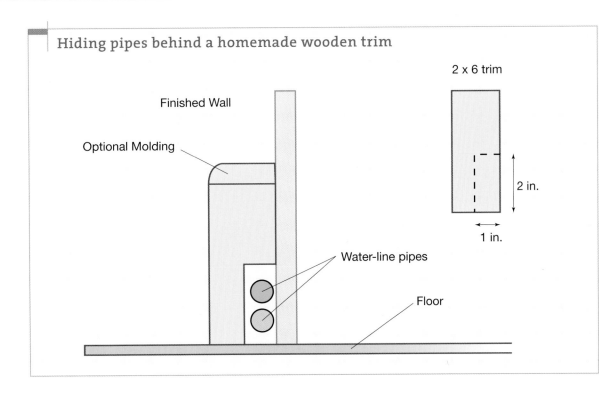

Finished Wall

Optional Molding

2 x 6 trim

2 in.

1 in.

Water-line pipes

Floor

This system of enclosing pipes is commonly used in log cabins—logs are solid. First, cut out a section of a 2×6 big enough to hold the pipes, stain the board to match the wall timbers, install the pipes, and cover them with the 2×6 trim piece, fastening it in place with screws. Add a molding strip if desired.

## Hiding pipes along a wall corner

Bring pipes up from basement to second floor by placing them in a corner.

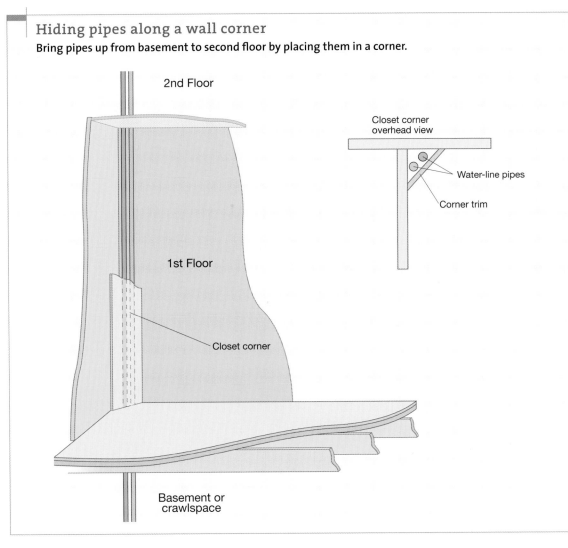

2nd Floor

Closet corner
overhead view

Water-line pipes

Corner trim

1st Floor

Closet corner

Basement or
crawlspace

This system of hiding pipes is applicable to remodeled homes with finished walls. The covering board's edges are cut at 45 degree angles to make them fit flush with the walls. Paint the board to match the wall, then fasten it in place with screws to allow access to the pipes.

This system of hiding pipes is applicable to studless and solid walls such as those in a timber-frame house. Start by gluing a 1×8 board to the wall with panel adhesive. It will receive the screws fastening the pipe cover board in place. Once this board is secure, proceed as shown for hiding pipes behind a homemade wooden trim (see p. 159).

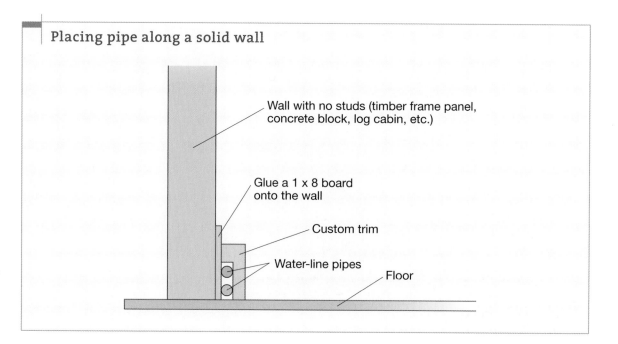

**Placing pipe along a solid wall**

Wall with no studs (timber frame panel, concrete block, log cabin, etc.)

Glue a 1 x 8 board onto the wall

Custom trim

Water-line pipes

Floor

### Cap the pipe end

Once the pipe is through the wall, cap the end or tape it up to keep debris out of the pipe. This also allows you to pressurize the pipes, provided you cap the ends securely with plug (for PEX pipe), solder (for copper pipe), or glue (CPVC pipe).

## Showers, Washers, and Refrigerators

The hot and cold lines for the shower have to come into the wall cavity where the shower (or tub shower) valve system is located. Carpenters typically put a stud in this area exactly where plumbers need the valve. To remove the stud, ask the carpenter first, use a recip saw to cut the nails between the stud end and the plate, and then lift the stud out. Do not smash the stud with a hammer and destroy it; studs are too expensive not to reuse whenever possible.

During the rough-in, cut the hole in the tub/shower or shower wall for the fixture and install it. I normally install stub-out pipes, or at

least male adapters, on the valve body before mounting it to the stall wall. Doing this on the shop table is a lot easier than doing it after the valve body is installed on the stall wall. This is mandatory for copper sweat pipe because if you sweat the pipes onto the valve body after it is installed on the stall wall, the heat will discolor the wall or ruin it. For copper sweat, install a union on the valve stub-out to make the connection from valve stub to pipe without sweating in place.

During the shower rough-in, also attach a drop-ear elbow for the shower head. Immediately behind the stall wall, where the showerhead is being installed in a stud cavity I dry-fit a nailer board. On this board I mark where the drop-ear elbow is to be installed so I have the showerhead where I want it, normally 6 ft., 6 in. above the floor and centered above the drain. I also mark the studs where the nailer is to be installed. I remove the nailer and install the drop ear with a pipe long enough to reach the shower valve assembly, and

The water lines to a shower, tub, or tub shower, as well as the valve itself, can be mounted to a simple metal-bracket. (Photo courtesy Sioux Chief Manufacturing.)

The wall on the left has a stud dead center that would block the installation of a spigot. The wall on the right is open in the middle—its stud is not in the way. When studs are in the way, cut their support nails with a recip saw and move them to the side.

then screw the board back into place where I marked the studs.

I rarely mount the valve body directly to the thin fiberglass stall wall. Instead, once I have cut through the wall for the valve body (the valve instructions give the size of hole), I glue 1× wood pieces around the hole, one small piece to each side and one above and below. The bottom one can be eliminated if the valve is for a shower only. I cut the hole and glue on the wood as soon as the unit hits the job site. This allows a day or more for the glue to dry. I attach the stub-out pipes to the wood to secure the valve assembly and put the handle on the valve assembly to finish it off on the front side of the stall wall. If tile is being installed, I do this step after the tile is up. For tile installations, be sure the valve body sticks out far enough into the stall so the handle will clear the tile by measuring and adding the thickness of the tile.

Remove the center valve first so the heat from the torch doesn't ruin its seals.

## Finishing the installation

The clothes washer pipes need to be finished off during the rough-in so the finished wall can be installed around the washer box. In an unfinished basement, leave the pipes and the washer box exposed on the wall, and do not be tempted to attach the washer valves (hose bibbs) to the pipe, leaving them unsecured to the wall. Use a washer box or attach a drop-ear elbow to the wall and secure the hose bibbs to the elbows. Typically, I mount a piece of wood to the wall and screw the drop ear to it simply because it is easier than fastening the drop ear to the concrete. Many washer boxes come with an integral valve system. If this is what you have, the box must be mounted to the wall.

Mount the washer box or hose bibbs immediately behind and above the back of the washer location. Typical washer height at the back is around 42 in. so the bottom of the washer box should be 43 in. off the ground, higher if you have the washer and dryer on a platform.

# Installing a shower-valve body

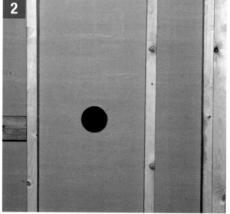

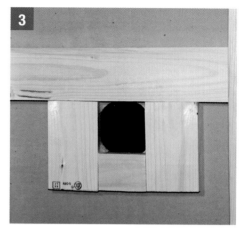

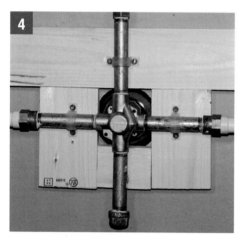

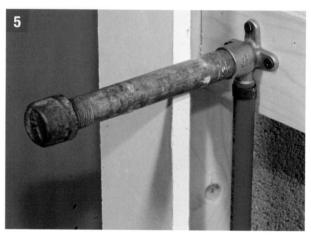

**QUICK REFERENCE**

**TECHNIQUES  p. 183**
For information about mounting a valve body
onto a fiberglass shower wall

**WATER LINES  p. 175**
For information about running water lines

**PIPE SUPPORTS  p. 176**
For information about pipe supports

**DRAIN STUB-OUTS  p. 155**
For information about stub-outs

**1** Drill the hole for the valve body, as specified in the instructions that came with the valve. The hole should be immediately above the drain and below the showerhead.

**2** Clean the area around the valve hole to guarantee adhesion of the support boards.

**3** Glue on boards and let dry.

**4** Install rigid pipes onto valve body and secure to boards.

**5** For a shower-head pipe, attach a drop-ear elbow onto a nailer between two studs and install a dummy ½-in. galvanized nipple. When the finished wall is installed, the wall will be drilled out or built-up around the pipe. Once the finished wall is up, the nipple can be removed and the showerhead pipe can be installed (not shown). For a tub/shower, extend the bottom pipe out of the valve assembly to the spout (not shown).

A clothes-washer box is not required. You can install just a hose bibb like this one. If you install a hose bibb, secure it firmly to the wall with a drop-ear elbow.

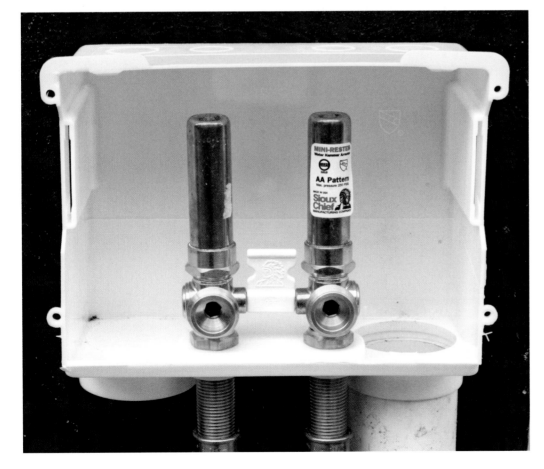

If installed within a finished wall, the clothes-washer box needs to be put in during the rough-in stage. Mount it inside a stud wall to a finished wall or against the block wall of a basement.

**200** | Installing
Whirlpool Tubs

**207** | Installing a Grab Bar

**210** | Plumbing a
Vessel Sink

**214** | Installing a
Vessel Sink Faucet

# Finish Plumbing

**A**fter the rough-in is completed comes the fun part: the finish plumbing. Now you will connect all the fixtures. Since the only plumbing items anyone will see are the fixtures, do not short your customers in this area. Regardless of the quality of the plumbing hidden in the walls and under the floor, if they see slipshod work on the outside they might assume you did the same throughout the job. In this chapter, I cover all the steps to wrapping up a job, from installing sinks and drains to creating a custom vanity. The last task on a job is to clean the faucets and sinks, leaving them sparkling.

## Kitchen Drains

What do I dislike about the common sink drains in the kitchen? Everything. They drain slowly, they breed bacteria, and, with more than a dozen slip joints, they're prone to leak. Once you get all those slip joints not to leak, they get bumped as people reach for supplies under the sink, and they start leaking again. I figured there had to be a better system—and I made one.

Most plumbers install **either a center drain or an end drain. Both tend to leak, but the center drain leaks more readily.**

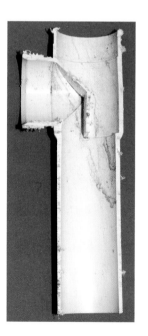

Whether **center drain or end drain, the water has to flow through this diverter pipe or something like it. The cutaway (*left*) shows the diverter, intended to prevent water flowing down the pipe from entering the side run. It reduces the ID of the pipe to less than ½-in., slowing flow and often causing the pipe to clog.**

## An improved drain

The first problem I solved was location. I put the drain and trap out of the way, flush against

Metal nuts along **the sink drain system corrode and sometimes cannot be removed by unscrewing. The mini recip saw, with its thin blade and tiny teeth, is good for cutting them off.**

the back wall. You can smash the drain with a hammer and it won't leak. Furthermore, water drains fast, keeping bacteria at bay.

I use a high-quality strainer—a Kohler 8801 Duostrainer®—the best on the market. Made of solid brass, it's quite heavy. Other strainers have rolled threads and the nut pops off when it's tightened onto the threads; the Duostrainer's threads are cut by a die, allowing a snug fit.

When I set the strainer into the sink bowl, I use clear 100 percent silicone as a gasket; I never use plumber's putty. I have replaced hundreds of strainers that were leaking because the supposedly non-hardening plumber's putty hardened and cracked. The disadvantage of the Duostrainer is its cost, about $35 each.

To **tighten or** remove a strainer, use a pipe wrench or a special tool designed for this. To keep the strainer from spinning, I insert needle-nose pliers into the cross-bar of the strainer from underneath and hold the strainer in place while I loosen or tighten it. If that fails, I use my mini reciprocating saw with its ultra thin blade—and slice through the tightening ring.

One of the worst things about the common strainer is the use of what I call "top hat" gaskets. These gaskets extend horizontally into the drain line immediately under the strainer (you can see them if you look straight into the strainer) and cut off about 50 percent of the water flow out of the sink. Even worse, this gasket becomes a host for bacteria, only a fraction of an inch away from dishes. I won't have these in my house.

Instead, I use fittings that grab onto the outside of the strainer threads underneath the sink. More specifically, I install a 1½-in. Fernco flex elbow, which gives me the maximum diameter drain hole allowed by the throat of the strainer and puts nothing in the waterway that can diminish flow or create a health hazard. Sometimes I use a PVC fitting with female threads and screw it onto the male strainer threads and then to the flex elbow.

I point the Fernco flex elbow straight to the back wall. Onto that goes a straight piece of schedule 40 pipe glued onto a PVC elbow at the wall. Then I connect that to a double Y fitting at the sink center and the trap immediately below. All the interconnecting pipe along the

I only use **a Kohler 8801 solid brass strainer. It is extremely durable, looks beautiful, and never leaks.**

One reason cheap strainers leak is their rounded threads. The tightening nut will sometimes pop off the threads rather than tighten and create a leak.

To install a **strainer, I always use clear 100 percent silicone caulk, not plumber's putty.**

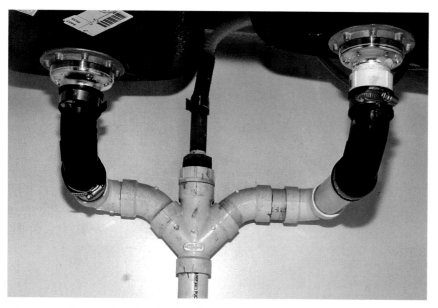

My custom drain system installed under a sink. The lower pipe feeds into the trap.

Here are all the parts to my custom kitchen sink drain: two 1 ½-in. flexible elbows (the two PVC female adapters are only used if I need to extend the drain lower for different bowl depths), two PVC elbows, a double Y, insert male adapter on top of Y, trap, and (not shown) a few lengths of PVC pipe to connect it all.

I connect the strainer to the drain assembly with a Fernco flexible elbow and point it toward the back wall. Grabbing onto the outside of the threads, and eliminating the gasket that extends into the pipe allows a full-flow output within the strainer drain.

Gaskets like this (*top*), with a flat top extending into the drain right under the strainer, are commonly used. These sometimes cut the drain flow by 50 percent. They also catch food particles and provide a breeding ground for bacteria (*bottom*).

back wall, along with the double Y and trap, is mounted snugly against the wall. With the trap here, the area under the sink is open for storage, and the pipe doesn't get bumped anymore.

Connecting my custom drain system to an existing drain line that is too high can be a problem. I sometimes have to cut off the old drainpipe within the wall so I have enough pipe on which to slip a flex elbow or T. The best way to connect it is to bring a new pipe up through the floor. I install an elbow for a direct connection to the trap output pipe, or a T if I want to continue a vent line. I have at least 3 in. of horizontal line between the trap and the elbow or T. This prevents the system from becoming a glorified S trap.

My custom drain system is too expensive to install on a low-bid job. On repair and renovation, however, I rarely have a problem talking owners into a high-quality strainer and drain system once they see first-hand how a low-quality system can leak and rot out the kitchen cabinetry.

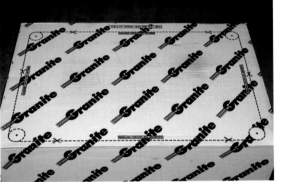

Most sinks come with templates to take the guesswork out of installing them. Tape the template on the countertop and cut. Each template corner shows a circle where the corners must be drilled with a spade bit to give room to start the jigsaw blade cut.

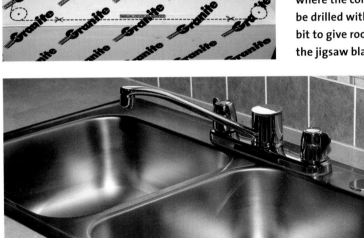

Stainless steel sinks account for 57 percent of the sink marketplace. Of those, the majority are drop-in models, like this one. To keep it shining, choose one with a high nickel content.

## Kitchen Sinks

Because there are sinks of every type and color imaginable on the market, the choice is best left to the home owner. I do tell my customers how to differentiate a good stainless steel sink from a cheap one. Low-quality sinks have shallow bowls, thin metal (21 gauge rather than the thicker 18 gauge), and not much nickel in the stainless, which will inevitably rust. To determine the amount of nickel in the sink you can only go by price: In general, the higher the price, the more nickel. A good stainless steel sink will cost around $200; better ones, $400. Forget the $50 models.

Never cut out the kitchen counter for a new sink unless you have the sink on hand, you're sure it is the proper one, and it's in good condition. Most sinks come with a template that you tape in place on the counter for the cut. In the past, we would lay the sink on the counter and draw a line around it; then we would cut ½ in. inside the line. Before cutting, look under the sink for any bracing, which you don't want to cut. If the counter is going to be tiled, cut the hole for the sink before the tile is installed.

The most common sink is a drop-in model. Simply cut a hole and drop it in. Some sinks, however, are designed with an under-counter mount; installing them requires a lot of work and should be left to the pros. Sinks are sometimes an integral part of the countertop. The ones I have seen scratch easily and become dull.

## Faucets

A kitchen or bathroom faucet, like a kitchen sink, should be the owner's choice. Again, I offer a few pointers. If a client regularly washes large pots and pans, he might want a high-arced spout. Or perhaps a model with a hand-held sprayer that pulls out from the spout. The check valve—a special one-way valve required by code on all pull-out sprayers—have been known to chatter, but they remain popular.

Does the customer want a single handle or two handles? Single is better. A single-handled faucet can be turned on and off with one hand, and it's easier for older users. If an owner wants two handles, I always recommend lever or cross handles, the old-fashioned handles that are in the shape of a plus sign. Handles that are smooth and round are more difficult to turn on and off by someone with arthritis. Plastic handles with lots of grooves collect debris and discolor. In addition, there are single-hole faucets, two-hole faucets, and a popular faucet that has no con-

necting body between the handles above the sink. The owner also has to choose a finish from the wide variety that are available.

As with the strainer, I never use plumber's putty when installing a faucet. Always use clear 100 percent silicone caulk, the kind that comes with a replaceable cap on the feed tip.

Installation within the small confines between the sink bowl and the cabinet wall is difficult. Often, even a basin wrench, that weird-looking plumber's tool that is made to fit in tight places, won't fit. I created a couple of tools that will fit in that small space and easily remove the faucet nut and one type of supply tube nut. I cut a cross in one end of a length of 1 ¼-in. PVC to use on the faucet nut. For the supply tube nut, I cut straight across the end of a piece of 1-in.

My custom tool (*top*) for removing faucet hold-down nuts (*bottom left*) and plastic supply tube nuts (*bottom right*). The cross is cut into 1 ½-in. PVC pipe (*center left and right*), and the opposite end is cut into a 1-in. copper pipe which is then bent to an oval to fit the supply tube nut. The rounded end of the copper pipe is then pushed into the PVC.

Although I use a flat bastard file to cut the cross-notches into PVC pipe, I use my solid-blade cutoff saw to cut the notches into copper pipe.

There are **two** types of plastic faucet hold-down nuts for the common 1/2-in. shank faucet: the cross with four wings and the cross with two wings. The PVC side of my custom tool fits both.

Simply insert my custom tool under the faucet and turn the faucet nut, removing it. Doesn't everyone wish using a basin wrench was that easy?

copper pipe and squeeze it into an oval. This reduces its diameter and allows it to grip the nut.

There are two types of supply tube hold-down nuts that my special tool can't remove. For these, I use a flare crow's foot tool, readily available online from companies such as Snap-On Tools (www.snapon.com).

A common crow's **foot** tool (*left and above*) will also work under a sink, but I had to grind its sides down to give it more room to turn.

**Flare crow's foot tools** (*right*) remove the metal supply tube nuts, both the old-style brass (*above left*) and the newer, smaller chrome nuts (*above right*).

## Dishwashers

Since most people are right-handed, dishwashers are normally installed immediately to the right of the kitchen sink. Typically, the rough-in width is 24¼ in. to 24½ in. If that size can't be accommodated, install an 18-in. dishwasher, which requires a rough-in width of 18¼ in. to 18½ in. Height is never an issue since all dishwashers are designed to fit under a common 36-in. kitchen counter.

Because air gap fittings in the drain line are not required by most manufacturers, bring the drain hose up high in a loop, to just under the countertop, and then drop it down just under the kitchen sink to interface with the kitchen drain immediately before the kitchen sink trap. Keep any slack in the drain hose behind the dishwasher.

The water line connection to the dishwasher is normally immediately behind the kick plate, on the left side. The water line can be bought as a kit: it comes with a long braided stainless steel flex line that has the dishwasher connection fitting (⅜-in. MIP angle) that screws right into the dishwasher. The opposite end terminates to a stop valve, which is not part of the kit, under the sink. Be sure to tap into the hot line.

Whenever you install a dishwasher, keep future maintenance in mind. To allow the unit to be pulled out from under the counter, get the longest dishwasher water pressure hose available and loop the slack behind the dishwasher; never cut the supplied drain hose. Do the same with the electrical cable—use a 12-ga. cable with ground on a 20-amp breaker on its own separate circuit—and make a large loop behind the dishwasher that can be pulled out easily. The electrical connection to the dishwasher is always behind the kick plate, on the right side. Connect the wires black to black, white to white, and cable ground wire to dishwasher frame or green wire.

Typical rough-in **width of a full-size dishwasher is 24 ¼ in.** For space-saver dishwashers—like this 18-in. Danby unit from Canada—the rough-in is 18¼ in.

I installed an 18-in. dishwasher a few years ago that lasted only a week longer than the warranty. The cost to fix it was within $30 of a new unit, so the obvious choice was to buy another one. That wasn't an easy proposition. Many of the 18-in. dishwashers sold in the United States are made by the same company as the one that died, regardless of whose name is on it, and could be expected to last about as long as the first one. But there's good news: I found a Canadian model (www.danby.com). It was much higher quality, with a stainless steel tub, and was about the same price as the one I initially installed. The cost of shipping it to Virginia—about $100—was well worth it.

High-quality and low-quality dishwashers (same price: about $300) seen from the bottom. Which is which is obvious. The high-quality unit (*left*) is from Canada while the low-quality one (*far left*) is made by an American company—it died a week after its warranty had expired.

This quality unit has two filters: a large stainless filter to catch the small stuff and a plastic coarse filter to catch the large. Both are easily removable for cleaning.

A quality dishwasher also has a stainless steel interior with separate water feeds to two sprayer arms—one beneath the upper rack, another for the lower rack. I do not recommend the more common telescopic sprayer that rises from the lower rack to spray the upper rack, because it doesn't clean as well.

Dense carpet-backer type insulation is preferred over loose, thin fiberlass, which is almost useless in noise reduction for dishwashers. Batt insulation is thick, dense, and lays like a blanket, all attributes that make it perfect for appliance noise reduction. Fiberglass, on the other hand, is loose, rips, and pulls back easily.

Secure the top of the dishwasher frame to the kitchen cabinet. This keeps the dishwasher to fall forward as the door is opened.

Under the front kick panel, the water connection is to the left (*top*) and the electrical connection to the right (*bottom*).

## Toilets

In the old days, no one cared about the amount of water it took to flush a toilet—most used 3 gal. to 5 gal. each flush. In contrast, by federal law, today's low-flow toilets take only 0.8 gal. to 1.6 gal. per use. Early designs of low-flow toilets didn't flush well because the manufacturers didn't redesign the entire system to use less water—they just cut back the water flow. Obviously, a toilet that was designed to flush with 3 gal. of water didn't flush well using 1.6. It would have to be flushed again and again. However, all of today's designs are designed for 1.6 gal., and most work satisfactorily. The flush is merely the first step in a good design, and there are other considerations in selecting a toilet.

This diagram shows **how water flows in a toilet.**
**(Photo courtesy of American Standard)**

## Selecting a toilet

Over the years whenever I replaced a stopped-up toilet that wouldn't clear, I would break it open to find the problem. Invariably, the waterway was too narrow and had a very rough finish. I also noted that the water didn't flow smoothly from the tank into the back of the bowl. Instead, it smashed into a flat surface of the bowl throat, which significantly lowered the velocity. And even that was rough and unfinished.

I have installed many toilets from various manufacturers, and I have always been on the lookout for a better one. I was searching for an "install-and-forget" toilet. Then I installed the American Standard Champion in my own house. It worked so well I tore it apart to find out why. That toilet addressed all poor designs I had seen in the past. And the manufacturer did it without consulting me, which means that others were also troubled by the same faulty design issues. Among other attributes, the Champion has a smooth waterway with a very

large diameter, a large tank-to-bowl water exit for a fast flush, and a tank-to-bowl attachment point that is up high so it stays clean.

## Pulling the toilet

Pulling a toilet can be easy if nothing goes wrong, or quite difficult if nothing goes right. The easy part is removing the water line and all of its water. A plastic margarine tub works well in getting any residual water out of the bowl, and an old towel will absorb leftover water in the tank and bowl. The most common problem is that the toilet bowl hold-down bolts spin, which prevents their removal. When this happens, I cut the bolts with my Makita mini recip saw. If the bolt moves or spins, I hold the upper tip with some cutters or pliers.

Before you pull the toilet, know where you are going to put it. I find it easiest to place it on an old towel and drag it out of the bathroom, or I just duck-walk it out (I make sure to have all doors open beforehand). Whatever you do, expect a mess.

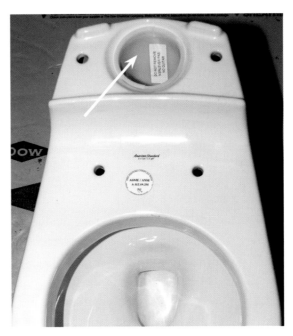

Two designs for **a good flush. The smooth plastic insert (*arrow, left*) where the tank connects to the bowl speeds water to the bowl, giving a fast flush. Second, a large, smooth evacuation hole, or porcelain trapway (*right*), in the bottom of the toilet bowl—this one measures 2½ in.—makes for a complete flush without stoppage.**

This old toilet was one of the first 1.6-gal. flush units. You had to hold the flush handle down for most of the flush cycle and occasionally had to flush twice. In addition, the rough surface of its waterway inside the toilet made it unsanitary and prone to stoppages.

If you have to cut the hold-down bolts to remove the toilet bowl, don't bother knocking the bolts down or turning them out with pliers. Just lift the toilet up to remove the bowl. The cut bolts will easily slide out of their curved slots in the flange.

Once you pull the toilet, attach heavy-duty bolts (*above*) to the flange to prepare it for the new toilet. Put a towel in the hole (*right*) to prevent anything from falling in and to keep the sewer gas from escaping.

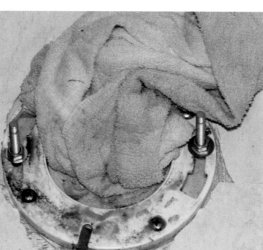

I don't mess around trying to loosen the nut on the bowl to the flange bolt. I simply cut the bolt with my mini recip saw, which takes only seconds. Once they're cut and the toilet is lifted, I replace them with new bolts to prepare the flange for the new toilet.

### Install a new toilet

For new installations, install the toilet flange 12 in. from the finished wall. If you screw it up you can buy a bowl that is made to sit 10 in. from the wall or 14 in. from the wall. Verify that this location is clear for at least 15 in. on each side, left and right from centerline.

Install the bowl's hold-down bolts onto the flange's two U-shaped cutouts. I never use the C-shaped slots that most other plumber's use because they usually spin, making removal difficult. I use 5/16-in. bolts (1/4-in. is standard) and tighten them onto the flange using a common nut on top. This way, the bolts cannot be bent

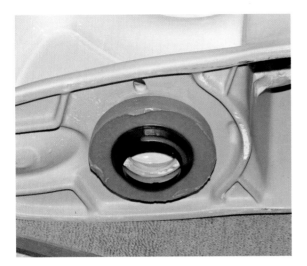

**You can put the wax seal on either the flange or the toilet. On the latter, it fits on what is called the "horn" of the bowl.**

over to the side as the bowl is set down over them. The flange should sit on the finished floor. If a tile floor is going in, the flange should extend above the subfloor by the measure specified by the tile installer.

I do not recommend any fancy type of flange or those that come with the center hole covered with thin plastic knock-outs. After you install the flange, if the toilet is not going in at that time, cover the hole with duct tape.

Set the wax seal onto the flange or the toilet. I use the type with a built-in funnel. If the flange is set deep in the floor, which sometimes happens, I set a common wax ring onto the funnel wax ring to extend the wax higher and compensate for the lowering of the flange.

As you set the bowl, always lower it dead center onto the hold-down bolts that extend up from the flange. If you get it off center and then bring it back, you'll ruin the wax seal by pushing it to the side, so have extra seals on hand.

All this assumes the floor under the toilet is flat. If it is not, make it so. You cannot allow the toilet to rock—either front to back or left to right. The movement will compress the wax ring, resulting in a gap that can allow water or sewer gas into the house.

**The old, hard-to-flush toilet was removed and replaced with a 1.6-gal. modern toilet that should be good for many years of reliable service.**

## Fine-tuning

All toilets need to be fine-tuned after installation. Flush a new toilet a few times and see how it works. In particular, note the water level in the tank. The water level should be around $1/2$ in. below the top of the overflow tube. If it comes up and flows into the overflow tube during refill, that's a sign that the refill mechanism will never turn off and needs adjustment.

If your toilet has a chain that goes to the lift flapper in the tank center, be sure it is the proper length. If it's too long, the flapper will close too soon, sometimes after only a two-second flush. Worst case is that the flapper won't lift at all and the toilet won't flush. Should the chain be too short, the flapper cannot seat properly. If the flapper never seats at all, the toilet will run continuously. I've never had a chain-type flapper that was properly adjusted right out of the box.

## Comfortable toilet seats

To be comfortable, what we sit on needs to be as wide as our hips. This is common knowledge to almost everyone—except those who design toilet seats. For some reason, they think the design of the toilet seat should follow that of the toilet bowl, not the human body.

After much research, I found a toilet seat that was properly engineered. Appropriately, the name of the seat is Big John ([www.bigjohn toiletseat.com](www.bigjohntoiletseat.com)). Based on first-hand experience, I can say that once you have used one of these, you'll wonder why we put a man on the moon before we got a comfortable toilet seat.

**The wide Big John toilet seat is more comfortable than a standard seat. Ample hip width should be a requirement on all toilet seats.**

> If the seat hinge nuts are in a space too small for your fingers, slip a washer onto the hinge's threaded bolt, then several large nuts, another washer, and finally a wing nut. This extends the wing nut down low enough for your fingers to turn it.

## Whirlpool Tubs

Whirlpool baths are the tubs of choice for many people. On average, the increase in house payment is insignificant and the presence of a whirlpool makes the house more attractive to buyers on resale. Forget about the 5-ft. tubs; they're not long enough for most people to lie back and relax.

**The massive soft bumpers (*top*) and the heavy-duty stainless steel hinge bolts (*bottom*) are two items I love on the Big John toilet seat.**

## Getting the old tub out

A steel, plastic, or fiberglass tub will lift out easily. Cast iron, on the other hand, is hard and heavy. Unless you have Superman to help you, I advise breaking the cast tub into small sections and removing it that way. Make at least two cuts with a diamond blade on a circular saw. Even then it will take a lot of muscle swinging the sledge. Wear safety glasses and gloves and protect everything. Warning: The broken shards will be razor sharp.

## When tub arrives

When the whirlpool arrives, immediately check it for damage. Keep it protected at all times. If possible, check for leaks and proper operation by filling the tub with a hose and running an extension cord (12 ga.) to check out the pump. If the pump has a 20-amp-only pigtail (meaning one slot on the plug is sideways), you will need a 20-amp-only receptacle to test it.

## Prep work

You need to build a frame around the lip of the tub using 2×4 stock. The instructions that come with the tub will give you an exact framing guideline. Assume a 300-lb. plumber is going to be standing on the lip and build the framing to suit. I usually install two sides only, leaving the other two sides open for sliding the tub in and out as the water lines and drain work go on. I frame in the other two sides only after all the work, except the drain connection under the floor, is completed.

You can place the tub on the tile, or you can build the tile up to it. I prefer to set the lip of the tub on the wood and set the tile to the edge of the tub. The weight is distributed more evenly if the tub is set on wood.

The question: how to remove an old, very heavy, cast iron tub? Answer: heavy work with a sledge hammer to break it into manageable pieces.

After the tub arrives, protect it by wrapping it with cardboard until it is installed.

It is a good idea to run water into the tub and get some power to the pump to verify there are no leaks and that the jet pump runs.

Check the walls and floors for plumb and right angles. Walls that are not at right angles are not a major problem if you lay the lip support 2×4 flat along the wall, like a counter. This gives the tub's lip plenty of room to be supported by the framing even if the wall is angling away from the tub.

The floor can be another problem. If it is sloping, you will have to shim up one side of the tub to level it. In one whirlpool installation, I had to add ¾-in.-plywood runners under the tub and then shim up one side by ½ in. Place the shims under the runners, not under the tub bowl. A tub sits on two runners, just like a snow sled. Try to have the shim be the length of the runner; do not support just one part. If you need to shim up ½ in. on one runner, cut a long wedge, tapered from ½ in. to next-to-nothing, for the desired length, perhaps 1 ft.

to 2 ft. or more. Once the tub is level, you can build the supports for the tub lip. An alternative to shimming is to pour a new floor with a self-leveling cement product, which is made for that purpose. That process takes a lot of time and trouble. It is faster and simpler to shim the tub than to level the floor.

Before you start the actual framing, determine where the whirlpool's drain and water lines are coming in. In many instances, the lines enter the tub in the middle rather than at one end as in a common tub. The tub's framing diagram will have a suggested faucet location. The drain however, will be fixed, and you will have to cut a large area for it under the floor, so pray that this location is not over a floor joist. If it is, move the tub to prevent cutting the joist.

Also consider future maintenance. Once the tub is installed, you have to be able to get to the pump for repair and upkeep. In addition, at this location (under the tub, next to the pump) you will need a receptacle outlet for the pump at a voltage and breaker specified by the instructions. You cannot tie into another existing circuit. If the tub has a heater, you need a second circuit. In this situation, I use a 12-ga. cable (20-amp circuit) to the pump along with a 20-amp receptacle (with a sideways slot).

**Once you know where the drain will go, cut a hole in the subfloor. The tub drain connection to the overflow pipe will be below floor level.**

When demolishing an old cast-iron tub, it can be quite messy and hazardous. As you smash the tub apart with a sledge hammer, razor-sharp shards of broken metal and dust will fly everywhere. For any demolition, wear appropriate gloves, safety glasses, a long-sleeve shirt, dust mask, and a hard hat. Also remove anything that could be broken by flying debris.

# Removing an old tub

## QUICK REFERENCE

**TOOLS p. 216**
For information about circular and reciprocating saws

**BLADES p. 234**
For information about using diamond blades on circular saws

**LAYOUT p. 153**
For information on distances between bathroom fixtures

**1** To remove the old tub, reach in and cut the water and drain lines with a recip saw. Also cut the drain line in the basement.

**2** Remove a row of tile and the trim from just above the tub, then use a car jack to lift the tub free of its mounting.

**3** Turn the tub to expose its weak side. Protect yourself, the floor (and everything else) from flying shards of broken cast iron.

**4** Pound the side until it breaks. With the sides gone, move to the front, back, rim, and bottom.

**5** Nothing left to do now except clean up the mess. Bottom line: This is easier said than done.

Always set the **faucet before you set the tub. Simply drill a hole in the tub and insert the threaded posts.**

Make sure you **have room for the water lines before you set the tub.**

Once the threaded **faucet posts are fed through, use a deep socket and tighten the nuts onto the post.**

Assuming the drain and faucet are going on the exterior wall, you have to install both before shoving the tub into place. Do not attach the drain tailpiece until the tub is in position (and then screw it in from below). Installing the faucet on the inside tub wall is better for the plumbing and access, but this means you may have to step over the faucet to get into the tub.

Most people want a high-quality, good-looking faucet for their whirlpool. When choosing a tub faucet that can deliver a lot of water fast, look for a high-flow model that is designed for a ¾-in. water line. Most of the major plumb-

Tub framing is **specified out in the tub's instructions. I build two mini walls, install the faucet, drain and water lines (if I can't get to them after the tub is in), slide the unit in, and level it as I build the last two walls.**

ing manufacturers make one. Expect having to connect the faucet to ¾-in. shanks. When I need flexibility, I choose ¾-in. stainless steel braid flexible pipe (similar to that typically used on water heaters). I may have to cut out more of the floor for the pipes since I will be moving the tub around during the installation. If the faucet is going toward the inside of the room (as opposed to an exterior wall), this eliminates the problem and you can connect the pipe directly to the faucet.

## Tub drain system

In new construction, you simply run a new 2-in. drain line to the tub. On a remodel job, you have to figure out where you want to tie into the existing drain line. For venting, you have several choices: run a new pipe for a vent, tie into a large drain line that is already vented, install an air admittance valve (AAV), or run an oversize drain line to a large pipe that is already vented. For this situation, a large, already-vented vertical drain line existed within 2 ft. of the tub.

You rarely have problems with a tub siphoning its trap dry due to improper venting because of the way tubs drain: first fast, then slow. If some of the trap water is removed, creating an air gap in the trap, it is refilled when the end of the tub draining occurs because the water drains out very slowly at that time.

## Using diamond core bits

To drill holes in tile for installing a grab bar or new faucet, I use diamond core bits, which are available from a number of different manufacturers. Such bits are also available, depending on bit size, at tool-rental agencies. *You cannot drill into tile with a carbide bit— you must use a diamond core bits.* These start at around $25 per bit.

A close-up shows a ½-in. cutter head (*left*) and the opposite end with a plug (*right*). The purpose of the plug is to keep water from flowing back into the drill if you drill up.

Diamond coring bits come with a wire to punch out the core. Here we have a ½-in. and a 3/16-in. core bit.

Larger core bits cannot use the small-V holder. But cradling the core bit in a hammer also prevents the bit from wandering.

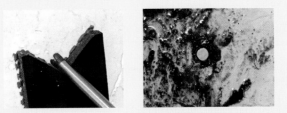

To use a small core bit, center it in the V holder (purchased separately), apply pressure and add water. A V holder can be anything that encompasses the bit to prevent it from slipping and wandering as you drill.

# Adding a tub drain

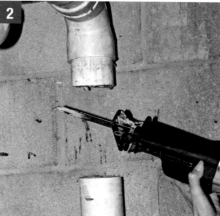

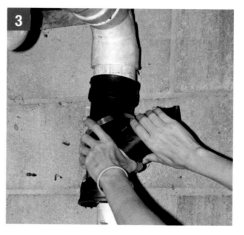

**QUICK REFERENCE**

**TOOLS p. 216**
For information about reciprocating saws

**MATERIALS p. 147**
For information about flexible fittings

**PVC PIPE p.142**
For information regarding PVC Pipe
and fittings

**VENTING p. 150**
For information about venting

**1** Using a 3-in. Fernco flex T, hold the pipe adjacent to the existing drain line and determine where to make the cut.

**2** Use a recip saw or a hand-held PVC saw to cut the old pipe.

**3** Compress the flexible T and fit it onto the cut ends of the upper and lower pipes.

**4** Orient the T in its proper alignment and tighten its upper and lower clamps.

**5** Insert tap pipes into the T fitting. Use a reducing bushing if needed.

**6** Attach pipes to tub drain, here using a 2-in reducer flex coupling to narrow the line to 1½ in. and a flex trap adapter fitting to make the final connection to the tub drain. Tighten all clamps.

## Exterior vs. interior walls

Building in a whirlpool tub—or any tub for that matter—within the interior of the room, means you need access to all sides to do the work, as you would with a kitchen-island sink. Most times, however, at least two sides of the tub will be against a wall, often with a long side against an exterior wall. And, more times than not, the whirlpool spigot is on this long side of the tub.

When the ends of the tub don't face open areas, you'll scrape your back on the spigot spout, and if the long side facing the room isn't open, you'll have to step over the spigot's spout and handles as you get in the tub. This leaves just one side on which to install the massive whirlpool faucet, and it needs to be installed before you slide the tub in. You'll also need to have a large enough hole in the floor so all the pipes can be attached to the faucet and drain after the tub slides in.

If you are using PEX pipe, install short stub outs of the flexible pipe that terminate below floor level before the tub slides in. When using stainless steel braided flex pipes to extend the faucet connections, also terminate them below the floor.

## Grab Bars

It is always a good idea to have a grab bar in a tub to assist getting up on a slippery surface. Even if customers don't think they need one, diplomatically point out to them that there may come a day when they do, either because of age or infirmity.

The first rule of installing a grab bar is to attach it to a secure spot. When I have the wall open, I try to note where there are three studs nailed together—the perfect place to screw in a grab bar. Usually I'm not so lucky—and then I'll use doubled studs instead of a triple. For finished walls, I start by using a stud finder to locate an existing wall stud. In many instances, though, I have to drill through tile to find the studs, which requires a diamond core bit of the right diameter.

A grab bar is an essential for safety, not just for seniors, but for everyone. Install them in every tub and shower. Choose from the many models available with different lengths, diameters and colors.

# Installing a grab bar

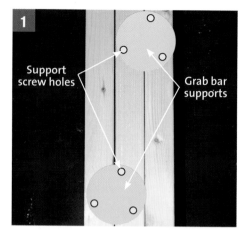

Support screw holes

Grab bar supports

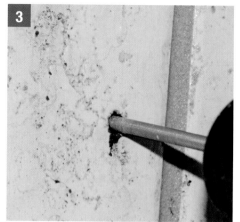

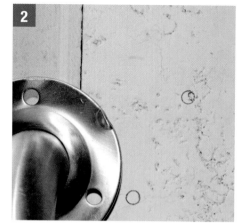

**QUICK REFERENCE**

**MATERIALS p. 207**
For information about grab-bar availability

**TOOLS p. 205**
For information about diamond-core bits

**PROCEDURES p. 205**
For information about supporting the core bit as it drills

**DRILLS p. 218**
For information about drills and bits

**1** Position the grab bar supports on the studs. These supports are 3 in. wide, and they can be mounted on doubled studs, but a triple is better. Position the triangle of holes on each support to be in solid wood. Mark each hole to be drilled.

**2** Verify the target location of the grab bar is plumb using a level. Place the grab bar against the wall and mark the screw holes on the tile.

**3** Using a diamond core bit suitable for drilling tile and of the proper size for the retaining screw, drill the holes.

**4** Attach the bar to the wall with retaining screws supplied with the bar.

**5** The grab bar is now securely attached to the wall.

## Cabinet-Style Vanities

To replace an existing vanity is simplicity itself. Simply cut the water lines from the faucet and disconnect the drain. If the water and drain lines come through the vanity bottom, you may have to cut the cabinet to free them. Next, look for any screws that attach the cabinet to the wall. There are usually two or three. Now all that's left to do is to cut through any old caulking, pry the cabinet away from the wall, tilt it up, and walk it out. Insert a new one of the same size.

Installing a new cabinet-style vanity is as easy as removing one. You have to remember only two rules: First, do not install the room trim until the vanity is in. Second, do not put the cabinet flush against a sidewall unless you have a special countertop for a corner. A common vanity countertop extends over the sides of the cabinet by at least an inch. If you want a corner unit to sit flush against the wall, you have to get a special countertop with a backsplash made for a corner.

Note the location of drawers when you buy a vanity. They may be in the way of the plumbing. Also, do not get a vanity that has a center vertical wood piece between the doors. It is unnecessary and does nothing but get in the way when you have to work on the plumbing.

Avoid vanities with **center posts like this one. The post is unnecessary and gets in the way of installing the plumbing underneath.**

Ripping out a **vanity is as easy as 1-2-3. Disconnect the water line and drains (*above*), remove any screws holding vanity to the wall, cut the caulk with a utility knife, and pull the old vanity out from wall (*left*).**

## Thinking Outside the Vanity

There are times when you can get creative. Those are the times I live for. To me, the common boxy cabinet-style vanity is the most boring piece of plumbing-use item. Most are made from pressed wood, which absorbs water like a sponge and then rots away. I'm glad to see that many vanity designers are finally offering alternatives.

One option is glass. Being see-through, glass makes a room seem larger. On the other hand, it is almost impossible to keep looking clean because it shows everything—rings from shampoo bottles, watermarks and fingerprints. Another option is to have the vanity design reflect the mood of the bathroom.

## Vessel Sinks

Vessel sinks are becoming more popular by the day. They are available in many models and styles. The one pictured below is a custom hand-beaten copper model from Oregon Copper Bowl (www.oregoncopperbowl.com).

Vessel sinks have a different installation procedure than is used for in-counter vanity sinks. Here I brought a 2-in. vertical drainpipe dead center under the sink, which would hook up with the sink's 1¼-in. tailpiece. That way, I could set the sink in place from above with its tailpiece extending into the drainpipe.

For this vessel sink, I had to drill four small holes through the vanity top for the threaded legs and one large hole for its drain. If the hole for a sink is too large for a diamond coring bit, use a jigsaw that has a dry-type tile-cutter jigsaw blade (cut the hole before you glue the tile down). Once the holes are cut, remove the sink and set it aside so it won't be in the way of the faucet installation.

Dry-type tile-cutter jigsaw blades, made by Edge Blades, are available at many large hardware suppliers. Unfortunately, these universal blades won't fit jigsaws that use proprietary blades. Bosch does make such a blade for its jigsaw, but I have found these difficult to locate in local supply houses.

**The old pitcher has been replaced with the modern bowl sink and faucet.**

**Vessel sinks have a center drain. Many also have threaded mounting legs to support and stabilize the fixture on the vanity countertop.**

## Custom vessel-sink installation

Though it may look difficult to build, it is not.
All this can be done in two days. For clarity,
the sidewall of the vanity is not shown in this
diagram.

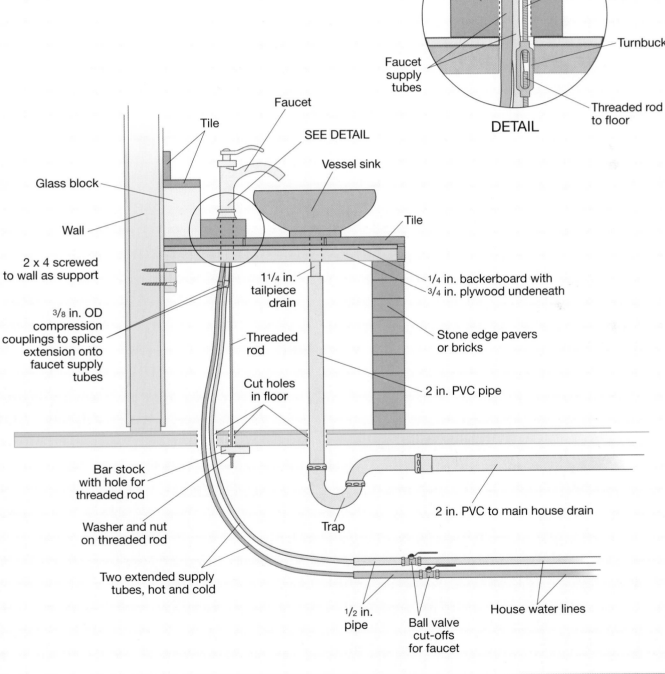

Faucet

Bored edger
or brick

Faucet
threaded rod
(faucet part)

Faucet
supply
tubes

Turnbuckle

Threaded rod
to floor

DETAIL

Faucet

SEE DETAIL

Vessel sink

Tile

Tile

Glass block

Wall

2 x 4 screwed
to wall as support

$3/8$ in. OD
compression
couplings to splice
extension onto
faucet supply
tubes

$1\frac{1}{4}$ in.
tailpiece
drain

$1/4$ in. backerboard with
$3/4$ in. plywood underneath

Threaded
rod

Stone edge pavers
or bricks

Cut holes
in floor

2 in. PVC pipe

Bar stock
with hole for
threaded rod

Washer and nut
on threaded rod

Trap

2 in. PVC to main house drain

Two extended supply
tubes, hot and cold

$1/2$ in.
pipe

Ball valve
cut-offs
for faucet

House water lines

## Picking a vessel sink

The style of vanity sinks has gone through a complete circle. In the olden days using a bowl to hold the water to wash your hands was commonplace. That evolved to a lav. Now we are back to using the bowl again, except that we have mounted it to the vanity counter and changed its name to vessel, vessel sink, or vessel lav.

As with most things, when you go shopping for a vessel sink don't judge the different models just by looks. You'll need to answer a few questions first. For example, will you want a vessel sink that sits on top of the counter or sits within the counter—it is a matter of taste. Will it be in a round or oval shape, or something entirely different, like a seashell or flower?

And what about the finish? It's hard to clean bowl sinks with a copper-patina, hammered-copper, or a polished-brass look. Others have problems with their coating being eaten away by such common but corrosive household products as tooth paste. Expect this to happen on any patina (coated metal) sink unless the manufacturer guarantees against it. The best bowl type for the least hassle as well as price is a common white ceramic sink. Its color stays, the white goes with anything, it is easily obtainable, and has a reasonable price. For a vessel sink more unusual and different, look in the catalogues or through on-line retailers—the sky's the limit. Indeed, you can even make your own of fired clay if you have access to a kiln and potter's wheel, or you have experience in working hammered copper.

Vessel sinks come equipped with and without built-in overflows. Having an overflow is nice (especially with small children) but making the cutout for it in an existing lav top is a hassle. In addition, you need to remember that a vessel sink with overflow will be thicker than one without because the bowl has to have double, hollow walls in parts so the overflow water can flow within. This may be the reason that many opt for no overflow.

Ceramic vessel sinks (*above*) look great. Sinks with overflows have hollow channels (*left*). Allow for them when cutting out lav tops.

Copper patina bowls look very pretty when new, but maintaining them is difficult. Toiletries may eat of the patina coating.

# Installing a vessel sink

**1** Turn the vessel sink over and note the holes required for the lavatory counter to accept the sink. This sink needs five holes, four for the threaded posts and one for the drain.

**2** Most sinks come with a template. Tape it in position on the counter (typically centered on the lav.)

**3** Using a diamond coring bit, drill through the tile for each leg. Stop drilling the holes as soon the bit is through the tile.

**4** Using a common twist drill, bore a hole through the backer board and plywood.

**5** Set the bowl's threaded legs into the holes and slide the bowl onto the tile. Trace a line around the drain where it touches the tile, then extend the circle 1 in. to 2 in. wider.

**6** Cut through the tile with a diamond hole cutter. Finish with a hole saw (not shown).

# Vessel Sink Faucets

Because of its height, a vessel sink needs a special faucet with a raised body so the spout will be high enough to reach the sink lip and extend into the sink. This faucet is a special extended-body faucet from Zoe, made especially for vessel sinks. Many such faucets are still not high enough if you don't recess the sink a little into the vanity. Instead, I install the faucet on a cut piece of masonry.

Before I could set the faucet on the vanity top, I cut and drilled this masonry piece, or edger, about 2 in. into the squared end behind the rounded end. Using a circular saw with a diamond blade (available at all large supply stores), it took about 10 seconds. Drilling completely through the rounded end (3 in. deep) with a 1¾-in. diamond core bit took about 3 or 4 minutes, drilling to a depth of ¾ in., chiseling out the core, then drilling again. Bottom line: Drilling though masonry to make a hole for the faucet supply pipe is no big deal.

After you install the faucet, replace the bowl. I found that the threaded rods that are an integral part of the sink fixture keep the sink in place quite nicely without the application of an appropriate adhesive. In theory, you are supposed to bolt the sink down, but I couldn't do that in this case since I have no access to the underside of the counter. I could have extended the bowl's threaded rods down to the basement or even mounted the sink to the counter (tightening it down to the counter) before I installed the counter. Bottom line: The sink was quite snug in the hole. It needed neither glue nor nuts to fasten the threaded rods attached to it.

## Installing the faucet

Drilling through the tile for the faucet pipes and hold-down bolt entails the same basic proce-

dure as cutting a hole for the vessel sink. Since I had lacked access space under the vanity top to attach any water lines, faucet hold-down nut, or cutoff valves, I extended all of them to the basement. I extended the faucet's supply tubes by splicing on 30-in.-long supply tubes. I did the same for the faucet's tie-down bolt by adding a 3-ft. (¼×20) threaded rod and custom rethreaded turnbuckle to match the faucet thread.

Vessel sink faucets **have extended stems so their spouts will be high enough to reach the lips of the basins. Sometimes these stems do not reach high enough. One option is to mount them on a piece of decorative masonry or cut stone such as marble or granite. Even taller bowl-sink faucets are available. They connect directly to the sink top instead of using a riser of decorative masonry.**

# Appendix

**P**lumbing requires a seemingly infinite number of tools and materials. The longer you stay in the trade, the more you will collect. Why? Because we always are in search of tools that make our work easier. This chapter contains a wealth of tools, those that are widely used as well as some designated for professionals only. The products in the pros-only section are listed there because the manufacturer wants the installer to be schooled in the product before installation, the material is not readily available to the general public (you have to get it from a wholesaler), or the installation tools are very expensive.

In addition, I've included a number of charts and tables pertaining to earlier chapters to help with understanding submersible pump installation procedures and how codes apply to the design of drains and vents. Lastly, ADA (American Disabilities Act) Guidelines are listed for those who want to go beyond the grab bar installation demonstrated in Chapter 8 to accommodate those with disabilities or handicaps.

# Tools

A list of all the tools used in plumbing would take an entire book. Most of the tools used in the trade are shown throughout the book in their place of use.

We all know the common plumbing tools: pipe wrenches and adjustable wrenches, torches and solder, glue and primer, drills and reciprocal saws. Levels. Crimpers and GO/NO-GO gauges. But we also need tools from other trades. Many tools such as chisels and saws one would think were the domain of carpenters. But if you work with plumbing you also work with wood. There may not be a carpenter on a job site to do what's needed so the plumber must put on his or her carpentry hat and get to work. The same is true of tile. A plumber must know how to work with tile because he may have to drill through it or replace some tile on rotted out drywall around a tub. In many small home situations, the plumber does it all.

## Cordless tools

Cordless tools have come a long way. Providing lightweight, portability, and safety, they have take the workplace by storm. Their only disadvantage is lifespan. Whereas a cordless tool may last you a lifetime, a cordless one dies in a few years.

## Corded tools

Corded tools provide the back-breaking work that need high torque and deep drilling. No job is complete without a right-angle drill and a reciprocating saw. For slab work you'll need a rotary hammer to get down through the concrete to install that drain pipe. For drilling into a block wall, you'll need a pistol grip hole shooter that can use spade bits and then be used as a rotary hammer drill for small diameter screw holes in block.

Pipe wrenches are **the mainstay of the plumbing trade. You will need all sizes.**

Adjustable wrenches are necessities. As with pipe wrenches, you need all sizes. The new designs with the wide handles (*top wrench—and complete set at photo bottom*) are easier on your hands than the old-style narrow design.

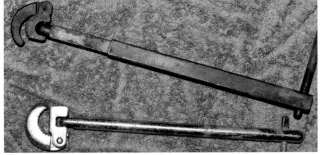

The commonly used basin wrench reaches into hard-to-get-to places to remove faucets. They work poorly, at best. I prefer to make my own, which work much better. See page 230 for details.

The circular saw pictured here has the blade on the left side of the saw so you can see the cut line more readily. It also has a quick-change blade mechanism so no wrenches are required. Use a circular saw to cut wood and, when fitted with a diamond blade, tile, block, and stone.

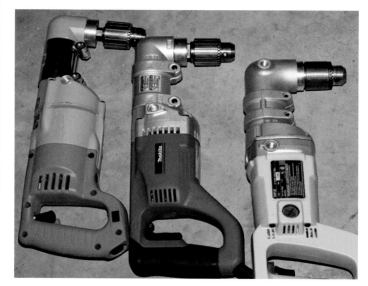

Tubular arm, right-angle drills are light and easy to use, especially overhead, but they have limited torque capability.

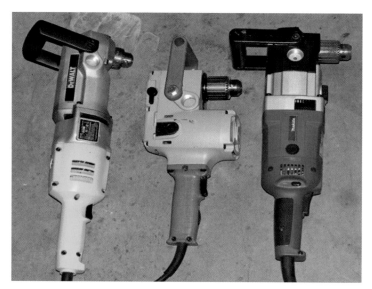

Heavy duty right-angle drills: DeWalt (*left*), Milwaukee (*center*), Makita (*right*)

A two speed control is common on heavy-duty right-angle drills.

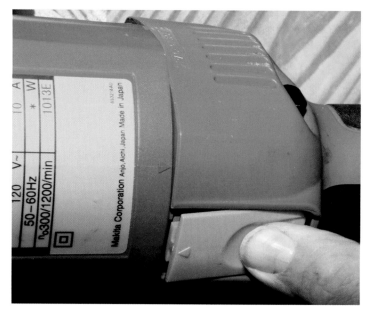

This heavy-duty drill has the capacity to pivot its handle.

Use a grinder to cut off the ends of screws that extend through wood.

A full-size recip saw (*left*) is required for fast cutting of all types of materials, from pipe to wood, while the mini recip saw (*bottom left*) is perfect for small cuts into metal because of its extremely thin blade (*above*).

# Specialty pipe wrenches

A number of specialty wrenches have been developed over the years. Sometimes they are developed for a specific need in the trade; at other times, I wonder what in the world was running through their minds.

Most plumbing suppliers only stock what sells—so if they can't sell a lot of it, they don't carry it. Even major plumbing wholesalers no longer stock a complete line of pipe wrenches. Thank goodness for the Internet—because soon you may have to order even the most common wrenches from cyberspace. Here are some of the good and not-so-good wrenches:

This specialty wrench has its head offset by about 45 degrees, which allows you a different angle to get to the pipe in tight locations. A common pipe wrench has its jaws set at 90 degrees to the handle.

This chain wrench was a good idea that got lost on the follow through. They give you a chain wrench for those really stubborn pipes you can't get loose. However, its handle is so short you have no leverage.

This aluminum wrench was developed just to be lighter but that comes at a higher cost. Its jaws are still made of steel.

A strap wrench--steel handle with cloth strap. I've had this tool for 15 years and still haven't been able to get it to work.

This specialty wrench has its jaws set exactly in line with the wrench's handle.

(Photos courtesy Ridge Tool Company)

This unique pipe wrench has no teeth. Being flat sided, it doesn't scar up the flats on a flat sided fitting.

A rubber strap wrench.

To work properly, rough up the smooth strap with sandpaper.

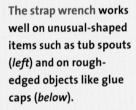

The strap wrench works well on unusual-shaped items such as tub spouts (*left*) and on rough-edged objects like glue caps (*below*).

# Wood bits

Plumbers use several different types of wood bits to open up studs and beams for water lines, drains, and vents. Spade bits are the most common. Kept sharp, spades bits can cut deep and fast. Bits with two end protrusions on their cutting surface drill faster and better than those with a common flat edge. Spade bits come in sets, and it's wise to store them in the original protective coverings to keep their cutting edges sharp. The two most common sizes used will be 3/4 in. and 1 in. When they are damaged, discontinue using them—they're generally inexpensive—and buy new ones. One problem you're likely to encounter with spade bits is that the bit sometimes jams between studs when you drill more than one stud at a time. For such jobs, it's better to use an auger bit.

Auger bits are used (in a right-angle drill) for deep cuts through several layers of wood or to cut through beams. The depth of their cuts are usually limited to 6 in. or less. Do not use auger bits in a pistol grip drill—the torque pressure the bit sends back to your wrist could sprain or even break your wrist. When the bit becomes damaged, sharpen or grind out the damaged area or buy a new bit. Auger bits are expensive so treat them with care. Some auger bits are made to cut through nails, such as Nailbiters by Greenlee.

For deep drilling, you can use long auger bits, long-shank spade bits, or any short auger or spade bit with a shank extension rod. Long auger bits tend to become jammed in long holes. To reduce the amount of drag, wax the sides of the bit or drill half the hole slightly larger than needed and then finish drilling the last half to the desired hole diameter.

**Self-feed bits and other Forstner-type bits remove all the wood away from the hole and can make a single, continous cut.**

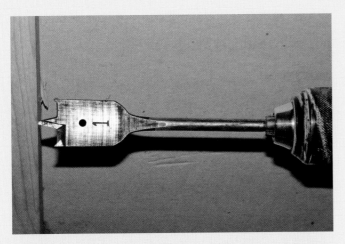

Spade bits are the most commonly used bit. They are inexpensive and cut fast when kept sharp.

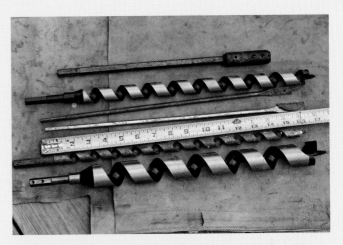

For deep drilling, use long auger bits, long-shank spade bits, or extension rods.

Always use a right-angle drill with self-feed bits. Be wary: if the bit jambs in the wood, the drill body turns with considerable force and could injure the user or break bones.

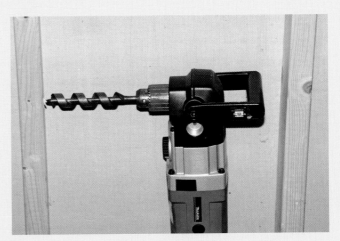

Short auger bits must be used with a right-angle drill and will fit, with the drill, in the cavity between studs.

# Extension cords

You can't do plumbing without extension cords. You'll need cords that are short, medium, and long. By short, I mean those that are only around 6 ft. long (12 gauge), which I use when my drill cord almost makes it to the outlet. Medium cords (12 gauge) are between 25 ft. and 50 ft. long. A long cord is 100 ft. or more, and should always be 10 gauge. Keep these long cords under control by winding them around an 8 ft. 2×6 with a notch on each end.

UL-listed extension cords now must be constructed with #16 gauge or larger wire, or be equipped with integral fuses. The #16 gauge wire is rated to carry 13 amperes (up to 1,560 watts), as compared to the former standard #18 gauge cords that were rated for 10 amperes (up to 1200 watts).

The chart shown here requires that you know the total amperage of all the tools you will use with the cord in the future. My rule of thumb on extension cord gauge is to always treat the extension cord as an extension of the house wiring—thus it should be 12 gauge cable. You'll never get in trouble using a larger physical size cable, but problems will occur if you use one that's too small. Remember, the larger the gauge, the smaller the diameter, the greater its electrical resistance, and the less power it will feed to the tool—which can burn up the cord or ruin the tool's motor.

Extension cords come with several different ends. I love the one that is lighted because

**Lighted-end cords** are my favorite—the second I pick it up I know if it has power.

**Multiple-end cords** are popular. It saves fighting over who gets power.

## Typical extension cord chart of ampere versus cord length

| Appliance Amperes | Extension Cord Length | | | | | |
|---|---|---|---|---|---|---|
| | 25' | 50' | 75' | 100' | 150' | 200' |
| 0–5 | 16 | 16 | 16 | 14 | 12 | 12 |
| 5.1–8 | 16 | 16 | 14 | 12 | 10 | — |
| 8.1–12 | 14 | 14 | 12 | 10 | — | — |
| 12.1–15 | 12 | 12 | 10 | 10 | — | — |
| 15.1–20 | 10 | 10 | 10 | | | |

**Auto locking cord** ends keep the tool's plug from pulling out.

it always answers the question of whether the power is on. Many prefer to have to have an end with multiple outlets. You can, however, have both. Mark your cord to make its ownership clearly visible. At a jobsite, many cords look alike, and marking it will make it clear who owns which cord.

## Levels

Though you can get by with one or two levels of different lengths, you will eventually have levels of every length. You can get common bubble levels and you can get electronic levels. I've had the latter and didn't like them. Life is complicated enough without having to figure out how to program a level. And heaven help me if I program it wrong and build a drain system accordingly. One fancy thing I do like on my levels is a magnet—sometimes it can act as a helpful third hand.

As plumbers, we are always building at a slope of ¼ in. per ft. You can either guess at the slope, or you can modify yoiur level shown in Chapter 6 to get a perfect ¼ in. per ft. slope every time.

Protecting your levels should be high on your priority list. It's possible to knock a level out of plumb. And always be wary of borrowed levels—their bubbles may be out of plumb. To check a level, set it down on a level surface. (Use a level you trust to determine where that is and be wary of trash that might accumulate on the level—such as dried concrete, dirt, or drops of paint or caulk.) Next, note the bubble's position. Then, flip the level over, end-for-end. If the level is reading right, the bubble should be in the exact same place. If not (and the bubble housing is adjustable), tweak it until it lines up the same on both sides.

Having a variety of lengths of levels aids when you work in tight locations or over long spans.

I protect my levels by building fitted CPVC sleeves to hold them.

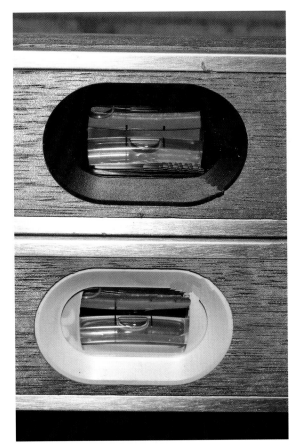

To verify a level's accuracy, flip the level end for end—it should read exactly the same both ways.

# Pipe and drain cleaning tools

Plumbing has always dealt with drain lines. We use water and then send it away. Every so often the fixture clogs or the drain clogs. To that end we have always created machines to unclog lines. Some are strictly mechanical—others are electrically operated.

This manual auger is inexpensive and has a revolving handle suitable for clearing sinks and small-diameter pipes.

This type of auger runs on AC power and is used to clear main lines. Its cutter head is made specifically to cut tree roots.
(Photos courtesy Ridge Tool Company)

This pistol-grip cordless auger works in the same manner as the manual auger above, but is battery powered.

# Marking your tools

Tools are expensive. Always mark your tools to prove you own them. I've found the best way to mark anything is to simply paint it some conspicuous, even outlandish color. That way, if someone else winds up with your tool, it is not by accident.

If someone starts using your pipe wrench, you want to be able to tell it from across the room. Spray paint works well, as do thick black letters from a permanent marking pen. If you want to be clever, hide your name on the tool in some out-of-sight place.

I spray paint my some of my tools an outlandish color to declare ownership.

Write your name on tools large enough to hold it.

## Pipe vises

There are many times when a plumber needs a third hand—one to hold the fitting and another two for the wrenches and fittings. It's called a vise. There are two basic types: chain and pipe. I prefer a chain vise because its smaller size allows you to work overhead and not just in front.

A pipe vise. It works well but takes up a lot of room and is more expensive.

(Photos courtesy Ridge Tool Company)

A chain vise. Works just as well as a pipe vise, but takes up less room.

## Using a pipe wrench

Using a pipe wrench does not come naturally. This is especially true when you use two simultaneously. There's also a good chance of the pipe slipping *in* the jaws instead of being grabbed *by* the jaws.

The teeth on a pipe wrench are curved one direction to grip onto the pipe.

To tighten, jam the left pipe wrench against your body (jaws facing away from you) and pull with the other.

To loosen, reverse the hold on the left pipe wrench (jaws facing toward you) and push with the other.

# Large-diameter hole cutters

Large diameter hole cutters are handy tools to have. The advantage of using circular hole cutters over a self-feed bit is that they require less torque to cut, cut through nails, and are much safer. And, they make a considerably neater hole than one made by a jig saw.

Always remember to cut the hole ⅛ in. to ¼ in. larger than the pipe requires. This prevents the pipe from rubbing against the hole and squeaking as the pipe expands and contracts.

You will need a considerable variety of hole cutters in the plumbing trades.

This is a removable arbor. It contains the pilot bit. This removable auger screws into any hole cutter with a matching center-thread opening. You'll need several hole cutters of different diameters, but just one arbor—which moves from cutter to cutter.

Some hole cutters have their arbor built into the cutter. These are more expensive than a hole cutter without an arbor. But it's not necessary to keep changing it out from cutter to cutter.

Insert the arbor into the center hole of a hole cutter and screw in.

Turn the arbor until the two alignment pins fit into the two alignment holes. Push the arbor forward to seat the pins in the holes.

If the alignment pins full out of the alignment holes, the arbor will jamb against the back of the hole cutter. To free it, use two large pipe wrenches and lots of muscle to free it.

# Cutting cast iron

Cutting cast iron has always been a pain. As far as I can tell, there are no good ways to cut it. The best compromise, if the pipe hasn't been installed, is using a solid-blade chop saw. This will give you a good clean but slow cut—always wear safety glasses. For faster cuts use a diamond blade.

If the cast iron is aready in place—used as a soil pipe for instance—try a chain snapper, but which takes lots of muscle. A diamond blade on a circular saw works well but it may not cut through the whole pipe. Snap the rest with a hammer, or grind it with a hand-held grinder.

A diamond blade on a circular saw works well to cut cast iron.

A chop saw with a solid blade works well when used to cut cast iron before it is installed.

Snap cutters use a chain that tightens around the cast iron pipe and snap cuts it when you close the handles. (Photo courtesy Ridge Tool Company.)

# Custom tools

In plumbing it pays to make your own tools when those provided by manufacturers fall way short of doing their job properly. A few were included throughout the book at place of use. Here is another one.

The problem: A basin wrench falls considerably short when it comest to its ability of getting a facet nut off easy and fast.

When applied, this manufacturer's tool for removing faucet nuts has a hard time staying on the nut. And you still have to get on your back and wiggle under the sink to use it.

To make a faucet-nut removal tool that you don't have to get on your back to use, place a faucet nut onto a 1 1/4-in. CPVC pipe (about 18 in. long) and mark where its wings lay on the pipe edge.

Using a flat bastard file, cut down into the marks about 1/2 in.

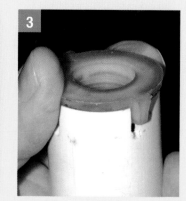

Test fit the faucet nut.

# Alternate Connections Systems

The RIDGID ProPress System uses a powered tool (cordless or corded) to crimp specially designed copper fittings that have an internal seal. Interchangeable heads allow one tool to crimp ½-in., ¾-in., and 1-in. copper pipe and fittings. The system works well but you have to get used to the weight of the crimp tool and it takes both hands to hold it. Most large plumbing wholesalers stock the fittings and tool. However, because the tool is very expensive and the fittings are $2 to $3 each, it is considered a professionals-only system.

## The NVent/PermaLynx system

The NVent/PermaLynx push-to-connect system for ½-in. to 2-in. K, L, or M copper does not require special tools. Simply cut the pipe, file off the sharp edge, and push the specially made fitting onto the pipe. The fittings have an internal O-ring and a stainless steel gripper ring. To prevent sharp edges, which can cut the internal O-ring seal and cause a leak, you can use the company's special tool to smooth out the pipe.

Once in place, the fitting can rotate in a full circle but it cannot come off. It is extremely

The RIDGID ProPress System crimper comes in two designs: corded (*left*) and cordless (*right*). Both have interchangeable heads and require special copper fittings. (Photos courtesy of Ridge Tool Company.)

NVent fittings allow a pipe to slip into a copper fitting without sweating. Once the pipe is seated in the fitting, it cannot be removed.

secure; the pipe feels as secure as it would be with a sweat joint. The fittings are more expensive than copper sweat fittings, but they don't leak, or require a torch, and the labor savings is substantial.

As you might have guessed, it takes no great intelligence or special schooling to simply push a fitting onto a pipe. However, the manufacturer considers this a pros-only device. The fittings are not widely available, and their price—approximately $4.50 for ¾ in. and $4.00 for ½ in.—makes them a little too expensive for residential systems under a bid contract. However, homeowners will love them for repair jobs as to get out of the creepy crawlspace or hot attic as soon as possible.

## Watts Radiant CinchClamp

This crimp system is for pipes from ⅜ in. to 1 in. Its band is made from stainless steel, but the method of crimping is the same as for copper bands. Simply slip on the ring, allowing for a ⅛-in. to ¼-in. gap between ring and fitting shoulder, and crimp.

The advantage of the CinchClamp system over one using copper rings is that the entire process is visible. A crooked crimp band, for example, will be readily apparent. With the copper-ring crimp system, the ring is hidden as the crimp is being made, meaning there is a great deal of guesswork, resulting in an occasional bad crimp. In addition, the CinchClamp is a ratchet crimper. (continued on p. 235)

# The RIDGID ProPress crimping system

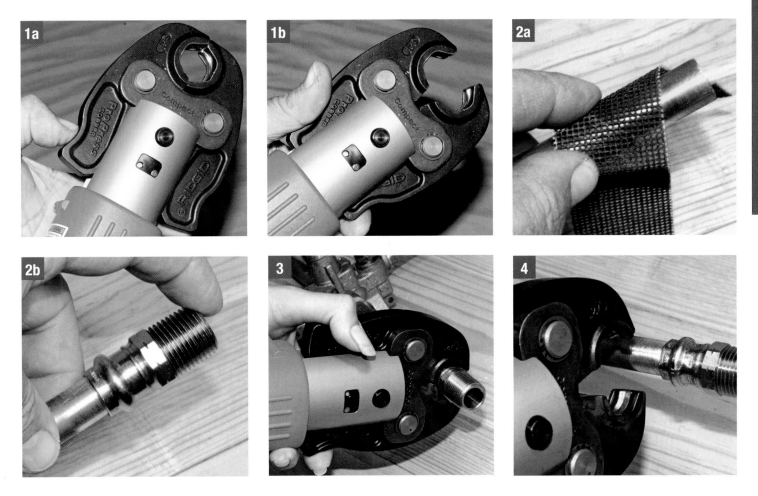

**1** Practice opening and closing the jaws. The crimper head has two ears. Press in on the ears (*1a*) to open the crimper head (*1b*).

**2** Sand the cut edge off copper pipe (*2a*) and insert fitting over a clean, smooth, pipe end (*2b*).

**3** Press in on tool's top and bottom ears to open jaw and let the jaw close around the fitting's raised edge. Pull the trigger and let the tool crimp the fitting.

**4** Push in ears and remove crimper.

# The NVent/PermaLynx system

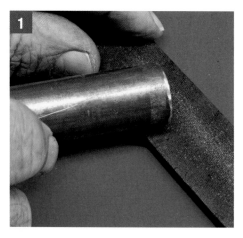

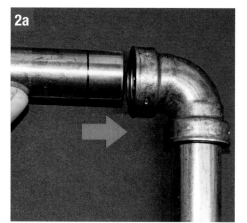

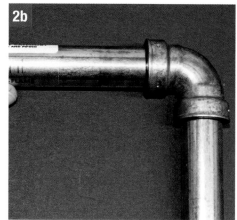

Photo courtesy NVent/PermaLynx

**1** Once the pipe is cut, remove any raised or sharp edges to avoid gouging or cutting the O-ring within the fitting, which may cause a leak.

**2** Mark the pipe so you will know that you have inserted it completely (*2a*) and then press the pipe into the fitting until you feel that it is fully seated (*2b*).

**3** This cross sectional view shows how the pipe fully seated against the fitting's O-ring. Photo courtesy of NVent/PermaLynx.

Once you start the crimp, you must finish the crimp before you can open the handle. This prevents accidentally reopening the crimper and screwing up the crimp.

Another advantage of the CinchClamp is that the stainless steel ring is a lot stronger than the soft copper ring. It is less likely to expand and cause a leak as was common with the old PB system with copper rings. The crimpers are smaller than copper ring crimpers, it takes less power to close the handle, and you only have to buy one. With a copper ring system, you may be buying a crimper for each pipe size.

**The CinchClamp system (*below*) is considered a more professional system since it uses stainless-steel rings instead of copper rings. (Photos courtesy Watts Radiant, Inc.)**

**The stainless CinchClamp ring (*top*) has a raised area that inserts into the jaws (*bottom*) of the CinchClamp crimper. Since only the raised area is in the crimper's jaws, the position and orientation of the ring is easily seen before crimping.**

# Crimping PEX fittings

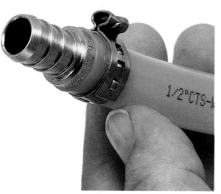

(Photos courtesy Watts Radiant, Inc.)

**1** Slide the stainless steel ring onto the pipe and slide the PEX fitting into the pipe.

**2** Slide the ring about ¼ in. down from the shoulder of the fitting. Insert the crimper onto the raised area of the ring and crimp. The crimper will ratchet—once you start you have to close the handles completely before you can open them again.

**3** Withdraw handle and observe crimp. Note raised area where the crimper brought the metal together.

# Charts and Tables

## PUMP TABLES

The table below shows the maximum depth you can submerge a pump and obtain a specific amount of water. If you have a ½-horsepower pump, for instance, you can sink it 120 feet to provide 5 gpm to 7 gpm at 50 psi. I usually install 7-gpm submersible pumps, and I try not to design for less than 5 gpm to 7 gpm at 50 psi. (If you go for a higher-gpm pump, you cut your maximum depth considerably.) I use the center column in the table as my guide. If a customer needs more water, and the well can supply it, I look at the right-hand column. Some submersible manufacturers have developed more efficient pumps that can exceed the conservative depths in the chart. To be exact, you have to look at the manufacturer's chart of the specific pump you are installing.

Though maximum depths for submersible pumps vary between manufacturers, this chart is typical of most pumps and provides a guide to avoid putting a pump in too deep. The deeper the pump is installed, the less water (gpm) it pumps and the harder it works.

### Maximum depth for submersible pumps

| Horsepower | Typical maximum depth in feet to get 5–7 gpm at 50 psi | Typical maximum depth in feet to get 8–10 gpm at 50 psi |
|---|---|---|
| ½ hp. | 120 ft. | 40 ft. |
| ¾ hp. | 200 ft. | 100 ft. |
| 1 hp. | 300 ft. | 160 ft. |
| 1½ hp. | 400 ft. | 240 ft. |

## Cable gauge for submersible pumps

You are limited in the cable distance from pump to breaker. The longer the distance, the more opposition the electricity sees in the cable and not enough electrical power gets to the pump which may burn out the pump.

Maximum cable length per gauge, in feet, from pump motor to service panel breaker for different voltage and HP pumps.

Using too small a cable gauge can burn out a submersible pump's motor. Use this table to verify the gauge required for a pump of specific horsepower (HP) and cable length (feet). Distance is measured from service panel to pump motor in the well.

### Maximum footage per pump and cable gauge

| Volts | HP | 14 ga. | 12 ga. | 10 ga. | 8 ga. | 6 ga. |
|---|---|---|---|---|---|---|
| 115 | ½ | 100 | 160 | 250 | 399 | 620 |
| 230 | ½ | 400 | 650 | 1020 | 1610 | 2510 |
| | ¾ | 300 | 480 | 760 | 1200 | 1870 |
| | 1 | 250 | 499 | 630 | 990 | 1540 |
| | 1½ | 190 | 310 | 480 | 770 | 1200 |

Use this table to compare different water lines mentioned in Chapter 4. Ignore manufacturer claims, which note only advantages without disadvantages. Listed here are both.

## Comparison of in-house water lines

| Pipe | Advantages | Disadvantages | Comments |
|------|-----------|---------------|----------|
| Copper, rolled | • Not damaged by UV rays<br>• Easily snakes through joists and studs without cutting<br>• Available in long rolls for running under slab<br>• Easy to thaw with a torch | • OD expands when frozen<br>• Expensive<br>• Corrodes when exposed to aggressive water<br>• Difficult and labor-intensive installation<br>• Must be reamed after being cut with tubing cutter<br>• Must be electrically grounded<br>• Hot-water pipes must be insulated | I no longer use due to problems with kinking and aggressive water. |
| Copper, rigid | • Not damaged by UV rays<br>• Resistant to damage<br>• Easy to thaw with a torch | • Requires joints to make long runs<br>• See rolled copper, above | No pipe is more beautiful. Should not be used with aggressive water unless the water has been conditioned. I expect copper to start making a comeback with the advent of push-on copper fittings. |
| CPVC | • Easy and fast installation<br>• Unaffected by aggressive water<br>• A nonconductor<br>• Heat is not as easily lost through pipe wall as copper.<br>• Available in long rolls for runs under slab (may have to be special-ordered). | • Cracks easily when frozen<br>• UV can damage plastic<br>• Not durable<br>• Tends to harden after it has been installed<br>• Cannot use common pipe dope on its plastic threads<br>• Plastic male/female fittings are prone to cracks and leaks | Currently my favorite pipe, though I have started using PEX on an experimental basis. |
| PEX | • Will take a moderate to hard freeze without breaking<br>• Quick installation<br>• Unaffected by aggressive water (but the metal fittings might corrode)<br>• A nonconductor<br>• Flexible; can be snaked around obstacles eliminating the need for elbows.<br>• Heat is not as easily lost through pipe wall.<br>• Available in long rolls for running under slab. | • UV rays can damage plastic<br>• Not durable<br>• Easy to install improperly<br>• Requires special, expensive tools for installation<br>• Tools are proprietary—each manufacture has its own<br>• No street 45s or street 90s | Delayed using PEX due to the problem with PB. I do like the red pipe and blue pipe system. It is flexible, but not as much as PB. |
| Galvanized | • Comes in 21-ft. sections (available in shorter lengths in some areas)<br>• Almost indestructible<br>• Unaffected by UV<br>• Easy to coat with a chrome or similar coating<br>• Easy to thaw with a torch | • Requires extensive experience to cut and thread properly<br>• Withstands a hard freeze without breaking but will split if the water stays frozen for long<br>• Rusts/corrodes from within. Smaller pipes can totally iron up in 6 months under some conditions. However, I have cut into galvanized pipes that were over 50 years old and they looked brand-new on the inside.<br>• Cut threads significantly reduce wall thickness and remove the zinc coating.<br>• Life expectancy is directly related to thickness of zinc coating which is not always well regulated. | Outdated. Only used as fittings and nipples, regardless of what main-line pipe is used in the house. Precut threaded sections can be obtained at most plumbing supply stores. |

Use the two DFU charts on this page to avoid overloading the pipes with fluid. Locate the fixture(s) on the drain line (*upper chart*), total the number of DFUs, and verify that the pipe will carry that capacity (*lower chart*). Experience has shown that it's best to stay far under the maximum DFU for a given pipe size.

## Typical drainage and venting DFUs

| Individual Fixtures | Typical number of fixture DFUs (may differ slightly per code authority) |
|---|---|
| Bar sink | 1 |
| Bathtub or combination bath/shower | 2 |
| Bidet | 2 |
| Clothes washer, domestic, 2-in. standpipe | 2 |
| Dishwasher, domestic, with independent drain | 2 |
| Kitchen sink, domestic, with or without disposer and/or dishwasher | 2 |
| Laundry sink, one or two compartments | 2 |
| Laundry sink, with discharge from clothes washer | 2 |
| Lavatory, single | 1 |
| Floor drain | 2 |
| Shower stall, 2-in. trap | 2 |
| Water closet, 1.6-gallon-per-flush gravity tank | 3 |
| Entire bath group (all fixtures within the bathroom) | 6 |

# DFU charts

## Maximum DFU per pipe diameter horizontal branch and stacks

| Pipe diameter | Maximum DFU |
|---|---|
| 1½ in. | 3 |
| 2 in. | 6 |
| 3 in. | 20 |
| 4 in. | 160 |

Bottom line: Keep your main incoming sewer/drain line at 3 in. and 4 in. Also keep your lines to the fixtures at 2 in. and 3 in. and you'll never have any trouble. You will always exceed code and never have a stoppage in the lines.

# Codes

There are more plumbing codes in the United States than there are states. The two most popularly used are the International Residential Code and the Uniform Plumbing Code. Listed are the most applicable code sections from each. These code references will remain applicable until the next revision of each code; after that, the numerical references to the code sections will differ.

## Plumbing Codes Reference

Blank boxes indicate specs not listed in code. For more detailed code listings see Code Check® Plumbing (Taunton Press)

| Application | International residential code section | Uniform plumbing code section |
|---|---|---|
| Pipe shall not be imbedded in concrete | 2603.3 | 313.2 |
| Placing sewer and water line in the same trench | 2904.4.1 | 609.2 |
| Pipe supports in trench (fully supported with no rocks) | 2605.1 | 314.3 |
| Pipe depth in trench (6 in. or 12 in.) | 2603.6 | 609.1 |
| Sleeving of pipe through wall | 2603.5 | 313.10.1 |
| 1/4 in. wrap on pipe at masonry penetrations | 2603.3 | 313.1 |
| protection required against freezing | 2603.6 | 313.6 |
| roof and wall openings must be watertight | 2606.1 | 313.8 |
| pipe support distances apart | T2423.1 | T3-2 |
| Fixture unit load | 3004.1, 3004.7 | T7-3 |
| Cannot drill drain pipe for connection | 3003.2 | 311.2 |
| Fireblock required at ceiling/floor penetration | 602.8, 321.3.1.2 | 701.1.2 |
| ABS and PVC cannot be glued together | 3003.2(5) | 316.1.6 |
| drain pipe slope | 3005.4.2 | T7-5 |
| main cleanout to be within 3 ft of bldg. wall | 3005.26 | |
| cleanouts required for runs | 3005.2.2, 3005.2.4 | 707.5 |
| cleanout size | 3005.2.5 | 707.10 |
| backwater valves | 3008.1 | 710.1, 710.6 |
| sump pumps | 3007 | 709, 710 |
| traps | 3201 | 1001, 1002, 1003, 1004, 1005 |
| Vent must be at least 2 pipe diameters behind trap (or it becomes an S trap) | 3105.4 | 1002.2 |
| Vent cannot be below trap weir (excluding toilet) | 3105.2 | 905.5 |
| Trap arm length cannot exceed distance in listed chart | T3105.1 | T10.1 |
| Side inlet vent OK of part of a dry vent | 3005.1.3 | |
| do not take fixture vent horizontal until at least 6 in. above flood rim of sink | 3104.4 | 905.3 |
| venting required | 3101.2.1 | 901.0 |
| vents to terminate above roof | 3102.1 | 906.1 |
| no flat (horizontal) venting | 3104.3 | 905.2 |
| vent slope | 3102.2 | 905.1 |
| minimum vent size (1 1/4 in.) | 3113.1 | 904.1 |
| Total vent area to be equal to or greater than drain size | | 904.1 |

## Plumbing Codes Reference (cont'd)

Blank boxes indicate specs not listed in code. For more detailed code listings see Code Check® Plumbing (Taunton Press)

| Application | International residential code section | Uniform plumbing code section |
| --- | --- | --- |
| vent size per fixture unit | 3113.3 | 904.1 |
| snow closure | 3103.1, 3103.2 | 906.7 |
| cross connections | 2902 | 602 |
| vacuum breakers | 2902 | 603 |
| pressure regulators | 2903 | 608 |
| minimum water service 3/4 in. | 2903.7 | 610.8 |
| minimum pressure | 2903 | 608.1 |
| steel plate required for protection | 2603.2.1 | 313.9 |
| water hammer arrestors required | 2903.5 | 609.1 |
| valves | 2903 | 605 |
| water supply material allowed | T2904.4.1 | 604.1 |
| air gap: flood line to spigot | 2902.2.1 | T6-3 |
| required valves, full flow | 2903.9.1 | 605.2 |
| dissimilar metals | 2904.14 | 604.1 |
| unions at water heater | 2801.3 | 609.5 |
| prohibited joints | 2904.7 | 604.1 |
| no gluing different types of plastics | 2904.12.2 | 606.2.2 |
| valve required at water heater cold side | 2903.9.2 | 605.2 |
| valve required at toilet | 2903.9.3 | n/a |
| fixture valves at distribution manifold if valves marked | 2903.8.6 | 610.4 |
| valve required at each appliance | | 605.5 |
| cutoff valve required on discharge side of water heater | 2903.9.1 | 605.2 |
| main valve required in house | 2903.9.1 | 605.2 |
| dishwasher air gap | | 807.4 |
| manifold sizing | T2903.8.1 | |
| required capacity at fixture outlet | T2903.1 | |
| procedure for sizing water service | 2903.7 | 610.8 |
| water pipe sizing per length of pipe | T2903.7 | T6-5 |
| access and working space | 1305 | 511 |
| water heater pans | 2801 | 510 |
| water heater combustion air | 2407, 1703.6, 1701 | 507 |
| prohibited gas water heater locations (bedroom and bathroom) | 2005.2 | 509 |
| gas heater 18 in. above floor | 1307.3, 2408.2, 2801.6 | 510.1 |
| seismic zone requirements | 1307.2 | 510.5 |
| protect from vehicles in garage | 1307.3.1 | 510.3 |

## Plumbing Codes Reference (cont'd)

Blank boxes indicate specs not listed in code. For more detailed code listings see Code Check® Plumbing (Taunton Press)

| Application | International residential code section | Uniform plumbing code section |
|---|---|---|
| gas water heater vents and flues | 1802.1, 1801.1, 1,2425.5, 2426.10.10, 2427.2.2, 2427.2.3 | 510.0, 518.0, 521, 515.0, 516.1 |
| reverse osmosis must use air gap | 2907.2 | 611.2 |
| laundry tub standpipe height (18 in. to 30 in.) | 2706.2 | 804.1 |
| no washer trap below floor | | 804.1 |
| washer trap min. 6 in. to 18 in above floor | | 804.1 |
| washer can drain into laundry tub | 2706.2.1 | |
| | | |
| T & P valves | | |
| T & P drain piping to be same size as outlet of valve | 2803.6.1 | 608.5 |
| T & P drain piping to terminate within 6 in of floor | 2803.6.1 | 608.5 |
| listed anti-scald/pressure balance valve required at 120 degrees | 2708.3 | 420.0 |
| T & P valve setting shall not be greater than 150 PSI or 210 degrees | 2803.4 | 608.4 |
| T & P valve to be in top 6 in.(by manufacturer) | 2803.4 | 608.3 |
| T & P required in water heater | 2803.1 | 608.3 |
| T & P drain piping may not run uphill | 2803.6.1 | 608.5 |
| No kinks or obstructions allowed in T & P drain | 2803.6.1 | 608.5 |
| End of T & P drain cannot be threaded | 2803.6.1 | 608.5 |
| T & P drain cannot have a valve | 2803.6.1 | 608.4 |
| T & P drain cannot discharge into pan | | 510.8 |
| | | |
| Islands | | |
| Cleanout required at the foot of island's vertical vent (if any) | 3112.3 | 909.0 |
| Cleanout required at the end of the horizontal branch to island | 3112.3 | 909.0 |
| Island type venting limited to sinks and lavs | 3112.1 | 909.0 |
| Island venting must use drainage type fittings only | 3112.3 | 909.0 |
| Island undersink vent pipe must rise up to just below bottom of counter | 3112.2 | 909.0 |
| Drain that serves island sink must serve no other fixtures upstream from vent | | 909.0 |
| | | |
| AAV | | |
| Permitted as individual vents | 3114.2 | |
| General install requirements | 3114.3, 3114.4, 3114.5 | |
| Must be accessible and ventilated | 3114.5 | |
| 6 in. above attic insulation | 3114.4 | |
| 4 in. above drain | 3114.4 | |

# Americans with Disabilities Act Guidelines

## Tubs, Showers, and Grab Bars

Although the 1990 ADA Guidelines are not required by code for residences, a large number of people in this country have a disability that prevents them from using a bathroom facility that the rest of us can maneuver with no difficulty. The guidelines cover a whole range of issues, but for our purposes, the bathroom is the main issue, specifically the safe entry and exit of tubs and showers. You may also be called on to deal with this issue either for personal reasons, such as a disabled or elderly family member, or professional reasons, such as a job you're hired to do. The drawings referenced in the guidelines below can be found at the government website, http://www.access-board.gov/.

**4.26.2* Size and Spacing of Grab Bars and Handrails.** The diameter or width of the gripping surfaces of a handrail or grab bar shall be 1¹/₄ in to 1¹/₂ in (32 mm to 38 mm), or the shape shall provide an equivalent gripping surface. If handrails or grab bars are mounted adjacent to a wall, the space between the wall and the grab bar shall be 1¹/₂ in (38 mm). Handrails may be located in a recess if the recess is a maximum of 3 in (75 mm) deep and extends at least 18 in (455 mm) above the top of the rail.

**4.26.3 Structural Strength.** The structural strength of grab bars, tub and shower seats, fasteners, and mounting devices shall meet the following specification:

(1) Bending stress in a grab bar or seat induced by the maximum bending moment from the application of 250 lbf (1112N) shall be less than the allowable stress for the material of the grab bar or seat.

(2) Shear stress induced in a grab bar or seat by the application of 250 lbf (1112N) shall be less than the allowable shear stress for the material of the grab bar or seat. If the connection between the grab bar or seat and its mounting bracket or other support is considered to be fully restrained, then direct and torsional shear stresses shall be totaled for the combined shear stress, which shall not exceed the allowable shear stress.

(3) Shear force induced in a fastener or mounting device from the application of 250 lbf (1112N) shall be less than the allowable lateral load of either the fastener or mounting device or the supporting structure, whichever is the smaller allowable load.

(4) Tensile force induced in a fastener by a direct tension force of 250 lbf (1112N) plus the maximum moment from the application of 250 lbf (1112N) shall be less than the allowable withdrawal load between the fastener and the supporting structure.

(5) Grab bars shall not rotate within their fittings.

**4.26.4 Eliminating Hazards.** A handrail or grab bar and any wall or other surface adjacent to it shall be free of any sharp or abrasive elements. Edges shall have a minimum radius of ¹/₈ in (3.2 mm).

**4.20 Bathtubs.**

**4.20.3 Seat.** An in-tub seat or a seat at the head end of the tub shall be provided as shown in Fig. 33 and 34. The structural strength of seats and their attachments shall comply with 4.26.3. Seats shall be mounted securely and shall not slip during use.

**4.20.4 Grab Bars.** Grab bars complying with 4.26 shall be provided as shown in Fig. 33 and 34.

**4.20.5 Controls.** Faucets and other controls complying with 4.27.4 shall be located as shown in Fig. 34.

**4.20.6 Shower Unit.** A shower spray unit with a hose at least 60 in (1525 mm) long that can be used both as a fixed shower head and as a hand-held shower shall be provided.

**4.20.7 Bathtub Enclosures.** If provided, enclosures for bathtubs shall not obstruct controls or transfer from wheelchairs onto bathtub seats or into tubs. Enclosures on bathtubs shall not have tracks mounted on their rims.

**4.21 Shower Stalls.**

**4.21.2 Size and Clearances.** Except as specified in 9.1.2, shower stall size and clear floor space shall comply with Fig. 35(a) or (b). The shower stall in Fig. 35(a) shall be 36 in by 36 in (915 mm by 915 mm). Shower stalls required by 9.1.2 shall comply with Fig. 57(a) or (b). The shower stall in Fig. 35(b) will fit into the space required for a bathtub.

**4.21.3 Seat.** A seat shall be provided in shower stalls 36 in by 36 in (915 mm by 915 mm) and shall be as shown in Fig. 36. The seat shall be mounted 17 in to 19 in (430 mm to 485 mm) from the bathroom floor and shall extend the full depth of the stall. In a 36 in by 36 in (915 mm by 915 mm) shower stall, the seat shall be on the wall opposite the controls. Where a fixed seat is pro-

vided in a 30 in by 60 in minimum (760 mm by 1525 mm) shower stall, it shall be a folding type and shall be mounted on the wall adjacent to the controls as shown in Fig. 57. The structural strength of seats and their attachments shall comply with 4.26.3.

**4.21.4 Grab Bars.** Grab bars complying with 4.26 shall be provided as shown in Fig. 37.

**4.21.5 Controls.** Faucets and other controls complying with 4.27.4 shall be located as shown in Fig. 37. In shower stalls 36 in by 36 in (915 mm by 915 mm), all controls, faucets, and the shower unit shall be mounted on the side wall opposite the seat.

**4.21.6 Shower Unit.** A shower spray unit with a hose at least 60 in (1525 mm) long that can be used both as a fixed shower head and as a hand-held shower shall be provided.

EXCEPTION: In unmonitored facilities where vandalism is a consideration, a fixed shower head mounted at 48 in (1220 mm) above the shower floor may be used in lieu of a hand-held shower head.

**4.21.7 Curbs.** If provided, curbs in shower stalls 36 in by 36 in (915 mm by 915 mm) shall be no higher than $1/2$ in (13 mm). Shower stalls that are 30 in by 60 in (760 mm by 1525 mm) minimum shall not have curbs.

**4.21.8 Shower Enclosures.** If provided, enclosures for shower stalls shall not obstruct controls or obstruct transfer from wheelchairs onto shower seats.

# Index